Praise for Hild of Whitby and the Ministry of Women in the Anglo-Saxon World

"Inman's hugely engaging and accessible book argues from a basis of solid scholarship for a more reliable reading of church history. Hild of Whitby emerges as an authoritative example of the widespread and diverse ministries of women in the Anglo-Saxon Church. Engaging in many liturgical, pastoral, and sacramental activities currently considered the sole preserve of the male priesthood in the Catholic Church, Hild challenges the deficiencies of a patriarchal system of ministry and governance by offering a more complete picture of the Church's tradition." —**Gemma Simmonds CJ**, Margaret Beaufort Institute of Theology

"At a time when women in the Church, and especially women in the Catholic Church, are asking fundamental questions about their place within an ordained ministry that has not only been an exclusively male preserve but one which has been profoundly male-oriented in its vision, it is important that we reflect on the ministry of women in the past and see what that tells us about the story of how we have come to where we are today. Anne E. Inman does just this in this book on Hild—its significance is not what it tells us about early medieval Northumbria but what questions we need to ask in the early part of the twenty-first century." —**Thomas O'Loughlin**, University of Nottingham

"Inman uses the best of scholarship and provides a solid context of the world of Abbess Hild to tease out what we can know of this important woman and her era. Her writing style is accessible to any reader. I highly recommend *Hild of Whitby and the Ministry of Women in the Anglo-Saxon World* for anyone interested in Hild and her era, and of the little-known contributions of women to early Christianity." —**Laura Swann**, OSB, author of *The Forgotten Desert Mothers* and *The Wisdom of the Beguines*

Hild of Whitby and the Ministry of Women in the Anglo-Saxon World

Hild of Whitby and the Ministry of Women in the Anglo-Saxon World

Anne E. Inman

LEXINGTON BOOKS/FORTRESS ACADEMIC
Lanham • Boulder • New York • London

Published by Lexington Books/Fortress Academic
Lexington Books is an imprint of The Rowman & Littlefield Publishing Group, Inc.
4501 Forbes Boulevard, Suite 200, Lanham, Maryland 20706
www.rowman.com

6 Tinworth Street, London SE11 5AL, United Kingdom

British Library Cataloguing in Publication Information Available

Library of Congress Cataloging-in-Publication Data

Names: Inman, Anne E., author.
Title: Hild of Whitby and the ministry of women in the Anglo-Saxon world / Anne E. Inman.
Description: Lanham : Lexington Books/Fortress Academic, [2019] | Includes bibliographical references and index.
Identifiers: LCCN 2019016778 (print) | LCCN 2019019644 (ebook) | ISBN 9781978700673 (Electronic) | ISBN 9781978700666 (cloth)
Subjects: LCSH: Hilda, of Whitby, Saint, 614-680. | Abbesses, Christian—England—Biography. | Christian women saints—England—Biography. | Monasticism and religious orders for women—England—History—Middle Ages, 600-1500. | England—Church history—449-1066.
Classification: LCC BX4700.H49 (ebook) | LCC BX4700.H49 I56 2019 (print) | DDC 270.2092 [B]—dc23
LC record available at https://lccn.loc.gov/2019016778

To David, my husband

Contents

List of Illustrations

Preface

This book is intended to be accessible to anyone who is interested in the ministry of women in the Anglo-Saxon world, as well as being of use to those who are, or who aspire to be, specialists in the Christianity of early medieval England. During the period of history under consideration, the written language in the West was Latin; therefore, the serious scholar will benefit from the occasional use of Latin quotations. Nonetheless for those with no Latin, it should be perfectly possible to skip over the Latin element with no detriment to the overall sense of the passage.

The main character is Hild, known today as St. Hilda, Abbess of Whitby, who died in 680, and it is beyond the scope of this book to look beyond the end of the seventh century. Neither is it within the scope of this book to give comprehensive coverage of Hild's many famous contemporaries. Rather the aim is to uncover as much as is possible of her life and responsibilities as abbess, and thereby provide a template for consideration of the lives and responsibilities of countless other abbesses, known and unknown.

It will be argued that abbesses once held positions of authority that were in many respects on a par with those of bishops and that they engaged in many liturgical, pastoral, and sacramental activities, which, in the Catholic Church, are now the sole preserve of the male priesthood. In the light of what we now know, this book will advocate an expansion of the telling of the constant tradition of the Church to incorporate the agency of its women leaders.

Introduction to Sources

BEDE: OUR MAIN SOURCE

Without doubt the most important source that we have for Hild's life is the *Ecclesiastical History of the English People* (*EH*), completed by the monk Bede in 731. This first-ever history of the English people was a remarkable work, linking together disparate pieces of evidence from a surprisingly wide range of sources and combining them into a compelling narrative whole. The broad sweep of this narrative is all the more impressive when it is remembered that Bede himself, a monk at Wearmouth then Jarrow, never left Northumbria.

It is as a historian that Bede made such a valuable contribution to the generations that followed him, including our own. Yet to contextualize this contribution it is important to recognize that Bede was first and foremost a monk. As well as works on chronology and computistics, he compiled lives of saints for the edification of his contemporaries, and he wrote commentaries on nearly every book of the Bible. For Bede, the Bible, as interpreted by the Church that Jesus founded, was the key to the right understanding of the world and its purposes. And it is into this wider understanding of the world through the biblical perspective that Bede's historical work is seen to fit.

Bede composed *EH* towards the end of his life, and it was while working on the *EH* that he also wrote his commentary on the *Acts of the Apostles*. D. H. Farmer, author of the 1990 *Introduction* to the Leo Sherley-Price translation of the *EH*, argues that Bede, who at first sight appears to be doing pioneering work without any obvious precedent, in fact owed much to previous historians, especially Eusebius. Eusebius's own *Ecclesiastical History*, which charted the spread of the Church from Pentecost until Eusebius's own time in the fourth century, had been translated into Latin by Rufinus.[1] Bede had access to this translation, and Bede's own project seems to have been a conscious attempt to do for the Anglo-Saxon Church what Eusebius had done for the Church as a whole. That is to say he attempted to incorporate the history of the spread of the faith in Anglo-Saxon England into the wider story that began in the *Acts of the Apostles*.

It is easy to detect in Bede's writings the strong pull of universalism, which took the form of a drive toward uniformity centered on Rome. This drive, which was gaining momentum in the whole of the western Church, would eventually spell the end of more diverse practices and relegate women to secondary rather than primary roles in Church's mission. Loyalty to Rome was deeply embedded in Bede's religious attitude, and from his Northumbrian base, he was able to maintain close contacts with the papal court.

Given this bias toward things Roman, Bede's treatment of Hild is all the more significant. Hild plainly does not fit into the patriarchal Roman mold, yet Bede's attitude toward her is one of huge admiration. Even so his bias toward uniformity can be detected as he tells her story. For example it is with obvious approval that he tells us that when she took over the organization of Streanaeshalch (Whitby) Abbey, she employed the same rule of life as she had established in her former monastery at Hartlepool. Maybe she did. Yet in fact there were considerable differences between monastic houses in the middle part of the seventh century, and it was later that the move to uniformity took hold. Perhaps the continuity of rule that he attributes to Hilda owes more to his admiration for her—an excellent abbess would have valued uniformity—than any concrete historical facts to which Bede had access.

This is not to say that Bede was not in fact remarkably responsible as a historian, thoroughly researching what he wrote, and meticulous in his use of sources. In his Preface to *EH*, he listed his main sources so as to demonstrate the accuracy of what he had written. He then identified Abbot Albinus of Canterbury as his principal authority. Albinus communicated with Bede through Nothelm, a London priest, informing Bede of the activities of Pope Gregory's missionaries in Kent and thereabouts.[2] Significantly, Bede saw the mission in Kent as Gregory's, rather than Augustine's mission.

Nothelm himself, who was to become Archbishop of Canterbury in 735, had actually visited Rome during the pontificate of Gregory II (715–731). This Gregory had been the librarian of the Roman Church, and Nothelm was given access to the Roman archives. There he found several papal letters, including three from Pope Gregory I. These, on the advice of Albinus, Nothelm brought to Bede. Bede quotes directly from Gregory's letter of encouragement to Augustine's party when they were tempted to abandon the mission they had been given to cross to England and convert the English. In it he urges them to carry on, saying that it would have been better not to have set out on their missionary journey, than to abandon it now that it had been begun.

Nonetheless Bede's account did suffer from lack of access to other letters of Gregory I. For example had he had access to Gregory's letter to Eulogius, he would have known that Augustine had been consecrated bishop before he reached England, rather than returning to Arles for consecration.

When Bede recalls the more secular aspects of history, the invasion of Britain by the Angles, Saxons, and Jutes, he relies on a work by the sixth-century British monk Gildas, *De Excidio et Conquestu Britanniae* (*On the Ruin and Conquest of Britain*). This was written around 540, in the wake of the fall of Britain to the Anglo-Saxons, which Gildas puts at 448 or 449.

In 446, the Britons had appealed to the Roman consul, Aetius, for military help against the invasions of the Scots, an Irish people based in Western Scotland, and the Picts, who inhabited much of northern and eastern Scotland. When this help was not forthcoming, Vortigern, who ruled much of Britain, invited in mercenaries from Saxony and Jutland (Denmark) to help repel the Scottish (that is to say Irish) and Pictish invaders. Gildas, who generally referred to Vortigern ("Great King") simply as "tyrant," regarded this move as utter folly because it resulted in the invasion of Britain by the Germanic tribes. For Gildas, the Anglo-Saxons had become an even worse threat to the civilized ways of the Roman British people than the Picts and the Scots.

Unfortunately for us, Gildas's *De Excidio* was more a moral tract, lamenting the lax standards of the Church of his day, than a work of history. Thus, it provides few exact names or dates, but an ample supply of biblical quotations, while dwelling on the sins of the British leaders. His criticisms may have influenced Bede's already negative attitude toward the British Church. Bede is far more concerned than Gildas to record events as they actually happened, though his underlying concern is always religious.

WELSH AND BRITISH SOURCES

There are two other sources in particular that should be mentioned here, and both are Welsh. Wales, of course, did not exist as the country we know today. The "Welsh" referred to here were those Britons who had remained Christian after the Fall of Rome and who inhabited what is now Wales as well as other parts of southern England. Bede saw the Welsh as uncooperative because they refused to submit to Augustine's—that is to say Roman—authority.

The first source, the *Historia Brittonum* (*The History of Britain*), was written by Nennius, a ninth-century Welsh monk. The second, the *Annales*

Cambriae (*The Annals of Wales*), is a chronicle dating from around 970. From both of these works come the legendary tales of King Arthur.

Ray Simpson, in his book *Hilda of Whitby: A Spirituality for Now*, includes Nennius among his primary sources.[3] Simpson thinks that Nennius, when he records the baptism of Edwin as having taken place at Pentecost rather than Easter "in this instance is probably more accurate [than Bede]." Simpson argues that "the divergent portrayals of these writers reveal a deeper, continuing divergence between two ways of incarnating the Christian Gospel—the Celtic and the Roman—which marked the whole of Hilda's life."[4]

I have chosen to go with Bede rather than Nennius because Nennius is notoriously, not to say frustratingly, unreliable as a historical source. He has been shown to have had a rather cavalier attitude toward the need for accuracy in relating significant names, dates, and events.

The way in which events are recorded in the second Welsh source, the *Annals of Wales*, is somewhat obscure, and of course, dates from more than three centuries after the time when Hild was active in Northumbria. There is no equivalent to Bede's account of Anglo-Saxon events when it comes to events in the Welsh area of Britain, and Bede himself, permanently hostile to the Welsh on account of their noncooperation with the Roman missionaries, had little time for Welsh sources. Bede's emphasis is very much on the refusal of the Welsh/British to preach the Gospel to the Anglo-Saxons. As Farmer remarks with regard to the *EH*, "The contrast between the energetic preachers from Ireland and Rome and the non-cooperative Welsh is fundamental for the whole book."[5]

Bede pretty well writes the Welsh bishops out of his story after they refused to accept Augustine's authority, though there are some further references that put British/Welsh Christians in a more or less negative light. The question raised for me is whether it was these Welsh/British bishops whose ministrations Wilfrid of York rejected when he traveled to the continent for his episcopal ordination. That question remains.

OTHER MEDIEVAL SOURCES

Another source that might be thought of as useful for an investigation into Hild's life is the *Anglo-Saxon Chronicles*. In its original version the *Anglo-Saxon Chronicle* was actually written about a century earlier than the *Annals of Wales*. It is generally thought to have been compiled on the orders of King Alfred the Great during the Viking invasions around the year 890. However, the compiler of the *Anglo-Saxon Chronicle* had access to Bede's *EH*, and thus copied rather than corroborated, many names, dates. and events recorded by Bede. For our purposes, it is therefore of less significance than Bede.

Another form of written record from the early medieval period, which proves more useful, is the calendars. The Church's calendar was organized around the two central mysteries of the Christian faith: the Resurrection of Jesus from the dead, celebrated at Easter, and the Incarnation, when God took on flesh in Jesus,[6] celebrated at mid-winter. The exact fixing of the date of Easter was a complicated affair, and as we shall see, of particular relevance for the life of Hild and central to the theme of this book. The commemoration of the Nativity, the birth of Jesus, was celebrated on the former pagan feast of the Unconquered Sun, December 25.

The Church's calendar, which had begun to take shape around the end of the fourth century, is particularly valuable for the historian because the accuracy of its dates and names was crucial to its purpose. The calendars would record the feast days of the saints, so that those who had lived an outstandingly holy Christian life could be venerated on the anniversary of their death, the day they entered fully into the feast of heaven. As these early liturgical calendars developed a useful source of historical information gradually built up. There are, for example, reliable calendars that confirm the date which Bede gives us for Hild's death as November 17, 680. The Feast of St. Hilda continues to this day to be celebrated on November 17.

The great number of women in early Anglo-Saxon calendars testifies to the significant role played by women in the mission of the Church at the time.

Not to be forgotten for the light they shed onto our period are the records of Church councils, both local and Church-wide. Local councils reveal that regulations regarding the rights and responsibilities of monastic heads were virtually identical, whether the head was an abbot or an abbess. Of similar interest are certain prohibitions curtailing the activities of women that began to infiltrate the rulings of various councils. It is evident that in many cases their purpose was to close down to women a number of activities and certain liturgical rites, which up to that time had been their responsibilities. A later theology that would consign women to a second-class status within the Church was beginning to condemn their previously orthodox practices.

GREGORY OF TOURS

Looking further afield, across the Channel, we find another outstanding church historian, whose writings have a bearing on our knowledge Hild's Anglo-Saxon England, Gregory of Tours. It is Gregory's *Historia Francorum* or *History of the Franks* that gives us most of what we know about the origins of the Frankish empire. The Franks, like the Romans and the Irish, were significant contributors to Anglo-Saxon thought and customs.

As we will see, in Anglo-Saxon times, when travel by sea was often safer than travel overland, the links between Frankia/Gaul and the Christian coastal regions of Kent, East Anglia, and Northumbria were close. We know that Hild, living in East Anglia, was about to join her sister in a monastery in Chelles in Frankia, before being persuaded by Aidan to return to Northumbria.

For us now, to cross the Channel from England to France is to enter a country with a foreign language that most of us are unable to speak, which has customs and a culture quite different from our own. Consequently it is perhaps difficult for us to appreciate the continuity of customs and culture that those who chose to travel between the Christian regions of Eastern England and Catholic Northern France were able to maintain. We should understand that Hild would have been more at home with family members in Chelles than in the many parts of Britain ruled by dynasties hostile to her own.

The Franks were a Germanic people who had long been encroaching into the Gallic lands of the Roman Empire. Book I of *The History of the Franks* by Gregory of Tours records this expansion. Book II treats of Clovis, who succeeded in uniting the Franks and, taking advantage of the Empire's disintegration, was able to establish himself as the sole ruler of the whole of northern Gaul by 494.

Most of the other Germanic tribes had adopted Arian Christianity, which denied that Jesus was fully God and equal to God the Father. Over the years of invasion, however, the Franks had gradually been influenced by Roman civilization. As a result, Clovis, on his conversion, embraced the Catholic faith, loyal to Rome, which held Jesus to be equal to God and of one being with the Father.

The Frankish population followed Clovis in embracing Catholic Christianity, and this served to ease the relationship between the Frankish invaders and the original inhabitants of Gaul/Frankia who still remained in the region. It also meant that Clovis gained the support of the clergy loyal to the papacy and thus solidified the pro-Roman sentiment of the Franks.

It was this Gallic or Frankish style of Christianity, strongly pro-Roman, that was first reintroduced to Britain by Bertha, Queen of Kent. And on this Christian community in Kent, Augustine and then Paulinus were to build, before Paulinus took the Christian message to Northumbria and converted Hild to the Christian faith.

The Frankish/Gallic influence on Anglo-Saxon Christianity, therefore, was one that reinforced Roman practices and underscored the unity of Christians around the pope. Through its heavy dependence on Gaul/Frankia, Britain was pretty well saved from entanglement in the Arian controversy. Although through that same influence it became very much tied up in the pro-Roman stance that would eventually win out against the Irish-style of Catholicism at the Synod of Whitby, hosted by Hild in 664.

Apart from this more general history provided by Gregory of Tours, two more specific pieces of information from him deserve brief mention. The first concerns Martin Bishop of Tours (d. 397) and the second Clotilde of Frankia. Book I of *The History of the Franks* includes the telling of the life of Saint Martin, who, as we will see, was a highly significant figure in the centuries that concern us, and one of the main inspirations for the extraordinary missionary spirit that gripped Britain and produced the likes of Hild. It is from Gregory in Book II that we learn of Clotilde of Frankia. Clotilde was the second wife of Clovis, and the first in a great line of female descendants credited with the conversion of their pagan husbands to Christianity. It is thanks to Gregory that we know how Clotilde had refused to rest until her husband renounced paganism in favor of Christianity. Chapter 4 of this book will explain how Clotilde's evangelization achievements relate to Hild's own story.

Thus, Gregory of Tours is a significant and reliable source for the background to Hild's own conversion. But more than that, Gregory gives us an insight into the Frankish style of Christianity that was to impinge on Hild in the initial stages of her conversion. He tells of that great saint and inspiration for mission, Martin of Tours. He opens a window onto the role of Clotilde in the conversion of the Franks and the subsequent conversion of the English.

SAINTS' *LIVES*

More can be learned about the conversion of the English through chinks of light that shine through the recorded *Lives* of Martin and other Saints. Saints were (and still are) regarded as both an advocate and an inspiration for the faithful here on earth. As a consequence, in the late seventh century, their deeds began to be lovingly recorded in Latin, the language of the Roman Church. There is available today an extensive collection of the *Lives* of saints written in the early medieval period.

Religious communities in Britain were already familiar with and inspired by the *Life of St Martin*, written by Sulpicius Severus. Also well-known was the *Life of St Anthony*, the fourth-century Egyptian hermit traditionally recognized as the father of monasticism. Anthony's *Life* was written by Bishop Athanasius of Alexandria (d. 373) and had been translated into Latin by Evagrius. The writing of *Lives* was to become very much part of the monastic endeavor. Ian Bradley, referring to the *Lives* of Celtic Saints, says that "the late seventh century saw the beginnings of what was to become a significant monastic industry, the systematic production of Latin *Vitae Sanctae* celebrating the lives and achievements of the Celtic Saints."[7]

These *Lives* are also called "hagiographies," a word with Greek derivations that simply means "writings about holy people." These early hagiographies were never intended to be historically accurate biographies. The aim was rather to provide inspirational examples of a holy Christian life, encouraging imitation, especially in the area of mission. It was an accepted convention to attribute miracles to holy persons as a means of reinforcing their reputation for holiness. And of course, there was always prestige to be gained by the region or the monastery or even the cause with which the saint was associated.

In addition, it is possible to detect a further stimulus toward the writings of these hagiographies. Notably, in the aftermath of the Synod of Whitby in 664, they seem to have been composed to make a point. A number of missionaries from Iona had been unwilling to accept the decision of the Whitby Synod to follow Roman rather than Celtic practices. This had led the hardline Bishop Wilfrid (d. 709) to speak out in the strongest terms against them, calling them heretics. Hence the urgent need in northern Britain to undertake the production of Celtic *Lives* written to safeguard the reputations of their leading figures, resulting in a significant number of Northumbrian compositions. During this period only one *Life* from the south of England survives: Felix's *Life of St Guthlac* (d. 714) who was from Mercia. It is possible that others may have been lost.[8]

Among those of Northumbrian interest were two concerning Cuthbert, monk and bishop of Lindisfarne, who died in 687. The first by an anonymous author was produced sometime between 699 and 705. By the year 721, this *Life of Saint Cuthbert* had been substantially rewritten by Bede. The historian Stephanie Hollis demonstrates the way in which this rewriting provides considerable insight into Bede's underlying bias against women in his *EH*. Hollis examines the way in which Bede downplayed or altogether omitted women's active contribution to the church's mission and their standing as coworkers alongside bishops[9]—an examination that will provide useful evidence for the gradual suppression of women's active ministry.

Hollis makes further interesting observations regarding another very early *Life*, that of Pope Gregory I, that is to say Gregory the Great. Gregory's *Life* was written at Whitby Abbey by an unknown author, possibly a woman, some time between 680 and 704 and contains the well-known story of Gregory's encounter with the Anglian slave boys, subsequently recorded by Bede. Hollis suggests that this *Life* "reflects a lingering resistance" to the increasing stress on hierarchical relationships and the growing tendency toward elitism among the clergy. Once again Hollis's study will provide useful information when we come to look at how the restrictions on women's active ministry were already beginning to take effect when Hild's successor and niece, Aelffled, was Abbess of Whitby.

Significant for our purposes is the *Life of Wilfrid*, Bishop of York, who impinged directly on the life of Hild and was, perhaps more than anyone else, responsible for the Romanization of the Anglo-Saxon Church. Composed by Eddius Stephanus, or Stephen the priest as he names himself, the *Life of Wilfrid* was circulating within ten years of Wilfrid's death. Although it is written with all the bias of a typical hagiography, its early date of composition speaks for the relative accuracy of recorded events. And the life of Wilfrid was, as we shall see, eventful.

Wilfrid was a highly combative individual, and Eddius delights in recording his more colorful clashes. For example, as Leyser points out, Eddius seems to relish reporting a specific incident when Queen Iurminburg of Northumbria stole and wore Wilfrid's reliquary—a story that Bede passes over in discreet silence. According to Leyser, this story has an air of verisimilitude about it because "it reveals tensions of a kind made familiar in Francia where aristocratic women, as portrayed by the historian bishop Gregory of Tours (c. 540-94), alternately love and hate their episcopal leaders."[10] The tensions between Iurminburg and Wilfrid provide an interesting contrast to the previous working relationships between aristocratic women like Hild and their bishops.

Before leaving this section on *Lives*, it is essential to mention the Life of Leoba, an Anglo-Saxon religious and relative of Boniface, the saint from Devon who was martyred in Frisia (the Netherlands) in 754. Leoba joined Boniface on his mission to the continent, and from the account given by Rudolph of Fulda in the early ninth century, we can learn something of the role played by monastic women in the conversion of those outside the monastery.

RECENT MEDIEVAL STUDIES

Recently there has been a significant increase in studies that shed light on Christianity in Anglo-Saxon England. A standard work is Henry Mayr-Harting's *The Coming of Christianity to Anglo-Saxon England*. Although his mention of Hild is disappointingly brief, he nonetheless provides a wealth of information pertinent to her life and times. In this category I would also put Thomas O'Loughlin's excellent *Celtic Theology*, which, without once mentioning her, likewise sheds much welcome light on the intricacies of Hild's world. Disappointingly O'Loughlin's two substantial sections on "women" have nothing to say regarding women's active participation in the Church's mission. Rather they deal with how Adomnán sought to protect them in times of war and how various regulations developed regarding marriage and sexuality.

These two authors exemplify a tradition that sees men as the main actors in history and mentions women in generally passive roles and only insofar as they provide the context for the telling of the stories of men. Such focus on the deeds of men is understandable because pretty well all early material we have has been written by men and specifically by men who have had an interest in writing out of history any public functions or authoritative roles exercised by women.

On the other hand, there are a number of scholars who have made it their job to recognize that women's activities have been written out of Christian history and to search all available sources in an effort to reclaim these women's lives. In their detailed research, they have uncovered what has been there all along: evidence that women and men together exercised leadership in the early medieval Church and that their sacramental and spiritual contribution forms an important component in the constant tradition of the Church.

A particular debt is owed to Joan Morris, who as early as the 1970s was uncovering the history of women with the jurisdiction of bishops in her book *Against Nature and God*. Morris follows the battles of abbesses to retain their quasi-episcopal powers, which lasted from the seventh century until Pope Pius IX finally suppressed the jurisdiction of the abbesses of *Las Huelgas de Burgos* in Spain, late in the nineteenth century.

In the 1980s, seminal articles by Peter Hunter Blair on Whitby and by Christine Fell on Hild were followed by extensive further research by a number of scholars. Subsequently Stephanie Hollis's *Anglo-Saxon Women and the Church* would prove especially useful. Hollis researches literature from the eighth and early ninth centuries and finds that before King Alfred, the eminence of abbesses was greater than after Alfred's reign. Their involvement in public affairs was greater before than after. Furthermore, it was at this time that there was a tendency in canon (church) law to increase the prestige and authority of ordained men with a corresponding reduction in the status of women, especially monastic women.

Sarah Foot in her magisterial work *Monastic Life in Anglo-Saxon England c. 600–900* seeks to uncover the reality of monastic life in early Anglo-Saxon England before the blanket imposition of the Benedictine Rule. Foot argues that the monastic aspiration before the tenth century should not be interpreted along the lines of later Benedictine ideals. Rather they reflected more of contemporary social attitudes. My argument will be that these contemporary social attitudes, though capable of their own forms of misogyny, were more favorably disposed toward the notion of women in positions of authority than the patriarchal Roman attitudes that were part and parcel of the imposition the Benedictine Rule. The subtitle of Foot's *Veiled Women*, Volume 1: *The disappearance of nuns from Anglo-Saxon England*, speaks volumes.

Barbara Yorke provides a vast amount of fascinating detail that helps to fill out the background to Hild's life and times. This is true both of her *Nunneries and the Anglo-Saxon Royal Houses* and *The Conversion of Britain 600–800.* Yorke provides an interesting insight into more recent ways in which the lives of women religious have been traduced. She comments that in anti-Catholic propaganda, nuns tended to be characterized as either hysterical or corrupt. However by the end of the nineteenth century, there was a tendency to look more favorably upon medieval monasticism. This, together with the beginnings of the movement for women's rights, led to renewed interest Anglo-Saxon monasteries, where women had evidently found scope for fulfilling activities and responsibilities outside the home. In 1896, Lina Eckenstein made a pioneering survey of female monasticism in the medieval west. Eckenstein saw the nun in the convent a precursor for the late nineteenth-century woman who persistently asked for "the right to self-development and social responsibility."[11]

Gary Macy, like Joan Morris, focused on what seems to have been the widespread practice of formally ordaining women. Macy found himself dragged into the question of women's ordination through a controversy not of his making. Quite accidently he found himself uncovering the hidden history of women's ordination. His writing on female clergy in the West has been invaluable.

Especially helpful in researching the background to Hild has been Part One of *Medieval Women* by Henrietta Leyser titled "The Anglo-Saxons: Studies in Evidence." Although Leyser's focus is the lives of women rather than the history of Christianity, the two are so completely intertwined in the period under consideration as to make general early medieval studies that include the history of women extraordinarily useful.

The focus on the lives of women in history generally has become a feature of broadcasting in Britain. The media have responded positively to one of the most significant developments in the field of historical research that began to take shape in the twentieth century. Up to that point recorded history was almost exclusively the history of men and men's deeds, interpreted from a male perspective. Now there is a serious determination to widen the focus of investigation to include the lives and works of women. And now women as well as men are undertaking historical research and interpretation.

This development has excited the interest of a wider nonspecialist audience. An outstanding example of this would be *The White Queen* 2013 on BBC television, which quite brilliantly portrayed the royal women Elizabeth of York and Margaret Beaufort as robust, powerful characters, who helped to determine the direction of the English monarchy in the late fifteenth century.

ARCHAEOLOGICAL FINDS

A few years ago, I had the privilege of walking over the ground at Jarrow with a group of theologians as Rosemary Cramp of Durham University brought to life Bede's monastery, based on insights from her archaeological research. When it comes to the sources of our knowledge of the early medieval world, we should not underestimate the significant role that archaeology has played in piercing the gloom that once pervaded our image of Anglo-Saxon England.

For example, a major archaeological find in East Anglia quite unexpectedly prompted a significant revision of our understanding of the so-called "Dark Ages." In 1939, as the sandy soil a few miles from the Suffolk coast at Sutton Hoo shifted, they revealed the outline of an Anglo-Saxon burial ship, laden with a startling abundance of treasures. These magnificent artefacts, weapons jewelry, utensils, and so on, worked in silver, gold, and other metals and encrusted with precious jewels, prompted a comprehensive rethink of the supposedly primitive and uncultured nature of life in Anglo-Saxon England.

More recent archaeological research, at the Sutton Hoo site and elsewhere, provides further evidence to challenge the notion that a pervasive gloom descended on Britain after the fall of the Roman Empire. These exciting discoveries have sparked a renewed interest in the period and caught the imagination of a wider audience. New scholarship has been made available in an accessible form to the non-specialist not only through publications but also through radio and television programs such as Melvyn Bragg's *In Our Time* series and Michael Wood's *In Search of the Dark Ages*.

The anthropologist and osteoarchaeologist Alice Roberts has likewise taken to the BBC to share her research into the origins of the Celtic civilization, while the archaeologist Max Adams, who has made a number of television programs as the *Landscape Detective*, has researched monastic geography in parts of Ireland and the Dark Age landscapes of the North of England. His book on the life and times of King Oswald of Northumbria, like that on the Celts by Alice Roberts, like the work of Rosemary Cramp at Jarrow are but three examples of the ongoing scholarship that continues to shed fascinating light on the not-so-Dark-Ages. Each contributes in their own way to uncovering the ministry of women in the Anglo-Saxon period and bringing to life that most influential of church leaders of her place and of her day: Hild of Whitby.

NOTES

1. D. H. Farmer, 'Introduction' to *Bede: Ecclesiastical History of the English People*, translated by Leo Sherley-Price, revised by R. E. Latham, with a new Introduction and Notes by D. H. Farmer (London: Penguin, 1990), 26.

2. Bede, *Ecclesiastical History*, 41–42. See also Bede Venerabilis, *Historia Ecclesiastica Gentis Anglorum* (Great Britain: Amazon), II-III.

3. Ray Simpson, *Hilda of Whitby: A Spirituality for Now* (Oxford: The Bible Reading Fellowship, 2014). "Bibliography" includes Nennius, *The History of the Britons* (Kessinger Publishing, 2004), 135.

4. Simpson, *Hilda of Whitby*, 28.

5. Farmer, *Bede: Ecclesiastical History*, 364 n. 72.

6. *Caro* is Latin for "flesh," from which we get the English word "carnal."

7. Ian Bradley, *Celtic Christianity Making Myths and Chasing Dreams* (Edinburgh: Edinburgh University Press 1999), 4.

8. Barbara Yorke, *The Conversion of Britain: Religion, Politics and Society in Britain c.600–800* (London: Pearson & Longman, 2006), 12.

9. Stephanie Hollis, *Anglo-Saxon Women and the Church* (Woodbridge, Suffolk: Boydell Press, 1992), 179.

10. Henrietta Leyser, *Medieval Women: A Social History of Women in England 450–1500* (London: Phoenix Press, 2002), 22.

11. Lina Eckenstein, *Woman under Monasticism: Chapters on Saint-Lore and Convent Life between AD 500 and AD 1500* (Cambridge 1896), vii and ix is quoted by Barbara Yorke *Nunneries and the Anglo-Saxon Royal Houses* (London: Continuum, 2003), 1.

Introduction to Hild: A Brilliant Light in a Dark Age

It was in that haunting period of European history known as the "Dark Ages" that a woman had a dream. Searching desperately for her missing husband, she found under her garments a most precious jewel, which "emitted such a brilliant light that all Britain was lit by its splendor."[1] The dream was fulfilled through the birth of a daughter. The brilliance of the jewel prefigured the shining example that would constitute the daughter's life. The daughter was to grow into the saint known today as St. Hilda of Whitby.

In mainland Europe, western civilization, newly Christianized, had barely escaped obliteration, but at the northern extremity of the known world, the light of the Gospel flickered spasmodically, with occasional shining bursts of exceptional brilliance. One such burst emanated from the life of an Anglo-Saxon woman, known in her own time as Hild of Streanaeshalch.

Hild was a woman with remarkable administrative abilities and personal qualities. The pinnacle of her career saw her as the abbess of a highly successful double monastery at Streanaeshalch, later known as Whitby, in Northumbria. Here Hild exercised an authority that in subsequent centuries would be reserved exclusively for men. Here, in 664, she hosted a synod that would prove highly significant for the future direction of the English Church because it pledged its allegiance to Rome and determined to adhere to certain Roman rather than Irish (also referred to as Celtic) practices. At this potentially divisive moment in the life of the nascent English church, Hild fulfilled the role of peacemaker or "peace-weaver."

Hild's influence and her reputation extended well beyond the monastery because people of all ranks, recognizing her goodness and her wisdom, sought her counsel. Shortly after her death, Hild was acclaimed a saint by the consent of those who knew her or knew of her. Like countless women before and after her, Hild had devoted her life to prayer, to love of neighbor, to service of the sick and the poor, and to hospitality for the traveler. The record of her illness during the last six years of her life serves to attest to her exceptional Christian devotion. Yet what marked Hild out as exceptional was not merely these saintly characteristics but also her pivotal role as influential ruler of one of the most powerful monasteries in England. Patrick Wormald comments, "it would be no exaggeration to say that Hilda was among the dominant figures in the early English church, and to an extent which later ecclesiastical history makes it difficult to envisage."[2]

Hild's assiduous attention to the education of those in her charge suggests that Hild herself was a woman of great learning. The unique contribution that the monasteries of the Dark Ages made to the future of European civilization was to keep alive the flame of learning. In this Hild excelled. From the *Ecclesiastical History of the English Nation* written by the Venerable Bede not long after Hild's death, we know that Hild was responsible for the religious formation of both the men and the women of her community. Her insistence on the study of scripture ensured an educated priesthood, and five men from her monastery went on to become bishops. The fertile ground of Hild's monastery also produced one of the most significant figures in English literature, Caedmon, regarded by many to be the first poet to write in the vernacular, that is to say the language of the common people: Anglo-Saxon. Furthermore, Hild's name was one of only two singled out in an appeal made to Rome in an attempt to have the bishop Wilfrid removed from the see of York; the other being Theodore Archbishop of Canterbury.

We know that Hild enjoyed a powerful position of ecclesial authority and leadership. It is also legitimate to surmise that her own scholarship fed into the interpretation of scripture in the seventh and eighth centuries and beyond. It is widely accepted that biblical manuscripts and commentaries such as those produced in the scriptorium at Streanaeshalch under Hild's direction were intended not so much to reflect as to shape a Christian culture.

> In their material form and intellectual content, biblical manuscripts and commentaries reflect the cultural context within which they originate. Yet their intention is not so much to reflect as to shape a Christian culture. . . commentators on the texts of scripture project visions of Christian culture (or counter-culture) in the diverse contexts of early and medieval history. . . . These texts reach back to the scriptural past in order to project the ideal future of an authentically Christian culture (or counter-culture).[3]

Thomas O'Loughlin beautifully describes the "theological products" of Britain and Ireland in the early medieval period as "fully a cog in the intellectual history of the western church."[4] I propose that Hild of Streanaeshalch's theological products, though lost to us in their originals, continue to exist anonymously, fully a cog in the intellectual history of the western, specifically the Roman Catholic, Church.

It is somewhat ironic that Hild at the Council of Whitby was unwittingly instrumental in the entrenchment of the patriarchy embedded in the Roman system that would in time smother the freedom to study, to interpret, and to feed their findings into the mainstream that women once enjoyed in the Irish-inspired Church and beyond.

In our own day, Hild is a saint who "belongs" more to the Anglican than the Roman Catholic communion. In part this is due to the fact that the Churches of the Reformation have tended to exaggerate the differences between the Celtic (Irish) Christianity and the Roman Christianity of the early medieval period to render Celtic Christianity more attractive to those hostile to Rome. In fact more recent historical research testifies to a great deal of mutual exchange between Christianity in the insular world (Britain and Ireland) and Christianity in mainland Europe. My aim is to rehabilitate Hild for the Roman Catholic Church, not out of hostility to the Roman Catholic tradition, but for it to be enriched by retrieving Hild's contribution to it. The ministries she exercised as a woman were fully a cog in the tradition of the Roman Catholic Church, which comes down from the apostles.

As the demand grows in our own day for women to be allowed to make full use of their gifts in the service of the Church, resistance to that demand most frequently takes the form of an appeal to tradition. The telling of that tradition has been somewhat selective, privileging some periods of history and some cultures above others. Furthermore there has been an understandable tendency to stress uniformity and continuity over diversity and historical development. Attempts to break free from a patriarchal system of governance and develop more inclusive models of service have been repeatedly quelled over the centuries. Ignoring the diversity of past practice, the current hierarchical male-only arrangements of the Roman Catholic Church in particular are defended by an appeal to continuity in the life of the Church from apostolic times to the present day. As this Church now finds itself hugely challenged by the deficiencies of a patriarchal system of governance, a more complete picture of the Church's history is called for. It is important that Hild's story is told.

It should come as no surprise that the sources for Hild's life are minimal. Bede plainly recognizes her significance, devoting to her life a complete chapter of the *Ecclesiastical History*. Yet his telling of Hild's story is inevitably colored by his sense that ecclesial authority belongs to bishops rather than monastic heads, and that it is men's more important work, on an altogether higher level than women's activity, that really counts in the conversion of

England. In this, Bede went along with thinking from Rome, to which he was completely wedded, and in the centuries that followed the patriarchy of the Roman system progressively reasserted itself over the entire western church. Thus, in a retrospective telling of history, in the absence of incontrovertible evidence to the contrary, the assumption would be that decisions were made, works written, ideas conceived, and official ministries undertaken by male rather than female figures. Female saints, like the women in the New Testament, were very much relegated to secondary importance after the leading male figures of Christian history.

It should come as no surprise, therefore, that nothing remains to provide evidence for the argument that Hild herself was likely to have produced her own written work, though not only for the reasons just given. Whitby was probably attacked in the Viking raids of 793, and the abbey was completely destroyed by the Danish invasions of 867. Building on the limited sources that are available on Hild herself, this book aims to give a full and accurate account of what we know of the woman Hild. Drawing on other sources, it aims to build up a picture of her times to draw the reader into a familiarity with and a proper appreciation of this truly great English saint.

NOTES

1. Bede, *Ecclesiastical History of the English People*, IV.23, 245–46. See also, Beda Venerabilis, *Historia Ecclesiastica Gentis Anglorum, Liber Quarto,* 21, CLIII.
2. Patrick Wormald, *The Times of Bede: Studies in Early English Christian Society and its Historian* (Oxford: Blackwell, 2006), 267.
3. University of Durham conference "Producing Christian Culture: Gospel Text and Gospel Commentary in Medieval Perspective" advertising material June–July 2013.
4. Thomas O'Loughlin, *Celtic Theology: Humanity, World and God in Early Irish Writings* (London: Continuum, 2000), 1.

Chapter One

The Anglo-Saxon Princess

By the time the Church was three hundred years old, the extraordinary account of the life of Jesus had broken the bounds of Judaism and spread throughout the whole of the Greco-Roman world. By 392, the Roman Empire, which at its height extended as far as Hadrian's Wall at its northern extremity, had outlawed paganism. Christianity had become its official religion. The first written records that we have that mention Christianity in Britain are by Tertullian around the year 200 and Origen around the year 240.[1]

The remarkable claims for Jesus of Nazareth, originally proclaimed in terms of a Jewish worldview, had been reexpressed through prevailing categories of Greek philosophical thought and took on some distinctly Roman characteristics. These broad cultural and religious categories—Jewish, Greek, Roman—were of course each highly complex in themselves; each made up of a multitude of different streams of thought. Equally complex was the overlap between the different cultures.

It was barely four hundred years after the birth of the Christian Church that Saint Patrick had toiled to spread the faith in Ireland. Perhaps surprisingly to us now, Patrick was Roman in outlook, rather than what we today would call "Irish" or "Celtic." It was the successors of Patrick who would develop the distinctly Irish or Celtic characteristics that would be so influential as the Gospel spread across Northern Europe.

CHRISTIANITY IN BRITAIN AT THE TIME OF HILD'S BIRTH

By the time Hild was born into a pagan Anglo-Saxon family in Britain, the Christian Church, barely six hundred years old, had endured two centuries of savage attacks by Hild's own ancestors, invading Germanic tribes that had swept down from Scandinavian lands outside the empire's boundaries. Yet despite the devastation that was wrought, the news that the crucified Jesus continued to live as the Son of God, with the promise of eternal life for those who followed him, still echoed throughout the known world. The Christian Church lived on.

It had long been thought that by the seventh century, as the invaders advanced after landings on the east coast of Britain, Christianity in Britain had been pushed back westward until what remained of the Romano-British Church was pretty well confined to what we now know as Wales. As a result when reference is made to the south of Britain, the terms "Welsh" and "British" are used synonymously. One explanation for this is that Bede, whose *Ecclesiastical History of the English People* is far and away our most important source, had his reasons for omitting the British from his account of the conversion of England.

In chapter 4, we will see how when Augustine, sent by Pope Gregory I to convert the English, arrived Britain, he had tried to enlist the help of the British bishops in Welsh areas. They had found Augustine disrespectful and declined to accept his authority. As a result, Bede, a whole-hearted supporter of the Augustinian mission, seems to have found it difficult to see any good in the British Christians. Max Adams puts it thus:

> One of Bede's difficulties was that, in traducing British Christians and tarring them all with the same brush, he found it difficult to discuss those British Christians in English territories who had kept faith alive against all odds; and so they have effectively been written out of the Bedan narrative.[2]

When the British are mentioned it is in a negative light.

We know that two centuries after Patrick, at a crucial turning point in Christian history, Hild would find herself at the confluence of Roman, Irish/Celtic, and Anglo-Saxon thinking, each in its turn reliant on the foundational spirituality of the eastern parts of the empire. Whether or to what extent the British contributed to the mix we cannot know.

As Hild was converted to Christianity, she necessarily imbibed its message and its way of life through the prism of her own Anglo-Saxon spirituality. Like so many other streams of pre-Christian religious ideas, Hild's Anglo-Saxon spirituality acted as the interpretive framework through which the significance of the Christ event could be understood. As Hild became one of the major players in the re-Christianization of Britain, she inevitably had recourse to her pre-Christian understanding of the divine. In this way Hild rendered the faith in the risen Jesus, Son of God, accessible to people of an Anglo-Saxon mind-set. Her Anglo-Saxon heritage then inevitably fed into the way in which the Christian proclamation was passed on and lived out. That is to say it fed into the Christian tradition.

HILD'S BIRTH AND THE DREAM OF BREGUSWITH

Working back from the date of her death, as recorded by Bede, the date of Hild's birth is reckoned to be 614. Bede gives an exact date for her death, which he puts at November 17 in the year 680, after she had spent thirty-three years—half her earthly life—in the secular world, and the other half in the monastery.[3]

There are reliable calendars which confirm the date which Bede gives us for Hild's death as November 17, 680. Nonetheless it is just possible that Bede approximated her age because sixty-six years is a highly telling life span, representing twice the length of the life of Jesus. We see that Bede also records Hild living for thirty-three years before entering the religious life and thirty-three years in the religious life. Thus, Hild's time on earth is seen by Bede as a twofold reflection of the time that Jesus spent on earth, a fact that served to underline the Christ-like nature of her life.

Perhaps, therefore, Bede was making a theological, rather than a historical, judgment when he recorded Hild's time on earth at sixty-six years. Bede's purpose is always to draw out not only Hild's exceptional holiness but also her legacy: the extraordinary expansion of the Christian mission in Anglo-Saxon Britain that resulted from her leadership of the Northumbrian Church. Nonetheless we do know that Bede had a great interest in and respect for the accurate use of numbers. It was largely his concern for precise science that caused him to oppose so vigorously the calculations made by the Irish Church to determine the date of Easter. He was an excellent mathematician and also careful to discover the truth of historical facts. On balance, it is reasonable to assume that the date he gives for Hild's birth—614—was in fact the year when she was born.

The early 600s, when Hild came into the world, was a period of continual warfare because the various rulers either sought to defend their territories or sought to extend their power and establish overlordship of several kingdoms. With the departure of the last Roman soldiers from Britain in 410, Anglo-Saxon settlements had begun to appear. By the early 500s, a small number of Anglo-Saxon kingdoms had been established in the south and east of Britain. As these kingdoms had spread across the whole of England, they eventually formed a loose-knit confederation under one of the kings, who acted as an overlord with the title of "Bretwalda." The historian Michael Wood defines the Bretwalda as an "over-king, a king who rules other kings", a "wide-ruler."[4]

The role of Bretwalda was hotly contested by the various kings and princes of the eastern coastal regions of England and of the southern extremity of what are now the eastern Scottish coastlands. It was a time when members of royal households and their retinue were frequently on the move, attacking or defending, banished or in hiding, taking or taken prisoner. As a result, members of high-ranking families were often widely dispersed. Furthermore, as alliances were built through marriage, daughters would leave their parents' household, only to find themselves with their retinue living in the household of their parents' former or potential enemies. Significant journeys, often by sea, would be undertaken simply to visit a sister, parent, or daughter. During military campaigns and their aftermath, children would be separated from their fathers and wives from their husbands. It was into this highly mobile, volatile, and violent situation, that Hild was born.

We know nothing of the origins of Hild's mother Breguswith. Hereric, her father, was nephew of the Anglo-Saxon Edwin of Northumbria, at a time when Northumbria ("North of the Humber") comprised the warring factions of Bernicia, north of the Tees, and Deira in the South. (See figure 1.1.) Hereric, like Edwin, belonged to the royal family of Deira. When King Ethelfrith of Bernicia invaded Deira, Edwin fled south, only to be pursued there by

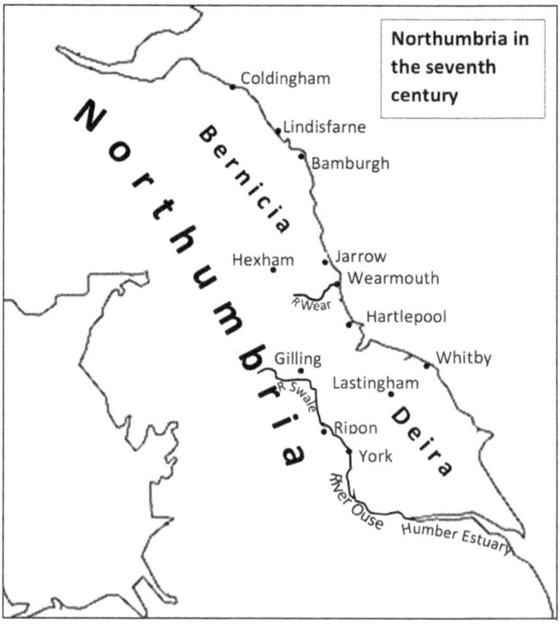

Figure 1.1. Map of Seventh Century Northumbria
Map by Eileen and Arthur Harrisson.

Ethelfrith in 613. Edwin fled again, eventually finding protection with King Redwald of East Anglia. It was most probably here in 614 that Hild was born.[5] Hereric, less fortunate than Edwin, never reached East Anglia.

We have it from Bede that when Hereric fled, he found shelter in Elmet, a small kingdom ruled by the British king Cerdic, near what is now Leeds. (See figure 1.2.) While under Cerdic's protection, Hereric was killed by poisoning.[6] It is not known whether Hereric was a prisoner in Elmet or was there of his own accord seeking refuge. Furthermore when we hear of his poisoning, we have to bear in mind, as Sylvia Mundahl-Harris reminds us, that "at the time death from violent internal pain was always put down to poisoning."[7] In truth, we know little about Hereric's death. What we do know is that at the time of Hild's birth, Breguswith was separated from Hereric, and Hild never saw her father.

Breguswith's distress at the absence of her husband during this turbulent period stands in stark contrast to her joy at the safe delivery of her second daughter, Hild. Bede illustrates these conflicting and traumatic emotions in a vivid experience that occurs in Breguswith's dreams. Breguswith was searching frantically for Hereric, with no success. Then she found a most precious necklace, a most valuable jewel, under her clothing and as she peered at it,

Figure 1.2. Map of Early Seventh Century Britain
Map by Eileen and Arthur Harrisson.

she saw shining from it a light so bright that it brought splendor to the very borders of Britain. (*Uerum cum solertissime illum quaesierit, extemplo se repperire sub ueste sua monile pretiosissimum; quod, dum attentius consideraret, tantifulgore luminis refulgere uidebatur, ut omnes Brittaniae fines illius gratia splendoris inpleret.*)[8]

The "most valuable jewel," of course, refers to Hild. Bede locates Breguswith's dream during Hild's infancy. Hild's brilliant life would effect such a transformation of pagan Britain into the new golden age of Christianity that her mother must have found great consolation for the loss of her husband in this most precious jewel.

HILD'S CONVERSION

Christianity had flourished in Roman and post-Roman Britain. As the Roman Empire declined and the Roman army withdrew from Britain, Roman practices, including its Christian religion, continued. Then, along the eastern part of Britain, "Christianity practically disappeared before the tide of pagan conquerors".[9] These pagan conquerors were, of course, the Anglo-Saxons, the likes of Edwin and his great-niece, Hild. It was to counter the paganism of the Anglo-Saxons that Pope Gregory in 596, and then again in 597, sent Augustine, an Italian monk (not to be confused with the great Augustine of Hippo), to convert the English.

The impetus for this missionary endeavor is memorably captured in a traditional story recorded by Bede that would be handed down with pride by the Anglo-Saxons. Seeing beautiful fair-haired slave boys in the market place in Rome, Gregory enquires whether they are Christians or ignorant heathens. When told that they are heathens from Britain and that they are called "Angles," Gregory comments: "That is appropriate. . . for they have angelic faces, and it is right that they should become joint-heirs with the angels in heaven."[10] Gregory's words have been paraphrased through the centuries of English history in the pleasingly neat phrase: *Non Angli sed angeli* ("Not Angles, but angels").

Bede goes on to recount that the slave boys came from the province of Deira. He would no doubt have been pleased to link Pope Gregory with Northumbria. In fact, the story itself, at least in its written form, has its origins in Northumbria, appearing first of all in *The Life of Gregory the Great*, written by an anonymous source at Whitby, sometime after Hild's death.

In 1616, the vagaries of war turned once again in Edwin's favor, and having killed King Ethelfrith, he was returned to power in Northumbria, where he would eventually become the Fifth Bretwalda. In 625 Edwin married the Christian Princess Ethelburga of Kent. Paulinus, who had been sent by Gregory to bolster Augustine's mission, was still in Kent. He was now made a bishop and accompanied Ethelburga to Northumbria where he remained as chaplain to the Northumbrian court.

Having had little success in converting the Northumbrian people, Paulinus exerted relentless pressure on Edwin himself, extolling the power of the Christian God. After a failed assassination attempt on his life, Edwin allowed his infant daughter, Eanfled, to be baptized by Paulinus, but still he held out regarding his own baptism. Carole Cusack describes how "Edwin frequently committed himself to conversion if a certain event came to pass, and just as frequently delayed accepting baptism until some further sign."[11] Bede records that Edwin "used to sit alone for hours . . . earnestly deliberating what he should do and what religion he should follow."[12] Eventually, when he could put off a decision no longer, Edwin put the matter into the hands of his council of advisers, or *witan*, and his pagan high priest, Coifi.

After Coifi declared himself immediately willing to receive the new doctrines of Christianity, another of the king's chief men gave that beautiful illustration of the advantages that Christianity could bring in the homely story that would resonate throughout English history. Addressing the king, he says:

> When we compare the present life of man on earth with that time of which we have no knowledge, it seems to me like the swift flight of a single sparrow through the banqueting-hall where you are sitting at dinner on a winter's day with your thegns and counsellors. In the midst there is a comforting fire to warm the hall; outside, the storms of winter rain or snow are raging. This sparrow flies swiftly in through one door of the hall, and out through another. While he is inside, he is safe from the winter storms; but after a few moments of comfort, he vanishes from sight into the wintry world from which he came. Even so, man appears on earth for a little while; but of what went before this life or of what follows, we know nothing. Therefore, if this new teaching has brought any more certain knowledge, it seems only right that we should follow it.[13]

The clinching argument, from Bede's perspective, putting the Christian religion on an altogether different plane from pagan practices, was its claim to teach how we came into being and what would be our ultimate destiny. A sixth-century sermon by Martin of Braga gives us an insight into the type of sophisticated arguments that might have been used. "He explains the pagan gods as devils, fallen angels in the Christian scheme, and emphasizes the reward that the new faith brings after death to people who have toiled all their lives."[14]

Hild was thirteen years of age on April 12, 627, when she was baptized along with Edwin, her great-uncle, in the Roman city of York. So to what extent would Hild's own conversion, being baptized along with Edwin, have been a free decision and personal commitment on her part? Bede, as we have seen, makes clear that conversion, for Edwin, was no snap decision. When he knew he could no longer prevaricate, he pondered the implications; he consulted Coifi and debated the matter with the *witan*. Edwin knew that this was not merely a matter of personal conversion. His expectation, indeed his gamble, was that his court would join him in converting to Christianity.

From this distance we might think that as a thirteen year-old girl, reliant on her uncle for protection, Hild would have had little say in the matter of her baptism. Yet there are a number of reasons for thinking that for Hild, too, her baptism marked a personal conversion.

First, it is important to pause here to imagine what it meant in seventh-century Britain for a girl to be thirteen years old. We find a different world from our own. Although some of the population lived to a quite considerable age, we know from archaeological evidence that life expectancy was in the thirties. The age of majority, accordingly, when girls as well as boys could legally take charge of inherited property, was usually either ten or twelve.[15] Thus, at the time of her baptism, Hild was considered an adult for legal purposes.

Furthermore, it was not uncommon in royal households for a queen or princess and her entourage to follow a different religion from the king or prince and his entourage. We already have the example of Edwin himself, who, before his conversion, followed pagan rituals, while his wife Ethelburga retained her own bishop, Paulinus, so that she might exercise her Christian faith. Edwin and Ethelburga were far from unusual in this respect, and indeed followed the example set by Ethelburga's own parents, Ethelbert and Bertha, the Frankish princess. Bertha's own chaplain was included the entourage she brought with her upon her marriage. In effect, she had already reintroduced Christianity into Kent when Augustine arrived bent on the same task.

We can suppose, therefore, that before her baptism, Hild too had been a target of Paulinus's evangelizing mission. She, too, would have been caught up in the discussions that took place within the royal family regarding conversion. She, too, would have experienced her baptism as a serious personal conversion.

HILD'S BAPTISM WITH KING EDWIN AND HIS COURT

The mass baptism of Edwin and his household, including his great-niece Hild took place in a new wooden church, speedily built for the purpose and dedicated to Saint Peter.

Had Hild and her uncle been converted in a less outlandish territory, they might well have expected the washing of baptism to have taken place in a purpose-built baptistery. While Jesus's own baptism had taken place in an actual river, the Jordan, the baptismal ceremony moved very quickly indoors. A separate baptistery would have been attached to the early Christian basilicas, like the one used by Pope Gregory in Rome. Even before that, when the newly formed Christian communities around the Mediterranean moved out of houses for worship and into purpose-built churches, it had been the practice to include a separate room or baptistery for the washing of baptism. Even the more elaborate house-churches might have included a baptistery, as in the house-church at Dura Europos in Syria, where, in 232, "two rooms were knocked into one. . . for the Eucharistic assembly and another room turned into a baptistery with canopied font and elaborate wall paintings."[16]

By the seventh century, although special baptismal churches with baptistery attached were a feature of the Gallic and Roman landscape, they were not generally found in Anglo-Saxon England. The Roman villa at Lullingstone, Kent, shows archaeological evidence of an early house-church, and one of the rooms may have served as a baptistery, but with the end of the Roman era in Britain, this would have fallen into disuse.

The wooden building in York, in which Edwin and his followers were baptized, would soon replaced by a stone structure, and over time it would be replaced by the magnificent York Minster that stands today. Recent excavations have dated the first Christian church on the site of York Minster at 627, the year of Edwin and Hild's conversion.

There would have been no place for the immersion in the hastily constructed church of St Peter in York in that year. So where did the baptismal washing actually take place? We know that after Edwin's conversion, Paulinus went on to baptize in the River Glen in Bernicia and the River Swale in Deira. We can safely assume that the baptism of Edwin and his people took place in the nearby river Ouse, after which the ceremony would have continued in the church itself. The day was Easter Day, April 12.

Hild's baptism must have made quite an impression on her. The Lenten fast and the liturgies leading up to Easter and baptism would have been serious affairs, in anticipation of the most sacred liturgies of the Christian church. We can only imagine the effect on Hilda of the long and stately procession to the river, the exhilaration of the cold river water on an April day, the clothing in a white gown, and then for the first time the splendor of the Easter liturgies in the Church. And all this would have been followed by feasting and joyful celebration.

The spiritual and emotional impact on the young Hild would have been intensified by the great significance attached to baptism in this period of Anglo-Saxon England.

> Baptism was a very serious step to take and was one of the most important rituals in the church of that time. Not only was it the sign of becoming a Christian and entering the church (early churches forbade any but the baptised to enter their sacred building) it was also a visible act of washing away all pagan error before entering the new life.[17]

HILD'S EARLY WOMANHOOD

Not a great deal is known about the exact details Hild's life from the time of her baptism in 627, until her entry into the monastic life in 647. Nonetheless, we can build up something of a picture.

We know that war was the constant background to Hild's life. We have seen how she was born while her entire family was scattered in exile from their kingdom of Deira in Northumbria. Yet two years after her birth, her great-uncle Edwin was not only back again as king of the whole of Northumbria, but he would soon be successfully taking the fight to Elmet, North Wales, Anglesey and Man. At the peak of his influence, Edwin was the Fifth Bretwalda. Through battle he had made himself the "wide-ruler" over all the Anglo-Saxon kingdoms. The question is: What would Hild's life have been like as a member of Edwin's court during this period of successful warfare and eventual overlordship?

An altogether unexpected window into the Anglo-Saxon world opened up in 1939 on the sands of the Suffolk coast at Sutton Hoo in East Anglia. There appeared in the sand the outline of an Anglo-Saxon burial ship. Upon excavation, no body was found, but "the excavators' notes for the dig revealed that a complete set of iron coffin fittings were discovered," suggesting that the ship had at one time contained a body. Wood believes that the ship had indeed contained a body, and that it was none other than Redwald, the Bretwalda who preceded and supported Edwin.[18]

Though evidence of the body itself was missing, what the ship did contain was a magnificent set of grave goods, comprehensively belying the supposedly primitive lifestyle of "Dark Ages" Anglo-Saxon England. This sumptuous find, deposited not long before Hild's own sojourns in East Anglia, testified to the enormous wealth of Anglo-Saxon families. As well as the impression of the ship itself, "long and elegant, which could be rowed or sailed," there were found:

> A helmet, a sword with gold and garnet fittings, a whetstone, a stand, a rod, spears, a battle-axe, a shield with bird and dragon figures, drinking horns mounted in silver, a set of ten shallow silver bowls with cross patterns, a large fluted classical bowl, three bronze hanging bowls, a pair of silver spoons, a lyre which had been taken to pieces before burial, a great silver bowl bearing the stamp of the Emperor Anastasius, nineteen pieces of beautiful jewellery set with garnets including a gold buckle weighing nearly one pound and a huge purse in which there were forty Merovingian coins from the continent.[19]

From this find and subsequent scholarship, we may assume that as an Anglo-Saxon princess Hild would have enjoyed considerable wealth and a highly cultured lifestyle. Hers would have been a comfortable and pleasant life until disaster once again struck, as the tides of war turned once more against Edwin.

In 632–633, Penda of Mercia, allied with Cadwallon, the British king of Gwynedd, invaded Northumbria. Penda was a pagan king, and Cadwallon was Christian. Bede stresses the horrible deaths and the ruthless savagery of the onslaught that spared no one, including women and children. He claims that their intention was to exterminate the entire English race. Bede's antipathy toward the Welsh comes to the fore as he expresses his abhorrence that a Christian king should have allied with a pagan to attack his beloved Northumbria.[20]

Edwin and his eldest son were killed; his second son surrendered, only to be murdered later at Penda's court.[21] Paulinus then took Queen Ethelburga back to her family in Kent, but Hild's movements are unclear. According to Benedicta Ward, Hild was "almost certainly part of the group of nobles who fled south with the queen."[22] Edwin and Ethelburga's small children were sent to Gaul, and Ward has Hild during this next period of her life in Gaul and in Kent. Other authorities suggest that she retreated to the royal stronghold at Bamburgh, which still held out against Penda.[23] This latter suggestion might explain the close links that Hild was to forge with Aidan at Lindisfarne.

What is clear, however, is that this drastic change of circumstances brought new Christian influences to bear on Hild, other than the Roman-style Christianity of Paulinus. When Edwin had finally defeated Ethelfrith in 616, Ethelfrith's sons had fled north into what is now southwest Scotland. At the time, southwest Scotland, together with parts of Ulster, formed the kingdom of Dalriada. This kingdom was regarded as Irish or Celtic, in contrast to the Pictish kingdom to its north and east.

In Dalriada, Ethelfrith's sons, Oswald and Oswy, had been converted to Christianity by the monks from the monastery on the island of Iona, founded by the Irish missionary St. Columba in the 560s. Oswald, in particular, would form a close tie with the Abbot of Iona, Ségéne, which would prove useful to Oswald when he returned to Bamburgh.[24] This he accomplished in 634 following a year of turmoil in Northumbria after the death of Edwin in battle against Cadwallon and Penda. At Bamburgh, Oswald held out against the relentless raids by Penda's forces, and by 635, he was the undisputed overlord of the whole of Northumbria: Bernicia in the north and Deira in the south. Determining to continue the Christian mission in Northumbria, Oswald immediately used his contact with Ségéne to invite a monk from Iona to come to help reinvigorate the Christian Church in his territories. Undeterred by the comprehensive failure of this first Ionan monk to make any headway with the English, Oswald asked for another monk, Aidan, to found a monastery in Lindisfarne.

Aidan was to have a significant influence on Hild, introducing her to Ionian spirituality, a spirituality that we might call "Irish" or "Celtic." He also had a direct influence on the course of Hild's vocation to the religious life. Aidan is famous for his rejection of worldly goods. A well-known story has it that his custom was to walk the lanes and engage those whom he encountered in conversation about the Christian faith. King Oswin, who succeeded Oswald in Deira for a while, was unwilling for Aidan to walk like a peasant and gave him a fine horse. Aidan promptly gave away the horse to a beggar.[25] His concern for the many peasants brought to ruin by continual warfare was undoubtedly a formative influence on Hild and her way of life both outside and inside the monastery.

Apart from her exact whereabouts, another intriguing question that remains frustratingly unanswered is whether Hild was married before her entrance into religious life. On the face of it, it seems unlikely that any woman of that period would have remained unmarried and outside the confines of a convent until the age of thirty-three years. Henrietta Leyser argues, "the probability is that Hilda was by now a young widow."[26] Yet as a royal princess, one might have expected to find some record of her marriage had such a thing taken place. Furthermore the number of suitable matches must have been considerably diminished by the loss of so many kings and princes on the battlefield.

Sylvia Mundahl-Harris has Hild continuing to live in Northumbria after Edwin's death, unmarried, probably engaged in charitable work among the poor and sick'.[27] On the other hand, Ray Simpson says that "the fact that Bede, who calls every woman he wishes to extol a 'virgin,' makes an exception for Hilda and describes her as a 'servant of God'" makes him think that Hild did marry.[28] Whether married or not, as we have already seen, according to Bede Hild spent the first half of her life "most nobly in secular occupations" and dedicated the second half "even more nobly to our Lord in the monastic life."[29]

Bede expresses the view, unremarkable for his time, that vowed celibacy is a higher form of life than any other. Nonetheless, what is striking is the value that Bede attributes to her "secular occupations". We have seen that Bede views Hild's life (thirty-three years in the secular world, thirty-three years as a vowed religious) as a twofold reflection of Christ's life. We know that the average life expectancy in seventh-century Anglo-Saxon England was in the thirties.

In Hild, we have in the first half of her life, a female saint held up as a role model for others, who is revered not for her life under religious vows, not for her role as a mother of children, not for her duties as a wife (though she may have been married), and not because she was an ignorant peasant girl to whom special visions had been granted. Here we have an intelligent, learned woman, revered as saint for her "secular occupations." Here we have a much-needed role model for many twenty-first–century Christian women!

NOTES

1. Carole M. Cusack, *The Rise of Christianity in Northern Europe, 300–1000* (London: Cassell, 1999), 88; Cusack cites W. H. C. Frend, The Christianization of Roman Britain, in *Christianity in Britain 300–700*, eds. M. W. Barley and R. P. C. Hanson (Leicester, 1968), 37.
2. Max Adams, *The King of the North: The Life and Times of Oswald of Northumbria* (London: Head of Zeus, 2013), 279.
3. Bede, *Ecclesiastical History* IV.23, 243; Beda, Venerabilis, *Historia Ecclesiastica, Gentis Anglorum, Liber Quarto* 21, CLI.
4. Michael Wood, *In Search of the Dark Ages* (London: BBC Publishing, 2005), 64.
5. Ray Simpson has Hild's birth taking place in Deira. Simpson, *Hilda of Whitby*, 12, 15.
6. Bede, *Ecclesiastical History*, IV. 23. Beda, *Historia Ecclesiastica, Liber Quarto*, 21.
7. Sylvia Mundahl-Harris, *St. Hilda and Her Times* (Whitby: Caedmon of Whitby,1997), 2.
8. Beda *Historia Ecclesiastica* IV. 21 [23] CLIII. See also Venerabilis Baedae, *Historiam Ecclesiasticam Gentis Anglorum Historiam Abbatum Epistolam AD Ecgberctum* Carolus Plummer, A. M. Tomus Prior Oxon II E. Typographeo Clarendoniano. 1896, 255–56.
9. Henri Marrou, Towards the Conversion of Northern Europe, in *The Christian Centuries: The First Six Hundred Years*, eds. Jean Danielou and Henri Marrou (London: Longman & Todd, 1978), 452.

10. Bede, *Ecclesiastical History*, II.1, 103.
11. Cusack, *The Rise of Christianity*, 103.
12. Bede, *Ecclesiastical History*, II.12, 128.
13. Bede, *Ecclesiastical History*, II.13, 129-30.
14. Cusack, *The Rise of Christianity*, 94.
15. The system of primogeniture (inheritance by the first-born male) was not introduced in England until after the Norman Conquest.
16. Peter G. Cobb, The Architectural Setting, in *The Study of Liturgy*, eds Cheslyn Jones, Geoffrey Wainwright, Edward Yarnold (London: SPCK 1978), 474.
17. Mundahl-Harris, *Hilda and Her Times*, 4.
18. Wood, *In Search*, 64.
19. Wood, *In Search*, 65.
20. Bede, *Ecclesiastical History*, II 20; Beda, *Historia Ecclesiastica*, II 20.
21. Mundahl-Harris, *Hilda and Her Times*, 6.
22. Benedicta Ward, *A True Easter: The Synod of Whitby 664 AD* (Oxford: SLG Press, 2008), 8.
23. Mundahl-Harris asks, "Did Hilda go with Ethelburga or did she retreat to the royal stronghold at Bamburgh, which still held out?" She concludes, "Hilda seems to have spent the next twelve years in Northumbria." Mundahl-Harris, *Hilda and Her Times*, 6–7.
24. Max Adams is tempted to see Ségéne, keen to expand the influence and interests of Iona, "as the motivating force behind the Bernician conversions." Adams, *King of the North*, 69. Henry Mayr-Harting, on the other hand, says that the monks of Iona came to Northumbria not because they wanted to, but because they were asked to by King Oswald, "It was an issue of obedience." Mayr-Harting, *The Coming of Christianity to Anglo-Saxon England* (Pennsylvania: Pennsylvania State University Press, 1991), 93.
25. Bede, *Ecclesiastical History*, III.14. Beda, *Historia Ecclesiastica*, III.14.
26. Leyser, *Medieval Women*, 24.
27. Mundahl-Harris, *Hilda and Her Times*, 7.
28. Simpson, *Hilda of Whitby*, 31.
29. Bede, *Ecclesiastical History*, IV.23, 243.

Chapter Two

The Forgotten Women of Early Monasticism

To come to grips with the second half of Hild's life, it is useful to understand something of the way in which monasticism had developed up to the point of Hild's entry. Broadly speaking, originating in the eastern side of the Roman Empire, there had been a tradition of monasticism in the home and a tradition of monasticism in the desert. Although this formative period predates Hild, it is significant in that, as in Hild's own time, women played a positive part in the making of monastic history, which has been overlooked in standard church histories.

THE TRADITIONAL ACCOUNT OF THE ORIGINS OF MONASTICISM

In the traditional account of Christian monasticism, the bias toward the actions of men is particularly acute. The story has gone something like this: In the primitive Church, when there were still alive people who had known Jesus in the flesh, Christians sought to emulate his passion and death through heroic suffering in the face of persecution, often to the point of martyrdom. With the gradual cessation of persecution and the admittance to the Christian Church of great swathes of the population, significant numbers of ardent Christians, desiring closer identification with their Lord and Savior, sought the solitude of the desert to concentrate on their struggle against the devil and the temptations of the flesh.

"The desert" in this context is not to be understood in terms of endless miles of barren sand, but rather desolate places in Syria and Egypt, on the fringes of population centers, strewn with the scattered the remains of previous habitation. W. H. C. Frend, who like most scholars identifies the beginning of Christian monasticism with Anthony of Egypt, explains that "the Egyptian climate, the nearness of the desert to the narrow strip of cultivable land flanking the Nile, and the presence of caravan routes whence hermits would draw supplies, made Egypt the obvious starting point for the monastic movement."

Frend's account is typical in tracing the beginning of the story of monasticism to Anthony of Egypt. Frend admits that before Anthony, many Christians had fled into the desert and that some of them had stayed there. The flight to the desert was not the sole preserve of ardent ascetics. The "crushing weight of taxation" in the third century meant that increasingly smallholders, unable to maintain a livelihood where they were, bolstered the numbers of those abandoning the city for the desert.[1]

"Even so," says Frend "it is with Antony (251–356) that the story of Christian monasticism begins."[2] In a similar vein in 1964, Henri Marrou states uncontroversially, "Monasticism first appears in history with St. Antony, the 'father of monks.'"[3] Yet again, in 1977 Bamber Gascoigne in his Granada television series on the history of Christianity points to "a crumbling cliff in the Egyptian desert [which] contains a group of caves in which there lived, in the fourth century, the man who is now regarded as the first Christian monk—St. Anthony."[4]

Julie Ann Smith, who has made an exhaustive study of the way in which the lives of vowed women religious were ordered in the early medieval period, points out that before retiring to the desert, Anthony had to make provision for his sister. According to Athanasius, his hagiographer, Anthony first established his sister with a community of virgins, "showing that women were living in religious communities even before the saint founded his prototypical monastery for men."[5]

MONASTICISM IN THE HOME

More recently, however, a new voice has been added to supplement the traditional account. Laura Swan argues that it is in the home, rather than the desert, that we find the beginnings of Christian monasticism. In this very early period, family members would order their domestic arrangements in such a way as to enable some to devote themselves entirely to prayer. Women were especially attracted to the Christian way of life, in which they could exercise freedom they did not otherwise have. As we will see in chapter 5, the involvement of the wider family in allowing certain members to live a life dedicated exclusively to God has close parallels to Hild's own experience. The solitary life of prayer, whether in the desert or the home, was viewed as a type of martyrdom.

In the very early years Christians "followed the Jewish custom of praying several times a day, and some began to pursue intense lives of prayer."[6] It made sense from the beginning that ardent Christians should seek to emulate Jesus's celibate lifestyle. During these early years, when Christians were persecuted, martyrdom was a common feature of the Christian way of life. Because Jesus himself had been crucified and then rose to new life, martyrdom very much made sense as the gateway to eternal life for Jesus's followers. The desire for martyrdom among the first Christians must be seen in this light.

Once the persecutions ended, "fasting, voluntary poverty and deprivations, silence, and deep prayer became a way of living a continuous martyrdom."[7] It was in the fourth century that monasticism, with its desire to subdue the urges of the flesh, really took hold as a major force in the Christian Church. From Eusebius, we have quite detailed knowledge of the daily life of those fourth-century monastics who stayed within the home. Frend writes:

> it is from. . . Eusebius of Emesa (*flor.* 330–350) . . . that we derive the most interesting picture of asceticism as it was practiced within the walls of the homes of prominent citizens in the first half of the century. The dedicated virgin read the Bible, observed daily hours of prayer, kept to a Lenten diet and wore distinctive dress.[8]

We also know that although the basic characteristics of this life—virginity, Bible-reading, the hours of prayer, fasting, and distinctive dress—were to remain remarkably constant through the centuries, original and diverse ways of living out this life nonetheless developed to accommodate the spirituality of the age. Laura Swan writes:

> The desire to be like Christ and to live as one in Christ led to experimentation in community living. Some lived in solitude on their family estates or rented small rooms on the edge of their villages. Others began to live together in small groups, frequently in the homes of the wealthy, whose dwellings were usually made up of a series of buildings that could easily accommodate followers and the inevitable guests. Although prayers were shared in a dedicated sacred space within a complex, most urban monastics frequented local churches as well.[9]

Original and diverse ways of living the monastic life continue to develop in our own day. Some elements are retained; some are lost. One aim of this book is to reconnect with those elements particular to Hild's time, which have been lost in a tradition heavily biased in favor of its male protagonists—a tradition that has tended to write out the part played by women.

A HISTORY THAT INCLUDES WOMEN

It was not only in the home that women played an important role in the development of monasticism. Women were there in the desert as well. Yet like the traditional accounts of so many aspects of Christian history, the telling of the history of desert monasticism focuses almost exclusively on its male protagonists. As Swan says, although "early church histories frequently make brief mention of women dwelling in the desert, living as urban solitaries, or residing in or near monastic communities. . . it is the stories of the men that are preserved and told."[10] When women are mentioned, it is largely because without them, it would not be possible to give a full account of the male saints.

Thus, for example, in relation to St. Jerome, Henri Marrou tells us that "his propaganda for the ascetical ideal met with great success, notably among a certain number of ladies, widows or virgins belonging to the highest senatorial aristocracy," and he names three women: St. Paula, her daughter, Eustochium, and St. Melania the elder.[11] That is the sum of the contribution of women to the origins and first developments of monasticism acknowledged by Marrou. Rather tellingly in another tightly packed chapter, this one on "Eastern Monasticism in the Fifth and Sixth Centuries," Marrou makes but one reference to women monastics with the words "not to mention communities for women."[12]

Research proves the traditional version to be but a partial account. For example, Swan in her book, *The Forgotten Desert Mothers*, records the lives of some of those desert mothers or "ammas," who shared the desert with their male counterparts, the "abbas." Swan reckons that women dwelling the desert outnumbered men two to one.[13] Despite the incontrovertible evidence to the contrary, with the occasional lapse of attention, it would be entirely possible to read a number of standard works on the early history of monasticism oblivious to the fact that women even featured in the history as a positive force.[14]

This distortion has only been compounded by the uncritical identification of certain male figures as founders of various women's religious orders. In a male-dominated society, it made sense for a male saint, especially a saintly bishop, to be the titular founder of a particular community for women. Yet there is no doubt that, in certain cases, women shared in or were mainly responsible for the work of establishing the community, formulating a lifestyle appropriate to its mission, setting the tone of its spirituality, and taking on the responsibilities of monastic head.

The downgrading of the agency of women is clearly at play in Marrou's chapter called "The Origins and First Developments of Monasticism." This chapter is full of factual information. St. Pachomius is credited with having "founded nine convents for men and two for women, the first women's convent having been established about 340 near Tabennisi by his sister Mary."[15] Jo Ann Kay McNamara reports that "Mary, Pachomius' sister, founded a community of women on the opposite bank of the Nile at Tabenisi."[16] In Marrou's version, however, although it is Mary who established the convent, its founding is attributed to Pachomius. Subtly the brother's role is exalted and the sister's diminished.

Swan continues this theme, while taking the argument one step further. She writes that "some [of the fathers] are even credited with founding movements that were actually begun by the women in their lives" noting also that "many of these fathers were educated and supported by strong women. . . many of our church *fathers* became prominent because of *women*."[17] A classic illustration of this phenomenon can be found in the telling of the lives of Basil of Caesarea and his lesser-known sister Macrina.

Norman Tanner follows the story of monastic leadership from Anthony to Pachomius (290–346), who like Anthony lived in Egypt, and thence from Egypt to Asia in the person of Basil of Caesarea, also called Basil the Great (330–379). In Tanner's, as in Marrou's account, the achievements of women monastics are downgraded or overlooked. Although Tanner acknowledges the importance of Basil's sister Macrina, as the "founder of female monasticism in the eastern Church,"[18] her role in the foundation of male monasticism is not mentioned. Yet Joan Morris states quite bluntly: "The Basilian Order was not founded by Saint Basil but by his sister Macrina. It was she who persuaded Basil to abandon the glory of the world. For four years he lived a monastic life under her guidance, giving himself to working on the land and toiling with his hands."[19] Basil's Rule is still today the basic monastic Rule for the Orthodox Church.

Macrina was born in 327, the eldest of ten children. Included among her younger brothers were Basil of Caesarea, Gregory of Nyssa, and Peter of Sebaste. It was Gregory, four years her junior, who wrote the story of her life. Gregory gives us a firsthand account of the transforming influence that Macrina had on Basil. In the following excerpt, the girl referred to is Macrina.

> The great Basil, brother of the girl we have been speaking about, came back from the school where he had been trained for a long time in the discipline of rhetoric. Although when she took him in hand he was monstrously conceited about his skill in rhetoric, contemptuous of every high reputation and exalted beyond the leading lights of the province by his self-importance, so swiftly did she win him to the ideal of philosophy that he renounced worldly appearance, showed contempt for the admiration of rhetorical ability and went over of his own accord to this active life of manual labour, preparing for himself by means of his complete poverty a way of life which would tend without impediment towards virtue.[20]

Kevin Corrigan, who translated Gregory's account of Macrina, tells us that "Gregory. . . calls her his teacher (*didaskalos*)" and that when Peter was born, Macrina personally took his education in hand and became everything for the child: "father, teacher, guide, mother."[21] Gregory records some of Marina's teachings in *On the Soul and the Resurrection* (380) in which, in classical style, Macrina ponders the nature of the soul and what happens after death. Intellectually gifted and well educated, above all in the Bible, Macrina was often referred to as simply "the Teacher."

Discussing the significance of the role of "teacher" in relation to St. Patrick, Thomas O'Loughlin comments that today few would give prominence to teaching in a list of church ministries.

> But in the early centuries of Christianity the teacher, as someone with a vocation and skill, was seen as one of the most dignified of ministers—indeed, being a teacher was seen as the primary occupation of bishops. For Patrick and his contemporaries, to be called as a teacher was to participate in the action of Christ by which Christ made his light known and so made the Father visible.[22]

If we take the view that Hild was not merely responsible for the education of those in her monastery, but was herself a teacher, then it is possible to find striking similarities between the life of Macrina and the life of Hild. We might argue that both were "Teacher," and in this respect both were accorded prominence on a par with bishops. As teachers, both were engaged in the primary work of the episcopacy. If we take the view that Hild herself did not teach, but merely determined what should be taught and to whom, nonetheless the striking fact remains that both Hild and Macrina were directly responsible for the education of several future bishops.

In Macrina's case, the future bishops she taught were her own brothers, St. Basil of Caesarea, St. Gregory of Nyssa, and St. Peter of Sebaste. All three acknowledged her as the primary influence in their theological education. All three were recognized as saints, and Gregory and Basil, especially, were to be revered as two of the most outstanding theologians of the early Church.[23] Furthermore Gregory of Nazianzus[24] and Eustathius of Sebaste, two other renowned "fathers" of the Eastern Church, were among those who came under Macrina's sphere of influence. Under her direction and impetus, they advanced toward Christian perfection.

Like Hild, Macrina was the head of a complex community, at the heart of which she formed and nurtured the monastic way of life. On the family estate in Annisa, Pontus, not far from the Black Sea, Macrina "lived with her household as one in Christ: servants and slaves treated as equals. She wore the same clothing, slept in a similar type of bed, made do with the minimum of necessities of life, and shared a table for meals."[25] Manual labor was highly prized in the community, psalms were prayed throughout the day, and the community came together occasionally for shared worship in the Church. Like Hild, Macrina was known to be an excellent administrator, skillfully managing resources in times of famine.

Corrigan tells us that "in Gregory's portrait of his eldest sister the genuinely human face of the great Macrina shines out to us across the centuries. As a result, a major influence in the history of Christianity begins to emerge."[26] Gregory's portrayal of Macrina can be seen as something of a precursor to the way in which Bede would describe Hild as a most precious jewel, a light so bright that it brought splendor to the very borders of Britain.[27]

In the case of Macrina, as in the case of Hild, her holiness, her learning, her teaching abilities, her gifts as spiritual director, her organizational acumen, and the way in which her light shines out across the centuries are endorsed by a key figure in the traditional account of Christianity. Just as Gregory of Nyssa extolled the virtue and powerful influence of a lesser known yet highly significant female figure, so Bede would proclaim the glory of Hild's life.

THE BENEDICTINE RULE

Basil's fourth-century Rule for the order founded largely by his sister Macrina became as we have seen the basic monastic Rule for the Church in the East. For the Benedictine Rule, the Rule that would become standard for the West, the Church would have to wait another two centuries.

Benedict was born the son of a Roman noble in Nursia on the Italian peninsular around the year 480. Having spent his boyhood in Rome, his outlook was necessarily influenced by the strict patriarchal system. Across the entire empire, of course, the notion of male superiority, of male headship, was standard; hence, the need for a community of women to have a nominal head who was male. Yet the patriarchal system that obtained in Rome had been refined to an altogether more comprehensive level.

The focus of Benedict's Rule, reminiscent of Macrina's insistence on manual labor, was on work as the first condition of growth in goodness. Benedict's Rule is usually judged in comparison with the harsh strictures of Anthony and other inhabitants of the Egyptian desert, his rule being less harsh and based on a more realistic appreciation of human nature. Described by Norman Tanner as "a masterly balance of high ideals and understanding of the human condition,"[28] it had the added advantage of being more easily adaptable to a colder northern climate.

Thus, as monasticism spread north, Benedict's Rule proved an ideal template for a basic monastic structure, which could be adapted according to specific local circumstances. It is clear from Bede's writings that he was familiar with Benedict's Rule, which would pretty well dominate the West by the end of the tenth century.[29] Nonetheless although this Rule was influential in seventh-century Anglo-Saxon Britain, it was very much the case that each community would work out the details of its own Rule, each developing its own ethos. Of particular significance for our purposes is the fact that by the seventh century and Hild's entry, against a general background male dominance, the strict hierarchy of the sexes that operated for Benedict had not penetrated monasticism in Anglo-Saxon Britain.

Benedict, like Basil, had a significant sister. In Benedict's case, his sister, Scholastica, was also his twin. Not a great deal is known about Scholastica, though it is likely that she established a monastery for women at Plombariola, about five miles from her brother's famous monastery at Monte Cassino. At any rate, she is considered to be the founder of the Benedictine way of life for women.

The contrast between the way in which Benedict related to Scholastica, when compared to the relationship that Basil, Gregory, and Peter had with their sister Macrina is stark. For a start, it was very much the case that Benedict was the one who directed Scholastica, rather than the other way round. It may well have been, of course, that Benedict was the most competent to give spiritual direction. Yet in all the accounts of their joint lives, there is the underlying assumption that it was in the natural order of things for brother to direct sister, man to direct woman. From what we know of Benedict, it is difficult to imagine that a reverse arrangement would have crossed his mind.

Jo Ann Kay McNamara describes how Benedict's patron, Pope Gregory I, greatly influenced by Benedict's rule, "tried to impose stability and claustration on all monasteries. . . . He banned women from male monasteries and all men but priests and supervised workmen from female communities."[30] So important to Benedict was the separation of the sexes that he ruled that his sister might visit him only once a year, and even then, they would meet at a nearby inn. Scholastica would not be allowed into the monastic grounds. Most famously, the story goes that when Benedict visited her, he refused to stay overnight at her monastery. Even when she was near to death, he refused her pleadings until in answer to Scholastica's prayers, a thunderstorm forced him to remain.

The whole tenor of Benedict's dealings with Scholastica, echoing the unquestioning assumption of subordination female to male, represents an indication of what was to come and what would be the hidden cost of the fateful decision of 664 at the Synod of Whitby to adhere to Roman rather than Irish practices. The story of Macrina and the story of Hild can only hint at what had been part of the tradition up to that time, and what, with some notable exceptions, was to be increasingly lost over the next thirteen hundred years.

NOTES

1. W. H. C. Frend, *The Early Church* (London: SCM, 1991), 189.
2. Frend, *Early Church*, 190.
3. Marrou, "Great Persecution to Medieval Christianity," in *The Christian Centuries: The First Six Hundred Years*, eds. Jean Danielou and Henri Marrou (London: Longman & Todd, 1978), 270.
4. Bamber Gascoigne, *Christianity: A History* (New York: Carroll & Graf, 2003), 29.
5. Julie Ann Smith, *Ordering Women's Lives, Ordering Women's Lives: Penitentials and Nunnery Rules in the Early Medieval West* (Aldershot, UK: Ashgate Publishing, 2001), 111–12.
6. Laura Swan, *The Forgotten Desert Mothers: Sayings, Lives, and Stories of Early Christian Women* (Mahwah, NJ: Paulist Press, 2001), 8.
7. Swan, *Forgotten Desert Mothers*, 8.
8. Frend, *Early Church*, 193.
9. Swan, *Forgotten Desert Mothers*, 8.
10. Swan, *Forgotten Desert Mothers*, 3.
11. Marrou, "Great Persecution to Medieval Christianity," 277–78.
12. Marrou, "Great Persecution to Medieval Christianity," 377.
13. Swan, *Forgotten Desert Mothers*, 3
14. Women were routinely portrayed by (male) ascetics in the guise of the devil, tempting them to sexual sin.
15. Marrou, "Great Persecution to Medieval Christianity," 275.
16. Jo Ann Kay McNamara, *Sisters in Arms* (Cambridge, MA: Harvard University Press, 1996), 70.
17. Swan, *Forgotten Desert Mothers*, 3
18. Norman Tanner, *New Short History of the Catholic Church* (London: Bloomsbury, 2014), 37.
19. Joan Morris, *Against Nature and God* (London: Mowbrays, 1973), 13–14.
20. Gregory, Bishop of Nyssa. Corrigan, Kevin (translator) "Saint Macrina: The Hidden Face Behind the Tradition" in *Vox Benedictina: A Journal of Translations from Monastic Sources* 5, no. 1 (1988): 13–43. *The Life of Macrina* by Gregory Bishop of Nyssa, translated by Kevin Corrigan of St. Gregor's Vita Sancta Macrina. By permission of Peregrina Publishers. http://monasticmatrix.osu.edu/cartularium/life-macrina-gregory-bishop-nyssa/. Accessed November 2, 2017.
21. Corrigan, "Saint Macrina," 13–43.
22. Thomas O'Loughlin, *Celtic Theology*, 40.
23. Gregory's and Basil's individual reflections on the Holy Spirit were hugely influential in the development of the doctrine of the Trinity after the Council of Nicea

in 325, and both Gregory and Basil were staunch defenders of the teachings of Nicea in the face of the Arian attacks.

24. Gregory of Nazianzus is commonly associated with Gregory of Nyssa and Basil, and the three together are referred to simply as "the Cappadocians."

25. Swan, *Forgotten Desert Mothers*, 129

26. Corrigan, "Saint Macrina," 13–43.

27. Bede, *Ecclesiastical History*, IV.23 245–46; Beda, *Historia Ecclesiastica* IV. 21 [23] CLIII.

28. Tanner, *New Short History*, 78.

29. Tanner, *New Short History*, 78.

30. McNamara, *Sisters in Arms*, 100.

Chapter Three

The Celts, Ireland, and Saint Patrick

Following the high point of desert monasticism in the fourth century, the ascetic life spread from Egypt, Syria, and Asia Minor to Western and Northern Europe in the early fifth century. By the beginning of the seventh century, the Irish had wholeheartedly embraced monasticism and developed their own distinctive practices. In many ways, Irish monastic life resembled monastic life in the Egyptian desert and the Middle East. We know that Irish monasteries had access to books that originated there. Meanwhile, as we saw in the last chapter, in the first half of the sixth century, a distinctly Roman strand of monasticism had emerged with the outstandingly influential person of Benedict of Nursia.

Thus, there developed in western Europe a Roman way of doing things and an Irish or Celtic way of doing things. It is in this period when Roman and Celtic ways prevailed in Britain side by side that Hild exercised her various ministries. The history here is complex because there were no rigid boundaries between the different traditions. Rather by the seventh century, there was an ongoing borrowing of ideas as members of Anglo-Saxon royal families traveled freely between Britain and Gaul with its Celtic ancestry, combined, as we will see, with Roman leanings. Meanwhile, missionaries were constantly on the move across Britain and Gaul, the Italian peninsular, the Holy Land, Syria, and the Egyptian desert. In matters such as scriptural interpretation, theological study, and liturgical and penitential practices, the Celtic/Irish appropriation of Christianity drew on what was already there in the Roman and Middle Eastern traditions. It then fed its own insights and practices into the Roman tradition, effecting a mutual exchange.

AN ELUSIVE CELTIC PAST

The term "Celtic," will recur frequently in the telling of Hild's story, not least because one of the most important events in Hild's life was the hosting of the Synod of Whitby in 664. Essentially what had to be decided at this Synod was whether the Northumbrian Church should embrace Roman or Celtic practices, both of which were operating alongside each other at the time.

In this context, the Celtic Church in Britain is sometimes used synonymously with the Irish Church. In the sixth and seventh centuries, the Irish/Celts were not confined to what we now know as Ireland but inhabited an area known as Dalriada (Dál Riata) based around Argyll in western Scotland.[1] It was from there in Iona that Aidan had set out for Lindisfarne to walk the byways of Northumbria spreading the Gospel as he went.

The term "Celtic" has a complicated history, which has been interpreted variously at different times and by different scholars. As I sought to pin down this elusive concept, I repeatedly came across warnings against misinterpretation—what should *not* be understood when the term was used. In particular there seemed to be two concerns: that what is now referred to as Celtic art should not be identified with the art of the ancient Celts and that the Celts of Dalriada should not be thought of as "ethnic" Celts. Then as reading material for a flight to Jordan, where I was able to experience the type of desert landscape to which the early ascetics were drawn, I picked up a recent publication by Alice Roberts called *The Celts: Search for a Civilization.*

Roberts acknowledges that the Celts prove difficult to define. The traditional view is that the Celtic "heartland" was an area in central Europe that included southern Germany, Switzerland, and eastern France.[2] Roberts thinks that the Celts predated even these ancient civilizations. Gravestones have been found in the Algarve in Portugal dating from the very start of the Iron Age, around 800 BCE. The use of the Celtic language itself in all probability goes back much further. The Celts were dispersed, following the death of Alexander the Great in 323 BCE and the breakup of the Macedonian empire. In the turmoil they migrated into Greece, into Asia Minor, and into Egypt.

It is not possible to know whether the Celts of the Diaspora shared an ethnic identity with the Celts of Central Europe. Until research further advances our knowledge, Roberts considers it reasonable to think of the Celts as "the people of central and western Europe, who do seem to have been united by some aspects of culture—most importantly, perhaps, by language."[3]

The Greeks and Romans used the word "Celts" to refer to those peoples of central and western Europe whom they regarded as barbarians. Thus, from the fourth century BCE, the names "Celts" and "Galatians" were used interchangeably. The Romans called the whole group "Galli" or "Gauls." By the first century BCE, a distinction had been made between the two groups by Diodorus of Sicily. Then Julius Caesar distinguishes the Celts as those who inhabited one of the three territories of Gaul.

Gaul was by then a mighty power, which Julius Caesar was determined to gain for the Roman Empire. Versingetorix, leader of the Celtic Averni tribe, formed alliances with the other tribes to become the supreme war leader of the whole of Gaul. In the end, the might of the Celts was crushed in the Gallic wars when Versingetorix was defeated by Caesar in 52 BCE. Gaul then leaned toward Rome, rather than the other Celtic tribes in Central and western Europe and adopted many Roman practices. With the fall of the Roman Empire, by the early sixth century, the Romans had lost control of Gaul, but much of Roman culture survived. Thus, when Hild's sister joined a monastery in Gaul/Frankia, and Hild considered whether to join her there, Gaul enjoyed a combined Celtic and Roman heritage.

When it comes to ancient Britain, the Greeks did not consider that Britons were Celts. Yet, the Roman Tacitus recognized similarities between the peoples of Britain and Ireland, which coincided with similarities to the Celts living on the continent. He identified a linguistic and a religious connection between Gaul and Britain. Given the strong maritime links between Ireland and Britain and the continent, Roberts argues that it was trade networks rather than Celtic invasions that brought Celtic culture to western Europe, including Britain. She is clear that "Britain was far from being a backwater,"[4] and she tentatively comes down on the side of there being what might be called a "Celtic" identity in Britain and Ireland; "the inhabitants of Britain and Ireland did indeed have a cultural identity, which we can perhaps call 'Celtic,' in common with their neighbors in western continental Europe."[5]

HOW IRISH WAS SAINT PATRICK?

Perhaps nothing illustrates how deceptive can be much of what we might think we know about Irish/Celtic history than the fact that Patrick, that towering figure of Irish sainthood, was not himself Irish.

Patrick, patron saint of Ireland, whom one might instinctively associate with Irish practices, was in fact more "Roman" than "Irish." It was the Irish who had enslaved him. We have no exact dates for Patrick, but reckon he was born sometime around the year 400, before or after. According to O'Loughlin's meticulous research, "all we can say is that a fifth-century date for Patrick's mission does not clash with any of the evidence."[6]

There is some debate regarding the exact location of Patrick's birth, but it could well have been one of the little settlements along Hadrian's Wall near

Carlisle.[7] He came from a well-respected clerical family and was proud of the fact that his father was a deacon and his grandfather a priest. Captured in his youth by Irish raiders, Patrick was taken into slavery, and during his years of captivity, he underwent a deep conversion. He escaped and traveled to Gaul, eventually returning to his home, but then felt compelled to return to Ireland to teach Christianity to the Irish.

Ireland had never been part of the Roman Empire, and its aristocracy was pagan at the time of Patrick's mission.[8] Yet evidently some of the Irish population were already Christian because Patrick was sent to be their bishop. We know that Patrick encountered considerable opposition from Christians already in Britain, southern Scotland, and Ireland. As we will see, apart from the warm welcome he received in Kent, Augustine encountered similar opposition from the Christians already in Britain when he was similarly parachuted in with episcopal authority over preexistent Christian communities.

THE GENIUS OF ANCIENT BRITAIN

When it comes to Celtic art, Roberts tells us that it was in the mid-eighteenth century that modern Celtic art was identified as such. It was inspired by the illuminated medieval manuscripts and carved stone crosses of the seventh and eighth centuries.

> Modern Celtic art, with flowing organic lines, stylized animals and complicated knotwork, draws its inspiration largely from the illuminated pages of mediaeval manuscripts and from carved stone crosses. In fact, it's that Christian art of Britain and Ireland in the seventh and eighth centuries AD which was first described—in the mid-eighteenth century—as "Celtic art."

According to Roberts, however, this modern Celtic art is not without a prehistory. Rather it is a "reimagining" of ancient Celtic artwork.

> But it does seem that this mediaeval expression of Celtic art was itself a reimagining of an ancient style.[9]

Many different styles of art flourished in Celtic lands across the centuries, but Roberts tells us that the particular style that is often thought of as "Celtic art" is one that was first identified on the continent at a place called La Tène in what is now Switzerland.[10] Metal objects recovered from La Tène exhibited the swirling patterns characteristic of modern Celtic art. "In the later centuries of the Iron Age in Britain and Ireland [the Iron Age in Britain is reckoned to have ended with the Roman invasion of 43 AD] . . . skilled metalworkers were producing their own interpretations of continental La Tène art."[11]

Roberts tells us that the earliest La Tène artefacts from Britain are two bronze scabbards, one found near Oxford dates from the mid-fourth century BCE and the other from Cambridge dates from the around 300 BCE. Metalworkers in Ireland in the first and second centuries BCE were being inspired by British La Tène objects, as well as by artwork on the continent. In a field near Snettisham in Norfolk, a great hoard of Celtic treasure has been discovered, including a twisted gold neck-ring, known as the Great Torc, one of the most magnificent pieces of jewelry from the Celtic world.

Roberts is at pains to stress the artistic genius and the originality of British metalworkers in the style of La Tène. "There is no way you can look at the British and Irish artwork as a barbaric imitation of a style emanating from a superior civilization."[12] Referring to evidence of mercury or fire-gilding on one of the torc fragments of the Snettisham hoard, Roberts says:

> Once again, we're reminded that Britain was far from being a backwater. The Celts here were culturally and technologically linked to their neighbours on the continent, especially to other Iron Age societies in western Europe—in Belgium, France and Spain. They were part of a much wider community linked by sea trade, on this Atlantic fringe of Europe—and had been throughout the Bronze Age, and even further back, into the Neolithic.[13]

The evidence from Roberts demonstrating that ancient Britain was no barbaric backwater is important for Hild's story in several respects. In a later chapter, I will discuss why the decision was made at the Council of Whitby to adopt Roman rather than Celtic practices. One of the main reasons was that despite the fall of the Roman Empire, Rome was still regarded as an attractive alliance in terms of political power and cultural advancement. To go with the Irish would have been to have risked insignificance in the greater scheme of European allegiances. There was a sense that what had been beyond the outer reaches of the northern extremity of the Roman Empire had always been and would always remain a backwater. It is important to remember that this is the historical narrative of the victors in the struggle for allegiance—the Roman party.

Another reason why it is important to recognize the genius of the people of ancient Britain is because there is a parallel between the way in which the cultural achievements of the Celts in ancient Britain have been disparaged and the way in which the achievements of Anglo-Saxon women, most notably Hild, have been blanketed out under the label "Dark Age Britain." Finally as archaeology continues to uncover the splendors of ancient civilizations previously regarded as backward or "barbaric," so rigorous academic study continues to uncover the significant leadership roles played by women in the first millennium of the Church's history, where traditionally the teaching has been that the absence of leadership roles for women reaches right back to the practice of Christ himself. The very archaeology that uncovers the one historical truth uncovers the other also, as demonstrated by the following example.

CELTIC WOMEN AND STATUS

In 2005, the body of a small child was found near Herbertingen in southern Germany, close to the Bettelbühl stream which runs into the Danube. By the girl's grave, next to the Bettelbühl stream, they found a burial mound containing two women together with magnificent treasures, providing us with "precious insights into the lives, society and culture of the early Celts."[14] Dendrochronological, or "tree-ring," dating revealed that the timber planks forming the chamber were felled in 583 BCE, and that in all likelihood this was the year that one of the bodies, that of a women in her thirties, was buried.

The quantity of gold associated with this body was "astonishing"; the quality of workmanship was "astounding." But for Roberts, the real impact of these objects came when she compared the finds from the burial mound with the finds from the child's grave. "The small fibulae [brooches] had exactly the same pattern as the large ones belonging to the woman in the burial chamber."[15] The jewelry that had been placed on the body of the little girl was like a miniature version of the woman's adornments. The intricately wrought golden brooches in particular were miniature versions of the woman's brooches, suggesting strongly that the two were mother and daughter.

Buried with the mother was a chamfron, a bronze plate that would have been attached over the front of a horse's head. The woman had been a horse rider. This fact together with the quality and quantity of gold artefacts demonstrated that the woman was among the elite of early Celtic society. From these graves, we learn that in southwest Germany, the higher echelons of early Celtic society were not exclusively reserved for men. "And not only was it possible for a woman to possess such high status, her children—including daughters—would inherit that status."[16]

Even more pertinently, there seems to have been what Roberts calls "ambivalence towards gender," which meant that it was possible for women to become leaders of men and to achieve the highest status in Celtic society.[17] In the north of Britain, there was a time in the mid-first century CE when Queen Cartimandua led a combined force of Celtic tribes that were loyal to Rome. Cartimandua appears to have ruled in her own right rather than through marriage. The most well-known example of a British warrior-queen is of course Boudica, who led the British rebellion against the Romans in 60 CE. Crucially, Boudica was described as riding into battle wearing a cloak and a gold torc. There is no hint in the description that it was unusual for a woman to wear a torc, the symbol of power associated with warriors or gods. Indeed on the continent torcs have been found together with female human remains.

Roberts's research is designed to uncover a lost civilization. In the process, it throws up important clues to the role of women in Celtic society. The stark contrast between this and the role of women in Roman society shows what might have been had Celtic rather than Roman attitudes prevailed. More importantly, however, it gives strong support to the argument that in the seventh century in Anglo-Saxon England and in Gaul/Frankia, women worked alongside men in positions of authority and leadership. In the countries of Europe with their own Celtic heritage, evangelized by the Irish missionaries, this was also the case. As in society so in the Church, we glimpse the way in which the Christian Church *did* organize its male and female workforce, before Roman patriarchy extinguished a once-legitimate way of living and spreading the Gospel message.

IRELAND: A QUITE DIFFERENT SITUATION

The situation in Ireland was quite different from that in mainland Europe. In other parts of the Western Church, though fragmented, structures of Roman governance survived. As MacCulloch describes the situation in Ireland, and the difficulties it posed:

> The island had no central authority, or (importantly) any memory of one, and instead there was a large collection of groupings (*tuatha*) headed by dynastic leaders. . . . No Christian episcopate had previously had to cope with anything like this since the Church had first formed its alliance with the powerful. . . . In puzzling out how the situation might become fruitful, the bishops realized that the Church could be rooted in Irish society by founding monasteries and nunneries.[18]

As a solution, this was to have profound implications for the Irish Church and its own missions to mainland Britain and mainland Europe.

The Irish Church found itself free from the constraints of the strictly patriarchal Roman system, and it would seem that this was the case both before and after Patrick. After Patrick, Christianity flourished, and within two centuries, another great Irish saint, Columba, had founded his several monasteries. Sometime in the 580s, Columba left the island of Ireland for Iona, a small island off the west coast of Scotland, where he reconstructed a monastery that was already there. The monastic center of Iona flourished, and its mission would extend to include all the north of Britain as far as the Orkneys. It was from Iona that Aidan, around the year 655, set out to convert the Anglo-Saxons by founding a monastery on the island of Lindisfarne off the coast of Northumberland. It was the missionaries who succeeded Patrick, the likes of Columba and Aidan, who maintained what we might think of as the distinctively Celtic or Irish forms of Christian life.

Building on common theological foundations, the Irish developed their own ways of doing things, some of which would feed into Roman practices. An obvious example here is the Irish practice of frequent and private confession. Other differences, notably the dating of Easter and the correct tonsure for male monastics, were to be settled at the Synod of Whitby in 664, hosted by Hild. On the surface, neither issue seemed to impinge greatly on the lives of female monastics. There were no strictly theological disagreements to be settled and certainly none to trouble women in particular. Nonetheless, the price that women were to pay for decisions such as the one at Whitby would be a heavy one. When to celebrate Easter, what sort of haircut was suitable for a man in a religious order, these were questions regarding how society should be ordered. Not mentioned, but very much at issue, was that in Roman eyes, no matter how society was ordered, there was no place for women in the public sphere. Under cover of the desire for unity in Christian practice, the subordination of women entailed in Roman patriarchy would eventually harden into a divinely inspired teaching.

When Aidan and Hild met, Celtic ways intermingled with Anglo-Saxon ways, only to be confronted by Roman ways which in that one crucial area of patriarchal governance would eventually win out over both. The lot of women in the Celtic and in the Anglo-Saxon world was more favorable toward women than their lot in the Roman world, where their status in the strictly patriarchal system was comprehensively subordinate.

Roman society was rigidly hierarchal and patriarchal, yet free women enjoyed considerable rights in the law, including the right of equal inheritance. Certain women, wives and mothers of emperors for example, could wield considerable power, but their main duties were in the household, and they were excluded from political office. Although a small minority of women actively participated in the religious ceremonies and festivals, significantly they were not allowed to participate in ritual sacrifice. In Celtic society, by contrast, women had been accustomed to a political role, often as war leaders, and naturally fell into leadership roles in matters of religion.

Thus, when the Roman way prevailed at the Synod of Whitby in 664, in one sense it was nothing essentially theological or doctrinal that was lost. What was lost was the legitimate, public role that women like Hild fulfilled—

a loss that could have been restored, had it not hardened into the theological imperative. As patriarchal structures squeezed out more women-friendly arrangements, the stories of women in the Christian tradition came to be included merely to fill out the background to the perceived main action, undertaken by the men. Ultimately, of course this did have an impact on theology because the exclusion of women from public ministry came to be presented as the unfailing tradition of the Church, and women were excluded on supposedly theological grounds from ministries that they had legitimately held.[19]

NOTES

1. Roman writers called the Irish the "Scotti," and it is from this appellation that Scotland gained its name. Barbara Yorke, *The Conversion of Britain 600–800*, 51–52.
2. Alice Roberts, *The Celts: Search for a Civilization* (Great Britain: Heron Books, 2016), 83–84.
3. Roberts, *The Celts*, 4.
4. Roberts, *The* Celts, 120.
5. Roberts, *The Celts*, 39.
6. O'Loughlin, *Celtic Theology*, 27.
7. Diarmaid MacCulloch, *A History of Christianity* (London: Penguin, 2010), 330, 1044 n.15; Wood, *In Search*, 42.
8. See Cusack, *The Rise of Christianity*, 65. Cusack points out the strange fact that Patrick was made a bishop because bishops were generally only sent to existing Christian communities. Certainly, Bede records, that Palladius was sent to "the Irish who believed in Christ." Bede, *Ecclesiastical History*, II.13 60. Cusack also suggests that Patrick and Palladius, who preceded Patrick as bishop, may in fact have been one and the same person.
9. Roberts, *The Celts*, 5–6.
10. Roberts, *The Celts*, 107–8.
11. Roberts, *The Celts*, 124.
12. Roberts, *The Celts*, 112.
13. Roberts, *The Celts*, 120.
14. Roberts, *The Celts*, 69.
15. Roberts, *The Celts*, 75–76
16. Roberts, *The Celts*, 83.
17. Roberts, *The Celts*, 195.
18. MacCulloch, *A History of Christianity*, 331.
19. When pressed on the matter of women's ordination in 2018, Pope Francis referred to the 1994 document *Ordinatio Sacerdotalis*, the apostolic Letter of John Paul II to the Bishops of the Catholic Church on reserving priestly ordination to men. This document states that "priestly ordination, which hands on the office entrusted by Christ to his Apostles of teaching, sanctifying and governing the faithful, has in the Catholic church from the beginning always been reserved to men alone."

Chapter Four

The Augustinian Mission

Toward the very close of the sixth century, Pope Gregory I in Rome, also known as Gregory the Great, sent an Italian monk called Augustine to Britain to convert the Anglo-Saxons. Augustine's mission is of particular significance for our story in several respects. First Paulinus, who as we have seen was to play a significant part in Hild's conversion, was sent by Gregory to join Augustine in his mission. Secondly it was Augustine, at Pope Gregory's insistence, who was the main power behind the drive to draw Britain into the Roman system of Church governance.

It was this drive toward the Romanization of Britain's Christians, beginning with Gregory and Augustine, that would culminate almost seventy years later in the momentous decision of the Synod of Whitby to comply with certain Roman practices. That synod, of course, was hosted by Hild. The decision was momentous, not so much because of the adoption of the Roman tonsure or the Roman calendar, but for the adoption as if by stealth of the patriarchy inherent in the Roman system itself. As the last chapter has already argued, the uncompromising form of patriarchy inherent in the Roman system would have a devastating impact on the status of Christian women as it steadily penetrated all parts of the western Church.

Augustine's mission is also significant insofar as it provides a further example of the way in which the contribution of women has come to be downgraded in the telling of history. We have it on the authority of Gregory himself that Bertha, Queen of Kent, was not only instrumental in supporting Augustine's mission—even essential to his mission getting off the ground at all—but also that Bertha herself might be regarded as ultimately responsible for the conversion of England. Yet, once again, in the traditional account of Christian history a powerful and influential woman receives mention only as a supporting character, rather than as an agent in her own right.

This chapter details the way in which the Augustinian mission made little progress in Augustine's lifetime. It was hampered by a certain rigidity, specifically by a determination to impose a system of governance that took little account of the reality on the ground—a rigidity that the Roman Church has yet fully to overcome. The first section of this chapter will consider the different roles of Augustine and of Bertha with regard to that part of the reconversion of England that had its origins in Kent.

BERTHA OF KENT

Pope Gregory in 596 and 597 sent Augustine to convert the English. But why was Augustine sent twice? Having set out in 596, Augustine and his party were not only afraid of the Channel crossing but were greatly alarmed by stories of the ferocious disposition of Britain's pagan inhabitants. Furthermore, none of the missionary party could speak the language of the Anglo-Saxons. Fear got the better of them, and they turned back.

Gregory however was insistent that the mission should go ahead and sent them once again. This time they hired interpreters in Frankia (roughly what is now France and what in Roman times was part of the larger territory of Gaul). Augustine and his fellow monks then crossed to Kent, *where they were met by an already well-established Christian presence*. We know that when Augustine crossed the Channel, he received a warm welcome and significant support from Christians already at Canterbury in Kent. And there can be no doubt that this well-established Christian presence centered on Bertha, Queen of Kent. As Henri Marrou records, "The missionaries found their path well prepared, thanks to the influence of a Catholic Frankish princess, Queen Bertha, who was the wife of Ethelbert, King of Kent."[1]

Thus, Bertha was central to the welcome Augustine received because it was she who as a condition of her marriage had a Catholic bishop[2] in her entourage. Relevant to our inquiry is whether Bertha was merely the passive instrument through which a Christian presence was established in Kent, or whether she herself was active in promoting the Christian faith. If, as I shall argue, Bertha was herself an active player, then how significant was the part she played?

When Augustine's party arrived at Thanet in Kent, Ethelbert, the King of Kent, ordered that they should be supplied with whatever they needed. He was already familiar with Christianity through his wife, who was given in marriage by her parents on condition that she would be able to practice her faith unhindered.[3] Not unusually for the time, Bertha is regarded as something of a commodity, passed from her parents to her future husband, with conditions attached. The active participants in this arrangement were her parents who set the conditions, among them Bertha's freedom to practice her faith, and Ethelbert who agreed to those conditions. Doubtless this is how the marriage contract was drawn up. What is not clear from Bede's account is to what extent, if any, Bertha herself was behind her parents' insistence on her freedom to practice the Catholic faith. Furthermore, it tells us nothing about how enthusiastically she availed herself of the freedom accorded her.

Stephanie Hollis in *Anglo-Saxon Women and the Church* gives a detailed study of Anglo-Saxon royalty, including the way in which king and queen were understood as "rulers together." The role of queen was specific, influential, and authoritative.[4] And as we saw in chapter 1, royal women in the early Middle Ages were powerful agents of evangelization. We already know from chapter 1 that Bertha's own daughter, Ethelburga, upon her marriage to the pagan Edwin, followed her mother's practice of taking among her entourage her own Catholic Chaplain, in this instance Paulinus—the very Paulinus who was instrumental in the conversion of Hild. We have also seen that it was common for a Catholic wife to practice her faith independently of her husband.

Bertha herself was the great-granddaughter of the hugely influential Saint Clotilde. Clotilde was the second wife of Clovis I, who by his death in 511, had greatly expanded the territory of the Franks and had brought the whole of the extended Frankia under his sole rule. It is Clotilde who is credited with the conversion of her husband. Gregory of Tours in his *History of the Franks* reports that Clotilde had refused to rest until her husband renounced paganism in favor of Christianity. Gregory puts into Clotilde's mouth the standard argument in favor of conversion:

> What have Mars and Mercury ever done for anyone? . . . they were certainly not worthy of being called divine, You ought instead to worship Him who created at a word and out of nothing heaven, an earth, the sea and all that therein is, who made the sun to shine, who lit the sky with stars.[5]

We hear Clotilde's voice preaching the gospel to her husband, and by implication, to the nation of the Franks. Clotilde can be seen as the first in a great line of female descendants credited with the conversion of their pagan husbands and therefore, their people to Christianity. As the first of the Germanic kings to convert to Christianity and the first sole ruler of Frankia, Clotilde's husband Clovis was a highly significant figure. Yet arguably more fundamental to the future of Christian Europe was Clotilde herself.

This pattern of the high-born Christian woman as the prime evangelizer who brings about the conversion of an entire tribe or kingdom is such a common feature of early medieval history that on these grounds alone it is not unreasonable to suppose that Bertha, Clotilde's great-granddaughter, far from being a passive convenience was in fact the prime mover in the conversion of Kent. As will become apparent, this supposition is further supported by a letter written to Bertha by Pope Gregory himself.

Before leaving Clotilde, however, it is interesting to note that there are many variants to her name. Among these variants is "Clothilda," incorporating the German element "hild," meaning "battle," which was to be the name give to the woman who can indirectly perhaps lay claim to being the greatest of Clotilde's descendants, the great Hild (or in its later Romanized form Hilda) of Streanaeshalch, or Whitby, the subject of this book. Thus, in more ways than one, Clotilde, the driving force behind the conversion of her country, can be seen to prefigure Hild, whose brilliance was to light the whole of Britain.

To return to Bertha and the conversion of Kent. Bede tells us that Augustine and his company assembled in an old church, dedicated to Saint Martin, which had been built during the Roman occupation of Britain. It was in this church that Queen Bertha went to pray.[6] Bertha was from Tours, and it is quite possible that, following the evangelizing zeal of her great-grandmother, Bertha was the driving force behind the restoration of the old Roman church just outside the ancient walls of Canterbury. This church still stands today; it is the oldest church in continuous use in the English-speaking world. On the south wall of the chancel, it is possible to see the stone lintel of the original door through which Bertha would have passed. (See figures 4.1, 4.2, and 4.3.) It is likely that Bertha was responsible for its dedication to Saint Martin. At any rate, the fact of her worshipping in this church together with her entourage (see figure 4.4) cannot but have been a factor in the establishment of a thriving Christian presence in the Canterbury area. And we know that it was from this thriving base that Roman Christianity would spread northward and eventually cover England in its entirety.

We know that Pope Gregory had high regard for Bertha's work of evangelization. In a letter to Bertha written in June 601, Gregory foresees that the conversion of the English, when it comes about, will be attributed to Bertha; and this on two accounts: First it will be her reward for the welcome and support she has already extended to Augustine on his arrival in Kent.

> For indeed our most beloved son Laurentius the presbyter, and Peter the monk, have brought us word on their return to us how your Glory has exhibited itself towards our most reverend brother and fellow-bishop Augustine, and how great succor and what charity you have bestowed upon him. And we bless Almighty God, who has been mercifully pleased to reserve the conversion of the nation of the Angli for your reward.

Figure 4.1. St. Martin's Church, Canterbury, where Queen Bertha worshipped. It is the oldest church in continuous use in the English-speaking world.
Photograph by David Inman.

Figure 4.2. The outer wall showing the stone lintel of the original Roman doorway, through which Queen Bertha and then St. Augustine would have passed.
Photograph by David Inman.

Figure 4.3. The original square-headed doorway, and a later rounded arch with a statue of Queen Bertha.
Photograph by David Inman.

Secondly the conversion of England will be attributed to Bertha through the conversion of her husband, which she has yet to effect. And here Gregory compares Bertha to Helena, the mother of Constantine—and of course it was Helena's influence through the Emperor Constantine (d. 337) that brought about the conversion of the whole Roman Empire. The letter continues:

> For, as through Helena of illustrious memory, the mother of the most pious Emperor Constantine, He kindled the hearts of the Romans into Christian faith, so we trust that He works in the nation of the Angli through the zeal of your Glory.

It is true that Gregory goes on to admonish Bertha for being slow to convert her husband:

> And indeed you ought before now, as being truly a Christian, to have inclined the heart of our glorious son, your husband, by the good influence of your prudence, to follow for the weal of his kingdom and of his own soul, the faith which you profess, to the end that for him, and for the conversion of the whole nation through him, fit retribution might accrue to you in the joys of heaven. For seeing, as we have said, that your Glory is both fortified by a right faith and instructed in letters, this should have been to you neither slow of accomplishment nor difficult.

Figure 4.4. Bertha at worship, from a stain-glass window of St. Martin's Church.
Photograph by David Inman.

Yet it is plain even as he admonishes her, that he attributes the future conversion of the English to the "zeal" of her "devotion"—seeing the conversion of England as her "great sacrifice to the almighty Lord."

> Wherefore strengthen by continual hortation the mind of your glorious husband in love of the Christian faith; let your solicitude infuse into him increase of love for God, and so kindle his heart even for the fullest conversion of the nation subject to him that both he may offer, out of the zeal of your devotion, a great sacrifice to the almighty Lord, and that the things related of you may both grow and be in all ways proved to be true: for your good deeds are known not only among the Romans, who have prayed earnestly for your life, but also through divers places, and have come even to the ears of the most serene prince of Constantinople.[7]

Thus, according to Gregory, Bertha's fame had spread throughout the Latin-speaking world and beyond to the very highest echelons of the Eastern Church. Yet while Bertha and her chaplain tend to receive but the briefest of mentions, it is standard practice to attribute to Augustine the introduction of Christianity into Kent and thence the whole of England.

A FLAWED PLAN

There can be no doubt that Augustine received welcome and support from Kent. It would be a mistake, however, to think that welcome was extended from further afield. The historian George Trevelyan says that "Augustine did not convert England. He converted Kent, founded the see of Canterbury, and made it the solid base for the subsequent spread of Roman Christianity over the whole island."[8] In Augustine's lifetime, the final victory of Roman rule over the whole of the church in England was by no means a foregone conclusion.

What is so interesting, however, because it is a pattern to be repeated, is that the plan to be implemented was so completely out of sync with the reality on the ground. As MacCulloch says:

> He [Gregory] envisaged his new Church rebuilding the structures of the old imperial provinces of Britannia Inferior and Superior, so there would be metropolitan bishops in the former colonial capitals of Londinium (London) and Eboracum (York), each with an apostolic flock of twelve bishops: all very tidy, and two hundred years out of date.[9]

Britannia Inferior was the name given to the more northern part of England, and Britannia Superior was the name for the southern part and Wales.

Thus, the Bishop of York was to have primacy in the north, and the Bishop of London in the south and Wales.

York, or Eboracum as the Romans called it, had indeed been a place of strategic importance in the year 71, when it was founded as a fortress of the Ninth Legion. The Emperor Constantius had died there, and it was there in 306 that Constantine had been declared Emperor. By the year 314, Eboracum had its own bishop, who along with two other bishops from England, was summoned by the Emperor Constantine to the Council of Arles in 314. The city reverted to paganism sometime after that, and it would not be until roughly twenty years after Augustine's arrival in Kent that we would hear of another person taking on the duties of the bishop of York. That person would be Paulinus.

We also know that it was not until the Synod hosted by Hild at Whitby in 664 that the whole of Northumbria, which included York, would undertake to follow Roman practices. Yet it was with London and with the Welsh, who incidentally were not restricted to what is now Wales, that the plan really came unstuck.

LONDON

London or Londinium, as it was called as part of imperial Rome, had been burnt to the ground by Boudica and her army in the year 60. After the defeat of Boudica it had been lavishly rebuilt reflecting the layout of a Roman town. By the middle of the second century it had replaced Colchester as the capital of Britain. However in the third century, along with the Roman Empire as a whole, it began to decline, and in 407, the last of the Roman soldiers stationed in London were recalled to Rome.

Thus, by 596, when Augustine first set out to implement Gregory's plan for Britain, London had been pretty well abandoned as a center of any importance for nearly two hundred years. Much reduced in circumstances, it had become a prize to be fought over continually by the kingdoms of Essex, Mercia, and Kent. It is apparent that as Gregory planned the Roman-style structures he sought to erect for the Church in Britain, he had little knowledge of the structures already in place.

Nonetheless in 604, Augustine consecrated Mellitus to preach among the East Saxons, that is to say, in Essex. This was at a time when London was the capital city of Essex. Thus, for a short period, London was a Christian center. However, when the Christian king Sabert of the East Saxons died, London reverted to paganism.

Bede tells the story that Sabert's three sons were demanding to receive the communion bread from Mellitus, believing that it had strengthening powers.

Mellitus refused this demand until they were willing to be baptized, as their father had been. This they refused, and when Mellitus stood firm, they drove him and the other missionaries out of London. In all probability some of the inhabitants remained Christian, but paganism was to be the dominant force in London and Essex until the reconversion to Christianity by Cedd in 653. Not until the twelfth century, with the Angevin monarchs, would London again become a capital city.

ROMANO-BRITISH CHRISTIANS AND THE WELSH BISHOPS

It has to be remembered that as well as Gallic Christianity, newly arrived with Bertha, and despite the invasions of pagan Germanic tribes, there remained in Britain many Christians who owed their faith to Britain's time as part of the Roman Empire. Thus, when Gregory sent Augustine, there were already in Britain Christians who owed their faith to having been part of the empire, which had fully converted to Christianity by the end of the fourth century. These remaining Christians were "the Welsh," although as already indicated, they were not confined to what is now Wales but occupied various territories in southern England. In all likelihood, there were still British Christians who owed their faith to the time of the Empire in the north as well.

Historians had assumed that Romano-British Christians had been pushed back westward by the invading Germanic tribes. Christians certainly flourished in Wales, while in Ireland and the west coast of Scotland, the Church had been greatly rejuvenated by Patrick and his successors. MacCulloch, however, provides the more recent historical consensus when he writes that "the British population had not been wiped out or driven to the far west. . . but had stayed put, while proving rather more able and willing to learn Anglo-Saxon than the Anglo-Saxons were capable of learning Celtic languages. . . . Many of these Britons would be Christian to some degree: Christianity did not come as a startling novelty to the inhabitants of lowland England in 597. So what," asks MacCulloch, "was different about Augustine's mission? Chiefly, but crucially, its emphasis on Roman obedience."[10]

After the withdrawal of the Roman army, these Romano-British Christians, that is to say, "the Welsh," had developed independently of the Roman traditions in mainland Europe. Augustine came to assert Roman or papal authority over them and to bring them into conformity with Roman practices. Augustine's attempts to win these Christians for a Roman-style Christianity proved singularly unsuccessful.

It must be stressed at this point that the Welsh Christians, though they rejected Augustine's overtures, were not basically hostile to Rome as the leading city of the Christian world. It was more the case that they had simply lost touch as a result of the Anglo-Saxon invasions. Nor did they reject the precedence of the pope as the first among Christian bishops. What they did not want was to be put in the position where their only option would be a blind obedience to the will of Rome as determined by Augustine.[11]

Gregory himself was not intent on bringing the Welsh bishops into strict obedience and conformity. He was far more tolerant of diversity of practice than later Romanizers like Wilfrid. In any case, he was probably unaware that there still were Christians in Britain. Gregory's aim was to convert the heathen nations into Christian ones, setting up episcopal structures over which he would naturally have jurisdiction. In this way, he planned to build up once more an empire that could preserve European civilization. And this time, the empire would be based on the sure rock of Christ and his Church. Bertram Colgrave puts it like this:

> Gregory may well have had in his mind the vague outline of a plan which could, if it succeeded, save both Rome and civilized Europe as he knew it. He saw the mighty world empire of Rome tottering to its fall, but instead of sitting by and waiting for the end, he conceived the idea of winning the young and vigorous nations for Christ and establishing a new Roman Empire, this time an empire based on the rock foundation of Christ and the Church. He saw Rome ruling a spiritual kingdom won, not by the sword but the tireless efforts of missionaries making dangerous and arduous journeys to the uttermost parts of the known world and risking their lives among heathen peoples.[12]

From Bede we have details of two notable and, from Augustine's point of view, unsuccessful confrontations with Romano-British or Welsh Bishops. Augustine was attempting to engage in a joint mission with them which he Augustine would lead. The very fact that Augustine was attempting a joint mission is evidence that the Welsh Bishops were in good standing with Gregory, once he was aware of their existence. Bede tells us that Augustine "summoned the bishops and teachers of the nearest British province to a conference."

At this conference, which probably took place in Gloucestershire by the river Severn in 602, the Welsh were not persuaded to abandon their own customs in favor of what was being presented to them as the universal practice of Christianity. First they wanted to consult with their wider community before committing themselves on such an important matter, but they did agree to a second and larger meeting.

This second meeting was attended by seven bishops and "many very learned men," mostly from the famous monastery at Clwyd, in the northern part of Wales. Bede recounts that they were advised by "a wise and prudent hermit" that they should judge Augustine by his demeanor. "If Augustine is meek and lowly in heart, it shows that he bears the yoke of Christ himself, and offers it to you. But if he is haughty and unbending, then he is not of God, and they should not listen to him. They should arrange for Augustine to arrive first and see whether, upon their arrival, he stood to greet them, or whether he remained seated."

Augustine duly arrived first and when the Welsh contingent made their entrance he remained seated. Immediately they became angry and accused him of pride, rejecting his arguments out of hand, "saying among themselves that if he would not rise to greet them in the first instance, he would have even less regard for them once they submitted to his authority."[13] Augustine, his mission thwarted, responded with a threat.

THE RIGIDITY OF ROMAN RULE

Setting aside the fact that Gregory's plan was two hundred years out of date, and the fact that there were already bishops in Britain, what we discover is a Roman way of operating that would be repeated well into the twentieth century. Bede records the content of a letter that Gregory sent to Augustine with a party, which included Paulinus and Mellitus, to assist Augustine's mission. In the letter Gregory says: "You are to consecrate twelve bishops in different places, who will be subject to your jurisdiction: the bishop of the city of London will thenceforward be consecrated by his own synod, and will receive the honor of the *pallium* from his apostolic See which, by divine decree, we at present occupy."[14]

It is not merely that a specific authoritative structure is being imposed, but this structure is presented as divinely decreed. Just as the writers of the Gospels had made a point of referring to the twelve among Jesus's followers, to indicate that the continuity with the twelve tribes of Israel, so Gregory sees significance in appointing twelve bishops for the North of England and twelve for the South and Wales to indicate continuity with the twelve apostles. The Roman system for the appointment of bishops is being tied into the Judeo-Christian tradition, so that to go against one will be seen as going against the other. And included as part and parcel of this tradition will be an insistence on a strict hierarchal system of patriarchy, which subordinates women to men.

This will happen despite the fact that in Jesus's lifetime, he rejected patriarchy and included outcasts and women in his circle.[15] It will happen despite the fact that in the first centuries of the Church, different forms of Christian churches or *ecclesia* (gatherings) flourished, where women and men worked together in leadership roles.[16] Early history and the practice of Jesus himself will be rejected with the imposition of Roman structure that subordinates women to men, when to go against the structure will be presented as going against the will of God.

As the authoritative Roman structure was imposed and eventually accepted by the Anglo-Saxon people, so in the nineteenth and twentieth centuries would it be imposed on the peoples of Africa and the peoples of Latin America—regardless of structures and forms of spirituality already in place. Obedience to authority would take precedence, while spiritual gifts which did not conform to the structures, specifically those of women, would be suppressed.

This process was played out in the centuries that followed the Synod of Whitby hosted by Hild. The leading role that she played in the spread of Christianity to the Anglo-Saxon world would not fit well into the Roman church of the future.

NOTES

1. Marrou, "The Conversion of Northern Europe," 457.

2. *Catholic* is used here rather than *Christian* to make the point that he was not an Arian bishop. Arianism was an influential form of Christianity, condemned as heretical by the Nicene Church and the Roman Church, but embraced by several Germanic tribes who overran the Roman Empire.

3. Bede, *Ecclesiastical History*, I.25; Beda, *Historia Ecclesiastica*, 1.25.

4. Hollis, *Anglo-Saxon Women and the Church*, 117.

5. Gregory of Tours, *The History of the Franks*, translated by Lewis Thorpe (London: Penguin Books, 1974), II:29, 140.

6. Bede, *Ecclesiastical History*, I.26; Beda, *Historia Ecclesiastica*, I.26.

7. Book XI, Epistle XXIX: To Bertha, Queen of the Angli [137], in *The Book of Pastoral Rule and Selected Epistles of Pope St. Gregory I (The Great).* Translated by James Barmby, edited by Paul A. Böer (Veritatis Splendor Publications, 2012), 571.

8. G. M. Trevelyan, *A Shortened History of England* (London: Penguin, 1987), 61

9. MacCulloch, *A History of Christianity*, 336.

10. MacCulloch, *A History of Christianity*, 338.

11. To understand how it was perfectly possible for the Welsh Christians to regard the bishop of Rome as the first among the bishops, and yet to reject Augustine's authority, see Hans Küng, "The Roman System," in Hans Küng in *Can We Save the Catholic Church? We Can Save the Catholic Church!* (London: HarperCollins, 2013), 65–105.

12. Bertram Colgrave, 'Introduction' to *The Earliest Life of Gregory the Great: By an Anonymous Monk of Whitby*, translated by Bertram Colgrave (Cambridge: Cambridge University Press, 1985), 1.

13. Bede, *Ecclesiastical History*, II.21, 106.

14. Bede, *Ecclesiastical History*, I.29, 90.

15. See Joan E. Taylor, in "Two by Two: The Ark-Etypal Language of Mark's Gospel," *The Body in Biblical, Christian and Jewish Texts*, edited by Joan E. Taylor (London: Bloomsbury, 2014), 58–82. Elisabeth Schüssler Fiorenza, "The Twelve and the discipleship of Equals" in Elisabeth Schüssler Fiorenza, *Discipleship of Equals: A Critical Feminist Ekklesia-logy of Liberation* (London: SCM, 1993), 104–16.

16. See Elisabeth Schüssler Fiorenza, "Women in the Pauline Churches" in *Feminism and Theology*, edited by Janet Martin Soskice and Diana Lipton, (Oxford: Oxford University Press, 2003), 203–26. Susanne Heine "Women, Tasks and Ministries," in *Women and Early Christianity* (London: SCM Press, 1987), 86–92.

Chapter Five

Hild Embarks on the Religious Life

At the age of thirteen, Hild had been converted in Northumbria by Paulinus, who was sent by Rome to assist with the Augustinian mission. Some five or six years later, her great-uncle, Edwin had been killed in the attacks on Northumbria by the pagan king Penda of Mercia, and like Ethelburga, Edwin's wife, Hild was forced to flee. Regrettably, beyond this point, we have no record of her specific activities or her whereabouts until she appears again at the age of thirty-three.

Perhaps she had remained for some time in Kent, having fled there with Paulinus and Queen Ethelburga after Edwin's death. Given the close links between Eastern England and Frankia,[1] Hild may have crossed the Channel and spent some time there. Perhaps her main residence had been in the north at Bamburgh, which returned to Christianity only a year or so after Penda's attack, or perhaps she spent much of her time in the south at the court of East Anglia, where she had been born and where her sister Hereswith had married the East Anglian king. What we do know is that in 647 Hild was to be found in East Anglia, preparing to join her sister Hereswith, who by now had left East Anglia and entered a monastery at Chelles in Frankia. Presumably Hereswith's husband had died, though the couple may have mutually agreed to part.

On the balance of probability, Hild herself had been married and widowed. If we knew to whom, it would help to locate her geographically, but there are no records relating any marriage she may have made. In view of her nobility, the lack of a marriage record would tend to argue against her having married at all. Yet, on the other hand, Bede, for whom virginity was a high accolade, never refers to her, as he does to other unmarried women as "virgin," which suggests that at some time she had been married.

HILD RESPONDS TO AIDAN'S CALL

When Hild resolved to take religious vows, the choice of Chelles was an obvious one. It was the accepted practice for women deciding to enter the religious life to join any female relatives who were already vowed religious. Once Hild had made her decision; for her to join her sister would have been the most natural thing for her to do. The more interesting question is why Hereswith should have chosen Chelles. The answer lies both in the paucity of opportunity in Britain and the close links between Britain and Frankia.

It was not until the 630s that the first religious houses for women in southern England were founded, and these with the support of the Kentish, rather than the East Anglian royal families. There was a foundation at Lyminge, which was probably established for Ethelburga when she returned to Kent after Edwin's death. We know of another monastery at Folkestone, which was endowed some time before 640 for Eanswith who was the daughter of Eadberht and Emma of Kent.[2] The famous double monastery at Ely in East Anglia was only founded by its first Abbess, Etheldreda, in 673. Etheldreda proved to be one of the great abbesses of Anglo-Saxon England, only to be followed by three further abbesses in the same mold: her widowed sister, Sexburga; Sexburga's widowed daughter, Erminilda; and her daughter, Werburga, who had custody of the church.

Although opportunities for women to enter the religious life were few and far between in England, this was not the case in Frankia, which had a much better established monastic tradition. And as we have seen, links between Britain and Frankia were strong.

The lack of religious houses in Northumbria was even more acute than in southern England. As far as we know, and this from Bede, the first vowed religious woman in Northumbria was Heiu, Abbess of a community at Hartlepool, which was in all likelihood not founded until sometime in the 640s. However moves were afoot that would remedy the situation and draw Hild to the very center of monastic expansion.

With the killing of Edwin, we left Northumbria at the mercy of the pagan ruler, Penda. Yet pagan rule here was short-lived. A Christian king named Oswald succeeded in quelling the many factions that followed Penda's attack. To understand Oswald's claim to Northumbria, we need to go back to that time when Edwin first ruled its southern kingdom, Deira, and was driven out by Ethelfrith, king of Northumbria's northern kingdom, Bernicia. Ethelfrith ousted Edwin and united the two kingdoms, forcing Edwin into exile. With the help of Redwald, king of the East Angles, Edwin returned to Northumbria and Ethelfrith was killed. For their own safety Ethelfrith's sons needed to be taken into exile. They escaped to Dalriada, in all probability under the protection of their mother, Acha. One of those sons was Oswald.

Oswald had then been educated on the Island of Iona at the monastery founded by Columba, where he had converted to Christianity. When Northumbria fell into a state of confusion after Penda's attack on Edwin, Oswald was able to return and claim kingship of the whole of Northumbria. He then made a determined effort to reestablish and reinvigorate the Christian faith that the Northumbrian population had first turned to under Edwin.

One of Oswald's most fruitful moves was to use his connections with the Ionan community to ask for a missionary to be sent to Northumbria. Success, however, was not immediate. The first monk to arrive was of an "austere disposition" and disliked by his potential flock. On his part, he found the English to be "an ungovernable people of an obstinate and barbarous temperament."[3] Oswald requested someone else. This time a holy and humble monk named Aidan was sent. Aidan founded the monastery at Lindisfarne, a tidal island off the Northumbrian coast. Lindisfarne gave Aidan and his monks sufficient seclusion to pursue the monastic life uninterrupted but at the same time the freedom to leave the island at low tide to engage with the general population. The causeway between the mainland and Lindisfarne can still be crossed at low tide to this day. (See figure 5.1.)

Aidan was to prove an inspiration to the people of Northumbria and have a deep and lasting impact on the path that Hild was to take. It was Aidan who was to alter the course of Hild's life as she made her preparations to

Figure 5.1. Lindisfarne Causeway
Photograph by KevinAlexanderGeorge on iStock

join Hereswith. Aidan persuaded Hild to return to Northumbria and enter the religious life there and become part of the Ionian mission. He wanted her to establish a new community.

It is not known what contact Hild had had with Aidan before entering her first monastery in 647. It is pretty clear, however, that between then and 651 when Aidan died, she was inaugurated into the Ionian spirituality and learned the principles of monastic leadership from Aidan himself. Hild's introduction to the Christian way of life had come through Paulinus with its Roman interpretative slant. As a high-ranking official of the Christian Church, it would have been natural for Paulinus to be concerned with his status. The Roman concern for the dignity of office with its attendant protocol is perhaps most plainly exhibited in the actions of Wilfrid—of which there will be more later—but Paulinus would have been very much in this same mold. Aidan, like Paulinus, was both monk and bishop, but Aidan's Irish background had given him a different take on the way in which a monk or bishop should behave. Aidan must have been very different from Paulinus. Paulinus would not have given away a good horse to a beggar and insisted on walking the byways on foot.

We must assume that during Hild's first years in the religious life she would have learned how to fulfill the role of abbess, and it was also during these years that Aidan's influence drew her to be fully immersed into the way of Irish monasticism.

It was very much the case, therefore, that Aidan had called Hild back to Northumbria to engage in the mission field, where the work was pastoral care, instruction, and evangelization. There must have been a great need to provide for the spiritual care of the lay population that had been converted with Edwin, but who may have received little instruction in the faith.

Paulinus, who had initiated their conversion, had returned south on Edwin's death, leaving James the Deacon at York to carry on his work. James continued in York for many years, teaching and baptizing and attempting to bring about liturgies with an appropriate level of singing. His attempts to reconvert the Northumbrians to Christianity seem to have been an uphill struggle. It was not until many years later that the number of believers was sufficient for him to begin to teach them to sing the music of the Church in the manner laid down by the Church in Rome and subsequently Canterbury. The proper chanting of the psalms was a particular concern to the Roman mission, and James had a wide knowledge of church music.

Central to the monastic life of course was prayer, strengthening the individual in the fight to subdue the body and overcome the temptations of the world, with a view to eventual union with God. As the medieval period proceeded, monasteries increasingly were devoted to either the entirely prayer-focused contemplative life or the active way of life, which focused on good works supported by prayer. In this later period, those wishing to devote their lives exclusively to prayer in an enclosed environment would join a contemplative order. There, separate from the world, their time would be divided between prayer and such work as was necessary to support their way of life. Those wishing to care for the sick, to teach, or to set out on preaching tours or missionary journeys would join an active order. No such division existed as Hild devised her Rule; contemplative prayer and pastoral work went hand in hand. Barbara Yorke writes:

> All Anglo-Saxon abbesses probably had some men as well as women under their control, and nunneries, even after the imposition of the *Regularis Concordia* [973], were probably never purely contemplative institutions strictly claustered from the concerns of the world. Abbesses not only had to oversee the spiritual lives of the religious subject to them, but also administer large estates and care for spiritual and secular needs of the many people who lived upon them. It is only occasionally that we can glimpse abbesses in narratives as estate managers, as briefly for Hild and Aelfflaed [Aelffled] of Whitby, but through charters we can see them acquiring land, and often exercising considerable acumen in arranging additional rights and privileges.[4]

It was during the earlier period when Penda continued to devastate Northumbria that Hild returned there. Despite the fact that Hild had been initiated into the faith according to the Roman principles of Paulinus, it was the Irish mission under the leadership of Aidan that Hild was now to join.

The fact that Hild responded to Aidan's called, indeed the fact that he called her in the first place, might seem to indicate that they had already formed a close bond. Their paths may have crossed. It was at least two years after Hild had fled from Penda that Aidan arrived at Lindisfarne. Aidan is famous for traveling the highways and byways of Northumbria on foot,[5] giving weight to the argument that Hild spent time in Bamburgh, the most obvious place for Hild and Aidan to have met. If she did go to Bamburgh, she would have been entering Oswald's kingdom, in the knowledge that Oswald's father and her great-uncle Edwin had been enemies to the death, quite literally. This is not perhaps as unlikely as it might seem to us, given the realities of her time. Mainly, but not exclusively, through marriage women often found themselves at the courts of the enemies of their own birth family. And Oswald was a Christian king.

Oswald in fact was to die at the hands of Penda in 642. Had Hild been at Bamburgh at this time, it is likely that it was then that she returned to the safety of East Anglia. At any rate, it was from East Anglia in the year 647 that Hild responded to Aidan's call and returned to Northumbria. Here she established her first monastery[6]—a small group of (presumably) women living together under vows and separately from the world—on just one hide of land on the north side of the River Wear.

Before taking up her post, Hild would have had to take religious vows herself, presumably in a ceremony conducted by Aidan. She would have vowed to live in poverty, chastity, and obedience for the rest of her life. In the first chapter, I attempted to convey something of the magnitude of the seventh-century baptismal ceremony—to glean something of the highly charged emotional impact, as the old life of paganism was visibly washed away through water. As we move on to consider Hild's entrance into the life of a vowed religious, we might do well to reflect on the fact that since St. Jerome in the fourth century, religious profession was often understood as a second baptism.[7] Baptism was marked by the taking off of clothes before going down into the water and the reclothing in a starkly different white garment upon coming out of the water into a radically new life. Similarly, the dramatic symbolism of religious profession was marked by reclothing.

On their entry into the cloister, in accordance with the vow of poverty, the monastic voluntarily gives up all possessions, even the clothes that belong to their previous state of life, marking a permanent break with their past state. With appropriate ceremony and ritual, as the past state of life is discarded, the new state is accepted through reclothing in the distinctive monastic habit. For women this will include a head covering; for men it will mean a new haircut with a tonsure or partially shaved head. As with the style of dress, the style of the tonsure was invested with great significance. So important was it, that, as we shall see in Chapter 11, the style of tonsure was one of the main issues at stake at the Synod of Whitby.

FROM THE MOUTH OF THE WEAR TO WEARMOUTH

The exact location of Hild's first monastery is not known. According to Mundahl-Harris "it is more than likely that it was very near to the site of the monastery of St. Peter's founded some thirty years later by Benedict Biscop."[8] Ray Simpson tries to pinpoint it more exactly and comes up with two suggestions:

> Where was this site by the River Wear? Dr. Victor Watts, a place name authority for that region suggested two possibilities—first, a site that later became Monkwearmouth, and second, the village of Westoe, about a mile south of today's South Shields. Dr. Watts suggested that the name Westoe is a compound

> of *stow*, meaning "a place of assembly, a holy place" and *wifa*, the Old English genitive plural of "woman."[9]

Simpson himself favors Monkwearmouth because Westoe is nearer the Tyne than the Wear. Monkwearmouth is an alternative name for Wearmouth, where Benedict Biscop founded his first monastery.

It seems to me that Hild's first community was indeed at Wearmouth. To set up his monastery, Biscop was given seventy hides of land from the estates of King Ecgfrith. Ecgfrith was the son of King Oswy, who had succeeded his half-brother Oswald to the throne. It was Oswald who had invited Aidan over from Iona and given him the island of Lindisfarne. It would have been Oswy who granted the one hide of land on the north bank of the River Wear where Hild set up her first community.

It seems altogether likely that Biscop's seventy hides granted by Ecgfrith included the one hide that comprised the first of Hild's monasteries. A "hide" of land was not a precise measurement, but an area comprising sufficient acres to support one household. Rather than earmarking a whole other portion of land for monastic purposes on the same north bank, it seems far more likely that Ecgfrith rededicated the land already given by his father, at the same time greatly adding to it. According to Sarah Foot, "charters, including documents which purported to establish a new minster on a given piece of land may [have served] only to regularize the status and landed possessions of a pre-existing community."[10]

Archeological evidence provided by Rosemary Cramp would seem to back up the theory that Hild's first community was indeed at Wearmouth. Cramp writes:

> Although it is impossible to map the exact boundaries of the individual vills, it is clear that the initial Wearmouth/Jarrow endowment must have swallowed up a large amount of land in what may have once been a large royal estate bounded on the west by the main roman road north, and on the north by Gateshead on the Tyne, on the south by *Cunecacestre* (Chester-le-Street) on the Wear, and on the east by the sea. Some of the landholdings of earlier and smaller monasteries such as Gateshead or Hilda's foundation on the north bank of the Wear may have been absorbed later by the twin monastery.[11]

From all the evidence, it is reasonable to infer that Hild's first monastery could very well have been at Wearmouth, and it would seem likely that in founding his monastery, Biscop took over the dwellings that had formed Hild's first community. The more interesting question is whether Hild's community had continued after her departure. Nothing is known of the community Hild left behind when she moved on to Hartlepool. It may well be that the small community flourished and that Biscop built on the still functioning community which Hild had founded.

At any rate, it is reasonable to assume that Biscop's monastic estate included the site of Hild's small monastery, whether or not it was still occupied. As to whether within the sizeable complex granted to Biscop, Hild's original community continued to exist, frustratingly there is no evidence to support the case either way. But given all that we know of Hild's reputation and the overall success of her monasteries, it seems not unreasonable to suppose that it did. At the very least, the probability that Biscop's monastic estates took over from the small beginnings of Hild's first community suggests an altogether different way of viewing the relationship between Hild and Bede.

It was on monastic lands that Bede was born in 673, presumably land belonging to Biscop's monastery because it was at Wearmouth that Bede, at the age of seven, was placed in the care of abbot Biscop for education. Thus, his entrance into the Wearmouth monastery was around the time of Hild's death in 680. Bede remained with Biscop for a few years, before moving to nearby Jarrow with Abbot Ceolfrid. The point is frequently made that Bede, from whom we have the record of Hild's life, was born during Hild's lifetime. Chronologically he was not far removed from her and those who knew her, but the evidence would seem to indicate a closer, more personal relationship.

We know that Bede was a great admirer of Roman ways and very keen that monasteries should adhere to a strict Rule. It would have been in the interests of his successors to emphasize these particular leanings. Yet we also know that Bede was greatly impressed by Irish spirituality. He was also a great admirer of Hild, describing her as a shining example of Christian living, comparing the light she shed upon others to the light of a brilliant jewel. Living in Northumbria when he did, he could not but have been impressed by the extraordinary accomplishments of the abbey at Whitby under Hild's rule, but perhaps there was also a more personal connection stoking his admiration for her.

At the age of around seven years, he would surely have heard of the death of the great celebrity of the age, Hild of Whitby. Almost certainly in the years that followed when the child Bede resided at Wearmouth, there would have been those for whom the memory still lingered of the first community to be planted there on just one hide of land, led by that same remarkable woman. There must have been some alive who, seeing her monasteries going from strength to strength, claimed her as their founding mother. And some of this strong, personal sense of Hild as not merely the "mother of all," but "our mother" must have rubbed off on the impressionable child, Bede.

LIFE AT HARTLEPOOL

Hild's first monastery was on the north bank of the River Wear, in what is Sunderland today. She was not to stay there long because in 649 she was appointed by Aidan to head the Abbey at Hartlepool, when Heiu moved south to Tadcaster. It was at Hartlepool that Oftor, destined to become bishop of Hwicce, was admitted to Hild's community. At Hartlepool, Oftor studied under Hild, before going with her to Whitby, and then finally leaving Northumbria for Canterbury, where he completed his studies.

Hartlepool was then known as "Heretu," or the place of the Hart. Bede writes of Hild's transfer to Hartlepool that she "quickly set herself to establish a regular observance," guided by Aidan and other men from his community, who would often visit her.[12] The "regular observance" that Hild is said to have set up plainly refers to the Rule which the community was to observe. It would have been very much a rule devised by Hild and specific to the situation at Hartlepool, following the principles she had learned from Aidan and his monks, though, too, there could well have been elements taken from the more Roman forms of monastic life that she had imbibed from her earlier contact with Paulinus. As Foot observes, it would be a mistake to imagine that, at this point in history, there was a set Rule that could be applied uniformly to each foundation.

Foot points to "a number of misconceptions about the essential nature of Anglo-Saxon monasticism in the period before the tenth century." Swayed by the writings of Bede and by the strictures of the monks who reformed the monasteries in the 960s and 970s, historians have tended to attribute to the early period of Anglo-Saxon monasticism a uniformity that clearly did not exist.[13] We know that Bede was familiar with and admired the Benedictine Rule and that he raised uniformity of practice to the level of a virtue. With his high regard for Hild and without firsthand knowledge of the particulars of Hild's Rule, it is likely that he assumed a set-up more Benedictine in character than was necessarily the case.

Julie Anne Smith, who has researched extensively into the various Rules that operated in the early medieval West, gives a sense of the complexity and the variety of Rules that existed, even before many were written down. Smith explains how up until the early sixth century, the Rule was tailored and sometimes repeatedly updated to suit the circumstances of each monastery or family of monasteries. Above all, the Rule was there to serve the spiritual development of those who followed it. In this early period, the Rule was to be found in the collective memory of the community rather than in anything written down.

> Up until the early sixth century monastic rules focused upon the spiritual development of the religious, and the daily practice of any individual foundation tended to be guided by the founder or abbatial incumbent. These customaries might be tailored continuously and seem seldom to have existed in written form, with the collective memory of the group as the repository for behavioural expectations.[14]

Smith also shows how, as Rules were formulated, various influences interacted with others from different geographical areas. At a most basic level, those who had sought communion with God in the desert had tended to be on a solitary quest, pursuing individual acts of heroism. Against this background, the foundational monastic Rule in the East, that of Basil and Macrina, was focused on ascetic guidance, rather than the functioning of the monastic household. In the West, Benedict's Rule was intended to counter the focus on individual feats of asceticism, with their tendency toward extreme forms of self-denial and the concomitant danger of spiritual pride. The focus instead was on humility, achieved through obedience to the Rule, and on shared communal living.

> The first known Western rule to specify the requirements for the daily practice of the members of a religious community was that of Benedict of Nursia (c.480–c.547). Benedict envisioned a fully communal life with all members fulfilling a prescribed daily round of prayer, work, eating and sleeping, performing all functions in unison and sharing all spaces assigned to those functions.[15]

According to the Eastern Rule, meditation on Scripture provided the basis for right conduct, whereas in the West, Benedict's Rule itself became an object of meditation.

A key concern, as various rules developed, was the question of whether, or to what extent, individual members were permitted to travel outside the boundaries of their own community. This was a concern whether it applied to men or to women, but generally speaking greater restrictions would be placed on the movements of women, especially as the centuries progressed.

It is sometimes written that the men in Hild's community were allowed to travel outside the monastery, while the women remained inside.[16] As John Blair remarks, "The problem is that we simply do not know what went on in the great majority of Anglo-Saxon religious communities, though it is likely that a high proportion of them were neither very regulated nor very enclosed."[17] What is crystal clear is that in Anglo-Saxon monasteries women and men were free to meet with each other for advice and encouragement in the service of their common aim. Their ease of interaction bore no relation to the refusal of Benedict to share his trials and aspirations with any woman, even his own sister, Scholastica.

How this ease of interaction came about is explained by Smith. Regarding England she says the following:

> In England the influences upon the development of monasticism were threefold. The major external influence on women's monasticism appears to have come from the Frankish nunneries which were part of the Luxeuil network with its

> Columbanian-Benedictine culture. There were also some elements of the Irish tradition which settled in the north of England during the missionary endeavours out of Iona. And the Benedictine tradition may have come firstly into Kent with the arrival in 597 of Gregory I's little missionary team of monks who it seems likely were Benedictines though this is never clearly stated.[18]

The missionary Columbanus had introduced Irish ascetic practices to Frankia around 591, setting up a monastic center at Luxeuil. Earlier monastic arrangements such as the Rule produced for the nuns of Arles by Caesarius (c.47–42), had required strict claustration, at least in part to ensure the safety of the nuns in a town full of dangers. Benedict had introduced a vow of stability for those following his Rule and had insisted that contact with the outside world was reduced to the minimum necessary for charitable works or abbey business. On the other hand, the missionary thrust of the Columbian enterprise required that both male and female religious leave the monastic enclosure and engage with the people of the surrounding area.

It would seem, therefore, that when Hild devised her rule, strands of different traditions came together. It is safe to assume that her mixed rule combined Benedictine elements—with each hour of the day allocated to its specific task to facilitate the spiritual growth of its members and the practicalities of communal living—with the freedom of movement associated with the Columbanian culture, necessary to fulfill the pastoral dimension of Aidan's mission.

Included in this mixture were elements of the Irish tradition, which prized harsh asceticism and solitariness. Yet combined with the solitariness of the life of prayer, there was in the Irish tradition considerable interaction with the local community. The absence of towns in Ireland, which had not known Roman occupation, meant that monastic heads fulfilled many of the functions that would have been undertaken by bishops, and it was the men and women of the monasteries who were responsible for much of the pastoral care of the population at large. Although there do not seem to have been double monasteries in Ireland,[19] it was the case that monasteries for women were accorded equal spiritual status with monasteries for men.

The equal spiritual status accorded to women and men transferred to Northumbria under Aidan, as did the practice of monastic heads functioning in certain respects with the authority and responsibilities of a bishop. In England, it was accepted that women were equals, perhaps even more gifted than men, in spiritual matters. It was also accepted that women could be rulers. Queen Seaxburh of Wessex, for example, "succeeded her husband Cenwalh in 672 and reigned for about two years."[20] Because the men among the nobility, if they had not already been slaughtered on the battlefield, were greatly taken up with war, those who ruled the monasteries tended to be royal women.

HILD ORDAINED AS ABBESS?

It would seem likely that when Hild took over at Hartlepool, the ceremony that saw her installed was an ordination. What was meant by "ordination" at this period in history will be the subject of further discussion in chapter 9. The ceremonies surrounding the ordination to the head of an abbacy underscores the fact that monastic heads fulfilled many episcopal functions. The ordination rites for an abbess show that the abbess had a miter placed on her head and that she received a staff from the bishop, both indicating episcopal responsibilities. Regrettably, there is no record of these ceremonies either at Hartlepool or at Whitby. We do know, however that in the early medieval period abbesses were, as Gary Macy puts it, "as ordained as any other clergy in this period." Macy gives the original Latin texts for several of the ordination rites for abbesses and abbots, discussing them in some detail.[21] Extant manuscripts giving the Mozarabic rite, that is to say the rite of the Visigoth Church of Spain, are of special interest because the oldest contain rites that were practiced as early as the fifth century.

Although there are certain differences between the Mozarabic rites according to whether they are performed for an abbess or an abbot, there are significant similarities.[22] Both rites begin in the sacristy with a vesting, or clothing. In the case of an abbess, we are told that she is vested by someone who has been dedicated to God (*Quando ordinatur abbatissa uestitur a deo uotis in sacrario ueste religionis*), and in the case of an abbot, it is the bishop who hands him his monastic clothing. In the case of the abbess (but not the abbot), a miter is placed on her head during the vesting (*et inponitur ei in capite mitra religiosa*).[23] The fact that the abbess wore a miter is highly significant because it denotes authority usually associated with a bishop.

The designated prayers differ according to whether the ordinand is male or female, "but at the conclusion of the rite, both received from the bishop a staff and a copy of the rule of the order as well as the kiss of peace from the bishop" (*Qua explicita osculatur eam episcopus, et tradit ei librum regule et baculum*).[24] Here again, the rite is replete with symbolism. The kiss of peace is an ancient and deeply significant gesture, and it is the bishop who offers it; the copy of the Rule symbolizes the abbess's authority over those under the Rule; and the staff, in the form of a shepherd's crook indicates that the abbess acts as shepherd of her flock, as Christ was shepherd of his flock. Like the miter, the staff denotes authority usually associated with a bishop.

It is not possible to say with certainty that any specific elements of the ordination service for an abbess that we have from the Mozarabic or any of the other rites were played out when Hild was installed as abbess. Yet on the balance of probability, given the considerable evidence for the widespread practice of such ordinations over several centuries including the seventh, I would guess that they were. It is also on balance likely that along with ordination went quasi-episcopal responsibilities. Hild would have been given the responsibility for several functions that would later be the sole preserve of male bishops. Once ordained abbess, in many areas of ecclesiastical life, she would have acted, and she would have been expected to act, as if she were a bishop.

NOTES

1. Frankia, roughly what is now France, and what in Roman times was part of the larger territory of Gaul. The territory of the Franks was greatly expanded under the rule of Clovis I (d. 511). Some sources use "in Frankia," and other sources use "in Gaul" to refer to the same place. For example, Bede, *Ecclesiastical History* (IV.23), refers to the monastery of Cale [Chelles] in Gaul, and Leyser, *Medieval Women* (24), locates Chelles in "Francia [Frankia]."
2. Sarah Foot, *Veiled Women I* (Aldershot, UK: Ashgate Publishing, 2000), 36.
3. Bede, *Ecclesiastical History*, III.5, 151.
4. Yorke, *Nunneries and the Anglo-Saxon Royal Houses*, 131.
5. Bede, *Ecclesiastical History*, III.5; Beda, *Historia Ecclesiastica*, III.5.
6. Sarah Foot tells us that in early medieval England all religious congregations apart from the households of bishops were referred to using the Latin word *monasteria*. Foot herself chooses to translate this as "minster," intending to cover a wide diversity of institutions, though recently scholars have begun to use the word "minster" itself in a specialized sense; see Sarah Foot, *Monastic Life in Anglo-Saxon England c. 600–900* (Cambridge: Cambridge University Press, 2009), 5–6. Henry Mayr-Harting notes that the word "monastery" in early English Christianity "might mean anything from the famous royal foundations or episcopal sees to the communities of perhaps three or four in the churches which served the pastoral needs of a scattered area" in *The Coming of Christianity*, 148. I will use "monastery" throughout to cover any group of people living together under vows. It was not until the tenth century that monasteries in England lost their flexibility on becoming more uniformly regulated.
7. Foot, *Monastic Life*, 40, referring to Jerome, *Epistola* 39, 3 (ed. Hilberg, I, 299), writes: "Entry into the monastic life was explicitly compared to the new birth of baptism by St. Jerome in the fourth century; writing to Paula about her daughter, Jerome reminded her that it was only four months since Blesilla 'by the grace of God was washed by a kind of second baptism, that of profession.' Many later medieval monastic writers echoed the same theme."
8. Mundahl-Harris, *St. Hilda and Her Times*, 9.
9. Simpson, *Hilda of Whitby*, 52 gives a reference to Christine Fell, "Hild, Abbess of Streonaeshalch," in *Hagiography and Medieval Literature: A Symposium*, edited by H. Bekker-Nielsen et al. (Odense: Odense University Press, 1981).
10. Foot, *Monastic Life*, 90.

11. Rosemary Cramp, *Wearmouth and Jarrow Monastic Sites* (Swindon: English Heritage, 2005), 37–38.

12. Bede, *Ecclesiastical History*, IV.23 244.

13. Foot, *Monastic Life*, 10–11.

14. Smith, *Ordering Women's Lives*, 120.

15. Smith, *Ordering Women's Lives*, 120.

16. For example, Mundahl-Harris, *St. Hilda and Her Times*, 9.

17. John Blair, *The Church in Anglo-Saxon Society* (Oxford: Oxford University Press, 2006), 3.

18. Smith, *Ordering Women's Lives*, 133

19. According to Smith (*Ordering Women's Lives* 132–33), "The only community which bore some similarities to a double house was at Kildare, but the men were governed by an abbot-bishop, and the women by an independent abbess and so does not conform to the model followed in Gaul and England."

20. David Williamson, *Kings and Queens of Britain* (Leicester, UK: Webb and Bower, 1991), 20. Henrietta Leyser comments that the responsibilities wielded by abbesses would have been "inconceivable without there being already a strong tradition of female command and spiritual expertise on which to draw" in *Medieval Women*, 13.

21. Gary Macy, *A Hidden History of Women's Ordination: Female Clergy in the Medieval West* (Oxford: Oxford University Press, 2008), 81 and Appendix 2, 143–56.

22. Elsewhere some rites were the same for men and for women. See Macy, *The Hidden History*, 81 and Appendix 2, 143–56.

23. José Janini, ed., *Liber ordinum episcopal [Cod. Silos, Arch. Monástico 4]*, Studia silensia 15 (Burgos: Abadia de Silos, 1991). XXIII Ordo ad ordinandam abbatissam (pp. 101–2), quoted in Macy, *The Hidden History of Women's Ordination*, Appendix 2,143.

24. Janini, ed., *Liber ordinum episcopal*, quoted in Macy, *The Hidden History of Women's Ordination*, 144.

Chapter Six

Life in Hild's Monasteries

Attempting to gain a sense of the atmosphere in Hild's monasteries, I am struck by the sheer vitality of Hild's communities. From small beginnings on the banks of the River Wear to the stunning achievements on the headland in Northumbria, Hild's project was blessed with such success as must have heartened her and all around her. No headway will be made into this lost world if it is viewed only through the lens of what was to come.

VITALITY AND SUCCESS

Hild ruled the monastery at Hartlepool for a number of years, always concerned to enforce a rule that would prove most conducive to a life of dedication to God and to the mission of the Church. She was then moved to a larger monastery at Streanaeshalch, later to be known as Whitby. There, she set to work to impose the same regularity of life, a task which she accomplished with great industry [*quod opus sibi iniunctum non segniter inpleuit*].[1] One gets a sense of an enormous energy that seems to have characterized all that she undertook.

This was a golden time, when women and men, like Hild with her coworkers and Aidan with his, labored together for the sake of the Gospel. Restrictions that would be placed on the movements of women were a thing of the future in Anglo-Saxon England at least. We may assume that Hild adapted her Rule according to the specific needs she encountered at Whitby. It was a time of joy at being part of a truly Christian community, in the heady days that constituted the Golden Age of Northumbria.

The flowering of Hild's monastery at Whitby must be traced back to the original seed planted by Aidan when he persuaded Hild to return to Northumbria, rather than follow her sister Hereswith to the convent in Chelles. Aidan had come out of Iona and made his base at Lindisfarne to convert the English back to Christianity. The site of this island monastery had been carefully chosen to provide seclusion, while the link to the mainland via the causeway at low tide enabled the monks to fulfill their mission to the outside world. In their seclusion, Aidan and his fellow monks demonstrated a rejection of worldly pleasures that would not always be imitated by those who followed them.

It was Aidan and his company who had initiated Hild into the Ionian way of monastic life. Aidan's attitude was essentially one of humility in the service of the poor. Rather than traveling by horse, he walked the highways to be on the same level as the peasant population. He eschewed the privileges of rank. Later commentators would call him bishop, yet this was not how he saw himself. Rather he was a traveling missionary, based at Lindisfarne.

The love of Jesus and the desire to serve him was the governing principal for all those who embraced the religious life with sincerity. The outward expression of this inner devotion varied considerably. There were those who felt it necessary to uphold the dignity of their station as officers of the Church. There were those who saw their role as humble servants, of the poor especially. Aidan fell into this latter category, and Hild's decision to choose Northumbria over Chelles is perhaps evidence that the humble servant model was the guiding principle of her life as well.

This chapter will explain the rich diversity of activity that pertained in Hild's communities. It will also discuss how that humble servant model was played out in Hild's life, given her high-born status and her ongoing involvement in the life of the ruling classes.

PERSONAL POVERTY AND MONASTIC WEALTH

From the beginning, monasticism had been associated with a renunciation of worldly attachments, combined with charitable giving to the poor. A significant inspiration for such a life comes from the Acts of the Apostles. "And all who believed were together and had all things in common; and they sold their possessions and goods and distributed them to all, as any had need" (Acts: 2.44). When Bede wrote the *Ecclesiastical History*, he was working simultaneously on a commentary on the Acts of the Apostles, and his description of the communal life at Whitby is doubtless colored by the description in Acts.

The reality would have borne out Bede's description. Those who entered Whitby would have handed over to the community any personal wealth or possessions, and if the monastery itself was rich, the inhabitants had no personal wealth. Their needs were catered for from the communal purse, distributed according to Hild's discretion. What these few lines from Bede do not cover is the question of whether the monastery itself was wealthy.

Bede says nothing detailed about the wealth or otherwise of Whitby Abbey, but he does go to some lengths to paint Lindisfarne as a monastery without wealth, when he records Colman's departure shortly after the Whitby Synod of 664. Apart from the church, Bede claims that the Lindisfarne monastery had very few buildings and owned no property except cattle. Whenever money was donated. it was immediately given to the poor because there was no need to accommodate important visitors, who only came to pray and to hear the word of God. Even when the king stayed for a meal, he asked only for the plain daily food of the brothers.[2]

There are several reasons to be cautious regarding this description. As Bede writes, he is troubled with what he sees as the excesses of some monasteries in his own day. His idealized picture of Lindisfarne is calculated as a reprimand to these excesses. However poor the monastery at Lindisfarne may have been when it was founded by Aidan at some time after 635, or when Colman departed from there around 664, some thirty-five years later by the turn of the century, it had produced one of the greatest riches of the age, the Lindisfarne Gospels. The scriptorium that must have existed for this magnificent masterpiece to have been created would not have been possible in a monastery without substantial possessions. The Lindisfarne Gospels feature today as one of the most famous illuminated books in the world, and its production at Lindisfarne is a sure indication that great wealth had been accrued over the years.

Monasteries were or came to be magnificent, status-conscious places, albeit individual monasteries might be poor, and individual monastics might live lives of genuine renunciation. One such individual was Cuthbert, who in the late seventh century moved to the isle of Farne from Lindisfarne to live the life of a hermit. In itself, Cuthbert's move is telling because we might have imagined that Lindisfarne itself was sufficiently cut off from worldly life as to provide seclusion for a hermit.

The story is told that one Christmas Day certain monks came out to Farne from Lindisfarne to celebrate the birth of our Lord with Cuthbert.[3] In another version of the story, Cuthbert left his hermitage on the isle of Farne and joined the monks at Lindisfarne for the feast.[4] Despite a sense of foreboding, Cuthbert continued with the feasting and engaged with the storytelling that accompanied the feast. Cuthbert's foreboding had been well founded because on the following day, a plague broke out at Lindisfarne. It is not clear whether Cuthbert's unease derived from the storytelling itself or from the feasting.

What is telling is that even for one who had sought solitude, the way in which he followed the Church's year included feasting on feast days, as well as fasting on fast days.

Assuming the monks went out to Farne island, what made the difference between Cuthbert's Christmas feast, and the feasting that *did* take place at Lindisfarne, at least in later years, was the presence or absence of "important people." Noble visitors required not just lodging but to join in the feasting. Their participation in the feasting, especially the stories they told, threatened to distract the vowed religious from their focus on the eternal.

A century after the production of the Gospels, the renowned scholar Alcuin, in one of his many letters, made a sharp critique of the lax living at Lindisfarne. His focus was on the feasting taking place there. For Alcuin, it was not so much the consumption of food and drink that were of concern, but rather the secular nature of the stories told and songs sung during the feasting. Alcuin thought it unseemly that those around the bishop's dinner table should be entertained by the lyre and the singing of secular songs.[5] He felt that the monks should take as their heroes the characters that came to life in the Gospels. They should dwell on the lives of the early martyrs and the monks of the desert. They should understand their own place in history in continuity with these heroic figures, not with the warriors of ancient sagas like *Beowulf*, whose ancestry could be traced to pagan gods. The problem was the generous hospitality extended to the many noble guests, whose secular values diluted the Gospel values of the vowed religious.

Cuthbert had feasted the Christmas feast with fellow monks. Plainly such feasting could have been tipped over into gluttony, drunkenness, or worse. Yet the real difficulty arose when members of royal families or the nobility more generally came as guests into the heart of the monastery. At times, Hild's monastery would have bustling with such guests.

FOSTERING CHILDREN

The provision of hospitality was an important function of the monastery. Feasts of one sort or another were an integral part of the Church, well embedded into monastic life. Wealthy patrons, family members, and all sorts of people would have been found as monastic guests.

Perhaps one of the most striking features of Hild's monasteries would have been the presence of children, not just on the outlying farms but at the very heart of the monastery. Hospitality extended to the fostering of children who would be consigned to the monastery's care. As we have already seen, at a young age, Bede was given into the care of Benedict Biscop. We know from

Bede that boys were given over to the care of nuns as well as monks. Bede tells the story of a little boy who was being cared for and educated by the nuns of Barking.[6] Monasteries like Hild's might well have fostered both boys and girls, but most famously when Hild was at Hartlepool, she was given the care of the infant Aelffled, daughter of King Oswy and Queen Eanfled.

It is easy to imagine the disruption that would have been caused by the presence of one loveable, helpless baby, demanding food and care at all hours. And with the arrival of this delightful, demanding package there would have been an entire set of people with a stake in the monastery's interests. An entire noble family would be intimately linked to the monastery, providing frequent and welcome visitors.

To appreciate how Aelffled fits into Hild's story, we return to Hild's great-uncle Edwin, who, in 616 had defeated his long-standing enemy Ethelfrith to gain control of the whole of Northumbria. Ethelfrith's sons who had fled north were converted to Christianity by monks from Iona. The sons had returned to Northumbria after Edwin had been killed by the pagan forces of Penda of Mercia. We have met them already: Oswald, who invited Aidan to Lindisfarne, and Oswy, who granted to Hild her first hide of land. On Oswald's death, the younger brother, Oswy took over as ruler of Bernicia; he married Edwin's daughter, Eanfled; and together they had a daughter. That daughter was Aelffled.

It was Oswy, who, in 655, finally defeated and killed Penda at a place called Winwaed in what is now South Yorkshire. The defeat of Penda was a victory as unexpected as it was great. Oswy had tried desperately to avoid this final showdown with Penda. As Mayr-Harting puts it, "Oswy tried every means of buying him off before entrusting the issue to battle in a last desperate gesture of survival."[7] His frantic attempts to avoid battle included offering Penda substantial treasure and gifts. When Penda refused, Oswy swore an oath, declaring that if the heathen would not accept his gifts, then he would offer them to the Lord. So he vowed that if he were victorious, he would offer his daughter to God as a consecrated virgin and give twelve estates to build monasteries.

Oswy was victorious. With Penda gone, he was able to reunite once again the whole of Northumbria and finally put an end to Penda's persistent and devastating attacks, Northumberland enjoyed more settled times, and Christianity was once again allowed to flourish. Aelffled, Oswy's daughter, then barely a year old, was given to the care of Hild, who was the Abbess of the monastery at Hartlepool.

Family ties figured prominently in determining the makeup of the monastery's residents. Hild's own relationship to Aelffled through Aelffled's mother, Eanfled, would have been a factor in the choice of Hartlepool,

Eanfled being the daughter of Hild's great-uncle Edwin. And, as abbess, Hild would be succeeded at Whitby by both Aelffled and Aelffled's by-then-widowed mother, Eanfled.

To have a royal princess in her care would have added significant prestige to her community. And Hild was to benefit further from Oswy's vow at Winwaed. Following his promise to give twelve estates to build monasteries, Hild received ten hides of land, which gave her around 1200 acres around Streanaeshalch,[8] which was to be known as Whitby. Oswy's interest in Whitby was thus further cemented.

FEASTING AND FASTING

To have a royal baby in its care would have greatly enhanced the reputation of any monastery. Furthermore, the family connection to the monastery meant that royal women like Eanfled had a place of security, which they could make their home when circumstances dictated. A constant theme running through this exploration of monastic life has been the way in which female members of the nobility followed their sisters, daughters, or more distant female relatives into the monastery to which they were connected through family ties.

Yet it was not only the women of the family who were linked to the monastery through these close ties. The monastery provided a place of burial for the family, through which it had been endowed, providing the monastery with yet another level of prestige. At Whitby would be buried Aelffled, her mother and father, Queen Eanfled and King Oswy, and Eanfled's father, King Edwin, as well as many other people of noble blood. Interestingly Bede's *Ecclesiastical History* makes no mention of Hild being buried at Whitby.

All this meant that at Whitby, there was a need to provide hospitality for many high-ranking visitors. In Hild's case we know that high-ranking visitors were not limited to family members. Hild's fame was such that she was sought out for her wise counsel by elite members of society from far and wide. Then there were the grand events, like the Synod of 664, which would have required considerable organization, not to mention financial resources, to meet the requirements of hospitality. I say "grand events" in the plural. Of course we know of only one, the gathering of 664 itself, but it is reasonable to assume that Hild's monasteries may well have provided the setting for other important political interactions.

The monastery, therefore, fulfilled two functions, which to some extent were at odds with each other. On the one hand, it provided a place where a person could embrace a frugal lifestyle, devoted to the worship of God and the service of the poor, and on the other hand, it provided a home for noble women especially, not all of whom necessarily felt called to a life of austerity, and a place where noble and royal persons had a vested interest and were frequent and welcome guests.

Hild's life well represents the dichotomy. Feasting in the royal household had been very much part of her life up until her entry into monastic life, when, by all accounts, her desire to cut herself off from worldly pleasures for the sake of the Gospel was genuine and wholeheartedly embraced. Yet her calling involved a significant amount of ongoing contact with the nobility.

THE POOR, THE SICK, AND THE DYING

As we have seen, in his idealized representation of life at Lindisfarne, Bede is anxious to show that in Colman's time, it had had not been corrupted by the desire for worldly possessions but rather embraced frugality. He then extends this interpretation to cover the wider practice of Christian life beyond Lindisfarne. Harking back to earlier days, he tells how teachers were only concerned to serve God. He then goes on to say that people flocked to the churches and monasteries because they desired to hear the word of God, not because they would be given food.[9]

Bede here is anxious to demonstrate that in earlier (better) times, it was spiritual hunger that motivated the population to respond to the holiness of those in monastic life. It was spiritual food rather than food for the body that drew the population to the monastery. In reality, the two were not mutually exclusive, and feeding the hungry was one of the most important functions of the monastery. Constant savage warfare had had a terrible effect on the ability of the peasants to produce and store food. There were insufficient laborers to grow crops and tend livestock, and those who did produce food would have had no way of protecting it from plundering armies.

Charitable giving, which was an essential element of monastic life, is most often portrayed in terms of alms-giving. The giving away of money to the destitute was a constant, if not daily, duty. Possessions were also to be given away, the most notable example being Aidan's horse.[10] Despite Bede's protestations, it is evident from the quotation that the monasteries also provided food.

The monastery would have provided refuge and succor for all classes of people. Along with the provision of hospitality and with alms-giving, the care of the sick was one of the most important of the charitable works expected of those who had devoted their lives to the Gospel. As we move on to consider how care of the sick would have been integrated into the monastic life, it is possible to build up a picture of the monastery itself, that is to say, the actual buildings that would have been constructed as Hild's mission grew from strength to strength.

As we know, Hild began the monastic life with only a handful of companions, and it must be supposed that the number of specialist buildings grew as the number of the community grew. As an absolute minimum, the original little group would have needed a place to sleep and a place to worship: sleeping quarters and somewhere to pray, that is to say, a church as soon as practicable. We know that in those first few years after her call from Aidan, he and others from Lindisfarne were in close touch with Hild, initiating her into the way of Ionian spirituality and monastic life. We must, therefore, suppose a place where visitors could be received and then later on a hall suitable for feasting. A place for food preparation would have made way for larger kitchens. Then there would have been a space set apart for the sick and the dying among the community. With no soap or disinfectant and little hot water, hygiene was poor and infectious diseases of all sorts spread quickly. By the time that Whitby was fully developed under Hild, the infirmary would have formed an essential part of the monastic complex.

On the basis of what we can glean from Bede's account of the activities at Whitby, and what is known of other monasteries of the period, Julie Ann Smith describes the monastery as it would have been at its height:

> So it is clear that Whitby was a complex set of buildings which provided accommodation for a mixture of male and female monastics, their servants, and novices, as well as the functional buildings for at least one church, scriptorium, infirmary, workshops for such necessary activities as textile production and metalworking.[11]

Sickness was a constant feature of life at this time, randomly striking down those inside and those outside the monastery. The plague swept through monastic houses in the same way in which it blighted the lives of the general population. Plague was by no means the only sickness, and where people from the peasant class lacked proper nourishment, they were more susceptible to illness of all sorts. Furthermore, the prevalence of war had left great number of men who had been maimed in battle.

Medical knowledge was virtually nonexistent, so death was very much part of life. From the 540s, a great plague had spread westward throughout the Roman Empire and further afield, with outbreaks of plague recurring right up to the eighth century.[12] By Hild's time, they had reached Britain, with a particularly virulent outbreak toward the end of 664, the year of the Synod of Whitby. Outbreaks of plague are recorded frequently by Bede in his *Ecclesiastical History*.

The story is told that, at the time when Ceolfrid was Abbot of Jarrow, an epidemic so severe swept through the monastery that only two monks were left who were able to sing the divine office with antiphons, Ceolfrid himself and a young boy. The young boy is widely reckoned to have been Bede.

We know from Bede's account of Caedmon's death that those who were sick or about to die were taken to a separate house or infirmary. Yet though Caedmon had been feeling unwell for several days, when he asked his attendant to prepare a place for him in the infirmary, the attendant was surprised to receive such a request. It did not seem to the attendant that Caedmon was on the verge of death.[13] The main work of the infirmary would have been care for the dying.

THE STUDY OF MEDICINE

Monasteries were to become renowned for their herbal remedies. This lay in the future. Nonetheless, even during Hild's lifetime, there began to appear indications that monasteries would become places of physical healing.

In chapter 9, which discusses Hild's role as Teacher, we will discover that one of her students, John, who would go on to become bishop of Hexham and then York, had studied medicine under Theodore, Archbishop of Canterbury, before going on to Whitby to further his education under Hild. Theodore figures prominently in the story of Hild's life, and more will be said about him later. For the moment, it is sufficient to consider his interest in medicine.

Born in Tarsus in 602, Theodore was most likely educated in Antioch (modern Antakya).[14] Theodore's method of interpreting Scripture was the same as that taught at Antioch. When he studied a biblical text, he used other fields of study, including medicine, to interpret them. Michael Lapidge detects in the biblical commentaries associated with Theodore at Canterbury "a persistent concern with explaining . . . the nature of the flora, fauna, minerals and precious stones mentioned in the Bible. . . . The ancillary disciplines of philosophy, rhetoric and medicine are often the sources of explanations."[15] Lapidge suggests that Theodore may well have attended the lectures of Stephen of Alexandria in Constantinople, an expert in many areas including medicine. Theodore's commentaries "contain extended discussion of various types of fever" as well as a discussion of lunacy, which both seem to follow Stephen's teaching.[16]

Theodore, therefore, appeared on the Anglo-Saxon scene not merely as the highest-ranking prelate as Archbishop of Canterbury but also a great scholar. Along with Adrian, the abbot of the monastery of SS Peter and Paul (later St. Augustine's), Theodore was the founder of the school at Canterbury. The most famous pupil of this school was Aldhelm. In a letter, Aldhelm gives the syllabus at the Canterbury school, and medicine does not seem to have been included. Nonetheless, we know that Theodore had a keen interest in medicine, and we know that he taught it to John.

Bede devotes five chapters to the miraculous healing powers of John.[17] Of particular interest is his account of the healing of a dumb youth with scabs on his head. John first tells the boy to show him his tongue and then he holds the boy by the chin and makes the sign of cross on his tongue. He tells the boy to say something and the boy's tongue is loosed. John then makes the boy repeat the letters of the alphabet, then syllables, then whole words, and then sentences. When the boy could speak, a physician was called in to heal the skin on his head. As the physician did his work, John prayed for the boy and gave him his blessing and the boy was cured, eventually growing a fine head of hair.

For Bede, thesc are miraculous events, and in describing the youth's exuberance at being able to express himself in speech, Bede makes allusion to the healing of the cripple by Peter and John in the third chapter of Acts.[18] We are also led to be reminded of how Jesus healed the dumb. At the same time, we glean from this tale how John, through his study of medicine, had gained insight into the physical and psychological workings of the human body.

Yet while, thanks to Theodore, the study of medicine was gradually finding its way into the curriculum of the monastic schools, we should remember that the actual practice of effective medicine was some way off.

AN OUTSTANDING CENTER OF LEARNING

It was only the monasteries that kept learning alive in the dark early medieval times of continual warfare and pagan advance. The monastery that Hild founded at Whitby was undoubtedly the main center of learning in Anglo-Saxon England before the appointment of Theodore to Canterbury.[19] Whitby would not lose its preeminence in Northumbria until after 674, when Benedict Biscop received land from King Ecgfrith to build the monastery and its well-stocked library at Wearmouth.

Of the many essential industries that facilitated the entire monastic enterprise, one of the most important was the copying of manuscripts. To provide for the liturgy, for theological study, and for missionary work, writings were needed, all of which had at some stage to be copied by hand. Styluses and book clasps have been excavated, providing evidence of a scriptorium, yet no surviving Whitby manuscript from the time of Hild's tenure has been identified.

Yet one of the most important pieces of writing from this period did come from Whitby during the time of Hild's successor, the Abbess Aelffled. This was the first *Life of Gregory*, "the source of two of the most famous legends of the Middle Ages, the Mass of St. Gregory and the story of Trajan's rescue from hell." According to Bertram Colgrave, this *Life* has "some claim to be the earliest extant piece of written literature produced by the Anglo-Saxons."[20] And despite the full title of Colgrave's translation, *The Earliest Life of Gregory the Great: By an Anonymous Monk of Whitby*, there is no reason to suppose that this was not written by a woman.

We may assume that Hild would have had the overall responsibility for ensuring that manuscripts were copied, and we can have some idea of the type of manuscripts these would have been. We know that Hild was responsible for the education of priests and bishops and sent them out to evangelize and to provide pastoral care for those who had converted to Christianity. Minimally these priests would have required some sort of Mass book or missal, including some Scripture readings and some basic liturgical prayers for other sacraments. The small pocket missal would have been high on the list of books to be copied.

It is reckoned that Aidan of Lindisfarne on his travels around Northumbria would have carried with him something like the Stowe Missal. The Stowe missal (found in Stowe House, Buckinghamshire) is an ancient Irish Mass book dating from around 800. It provides an excellent example of the type of book that would have been taken on their journeys by priests and bishops at the turn of the ninth century.

The Stowe missal contains "extracts from the Gospel of St. John, the ordinary and canon of the mass, a few variable prayers and scriptural readings which would do for any mass, a few prayers for special masses, e.g. of the dead, and orders for the administration of baptism and extreme unction."[21] The beauty of such a composition is that it contained in one volume all that was essential for the traveling priest. How much more useful would this small book have been for those who, like Aidan, chose to walk the footpaths, rather than ride on horseback, and thus had to carry with them everything they needed.

Thomas O'Loughlin describes how one missal would differ from another, while retaining the essentials.

> In the earlier period missals had no definite shape as books and their form depended on the particular conditions of when and where they were commissioned and the availability of resources. As to their contents there was a similar variability, not just because no two manuscript books have ever the exact same text, but because the nature of their production allowed for variations and additions to be made with minimal difficulty. Then when that missal was used as

> an exemplar for another book, all its accretions would be transmitted to the new book as its basic text.[22]

Although no copies of a missal survive from Anglo-Saxon England, we can be confident that when Hild herself sent out priests and bishops on mission, at a minimum she would have provided them with a missal of some sort. No one missal would have been an exact copy of another. Decisions would need to be taken as to what should be included, what should be adjusted, and what should be left out, according to the particular requirements of the priest for whom it was intended and according to what materials were available to be copied at the time of writing, and indeed, what new liturgical compositions had become available. It would seem quite plausible to suggest that at least some of these were decisions taken by Hild herself.

At its height the monastery that Hild founded at Whitby was a thriving hub of prayer and work of various sorts, with the core focus on the worship of God, the love of neighbor through hospitality, alms-giving and care for the sick, and the proclamation of the Gospel. With its monastic buildings proper at the center, including the all-important scriptorium, the entire monastic estate operated like a parish. Within its boundaries, all the essential industries necessary for the quasi-parish community to flourish were present. And flourish it did!

NOTES

1. Beda, *Historia Ecclesiastica*, IV.21 [23] CLII
2. Bede, *Ecclesiastical History*, III.26; Beda, *Historia Ecclesiastica*, III.26.
3. Mayr-Harting, *The Coming of Christianity*, 225–26.
4. Sarah Foot, *Monastic Life*, 236, following Colgrave, ed. and trans., *Two Lives of Saint Cuthbert: A Life by an Anonymous Monk of Lindisfarne and Bede's Prose Life* (Cambridge: Cambridge University Press, 1940), 246–47.
5. Aidan had eschewed trappings of clerical status and saw himself as a traveling missionary based at Lindisfarne. By Alcuin's time, the status of bishop enjoyed by the Lindisfarne abbot was all-important—at least to Alcuin.
6. Bede, *Ecclesiastical History*, IV.8; Beda, *Historia Ecclesiastica*, IV.8.
7. Mayr-Harting, *The Coming of Christianity*, 99.
8. Mundahl-Harris, *St. Hilda and Her Times*, 10.
9. Bede, *Ecclesiastical History*, III.26 194; Beda, *Historia Ecclesiastica, Liber Tertius*, 26, CXIV.
10. See Chapter 1. Bede, *Ecclesiastical History*, III.14. Beda, *Historia Ecclesiastica*, III.14.
11. Smith, *Ordering Women's Lives*, 133–34.
12. MacCulloch, *A History of Christianity*, 436.

13. Bede, *Ecclesiastical History*, IV. 24. Beda, *Historia Ecclesiastica, Liber Quartus*, 22.

14. Michael Lapidge, ed., "The Career of Archbishop Theodor," in *Archbishop Theodore: Commemorative studies on His Life and Influence* (Cambridge: Cambridge University Press, 1995), 3.

15. Lapidge, *Archbishop Theodore*, 5.

16. Lapidge, *Archbishop Theodore*, 18.

17. Bede, *Ecclesiastical History*, V. 2–6; Beda, *Historia Ecclesia*, V. 2–6.

18. Bede, *Ecclesiastical History*, V.3; Beda, *Historia Ecclesia, Liber Quintus*, 2.

19. See Peter Hunter Blair, "Whitby as a Centre of Learning in the Seventh Century," in *Learning and Literature in Anglo-Saxon England*, edited by Michael Lapidge and Helmut Gneuss (Cambridge: Cambridge University Press, 1985), 30: "During the middle years of the seventh century, Whitby was unquestionably the preeminent center of learning in Anglo-Saxon England."

20. Bertram Colgrave, ed. and trans., *The Earliest Life of Gregory the Great: By an Anonymous Monk of Whitby* (Cambridge: Cambridge University Press, 1985), v.

21. Mayr-Harting, *The Coming of Christianity*, 244.

22. O'Loughlin, *Theology*, 130–31.

Chapter Seven

Hild the Confessor

While the whole of the Christian world relied for its spiritual nourishment on the weekly celebration of the Eucharist as a background to its entire life, for many centuries, including the seventh, the core focus of pastoral care seems to have been not so much Eucharistic as penitential. In other words, in line with the practices of the early desert mothers and fathers, it seems that the emphasis was on confession of sins and the performance of penances, rather than the Mass. Thus, when Aidan called Hild to serve the Northumbrian Church, an important part of her ministry would probably have been to hear confessions and set penances. In doing so, not only would she have been fully a cog in the tradition of the Roman Catholic Church, which comes down from the apostles, she would have also played a leading role in the shaping of the tradition at a time of significant development in the way in which the sacrament was practiced.[1]

To appreciate the part that Hild played in the shaping of sacramental confession, it is necessary to set out, at least in outline, the complex history of the reconciliation of sinners.

THE EARLY CHURCH

In the New Testament, we find that the earliest Christians were exhorted by James: "confess your sins to one another" (James 5:16). This sentiment is echoed in the Didache, a text originating probably in Syria in the early part of the second century. "In the church you shall acknowledge your transgressions, and you shall not come near for your prayer with an evil conscience."[2] Thus, it would seem that lesser sins were in some way treated by the Christian community as they assembled to pray.

It was baptism, of course, which was the fundamental sacrament for washing away a person's sins, as it continues to be to this day. The Church teaches that the grace imparted at baptism is sufficient to keep a person from serious sin. Thus, when the baptized went on to commit what have traditionally been called "mortal sins"—sins that bring death to the soul—the early Church took a very serious view. The sinner was barred from the Eucharist and was given severe penances to perform before being allowed back into the Christian community. Reception of the Eucharist (communion) following the period of penance would be the sign that the sinner had been reconciled with the community and with God.

By the end of the fourth century, there were three mortal sins especially at issue: murder, adultery, and apostasy, or denying the faith. The last was hugely damaging to the Church in times of persecution because it often meant the betrayal of other Christians and their torture and death if they themselves refused to apostatize, that is to say if they refused to deny their Christian faith and worship pagan gods. The confession of these sins was a public affair, as was the enactment of the penances prescribed, before the penitent was reconciled and publicly welcomed back into the Christian community. In Rome, the solemn ceremony of reconciliation took place on Holy Thursday. This sacramental forgiveness was allowed only once after Baptism.

A NEW SYSTEM FOR CONFESSION

In the fifth and sixth centuries, a quite different dispensation for the confession of sins and their sacramental forgiveness began to take hold thanks to a Celtic spirituality that flowered in the numerous Irish monasteries that were founded and flourished at this time. Thomas O'Loughlin, who has written extensively on the topic, is clear about the novelty of the new system. The proponents of Celtic penitential practices were "part of a new system that broke radically with the practice of penance in the Church at the time."[3] The whole penitential process, rather than being played out in public, was a private affair, which could be repeated many times. Furthermore, it treated not merely of extremely grave sins but also lesser sins. These lesser sins would later be termed "venial" sins, in contrast to grave or "mortal" sins.

There was a further innovation in the Irish practice of frequent confession. It was not only the frequency of confession that was innovative but also the carefully worked out tariff of penances that were given and the advice, tailored to the individual, as to how further sin might be avoided. Such advice might be one-off and in depth, or with frequent confession, could form the basis of ongoing spiritual direction.

In Celtic monasteries, sin was seen not so much in terms of grave deeds that cut a person off from the grace received in baptism, but rather sin was seen as everything that impeded a person from living a life of perfection. In their fiercely demanding ascetic lives, Irish monastics sought to be free of those daily lapses that hindered union with God through contemplation. In pursuit of this aim, they developed a sophisticated system of penances that were codified in various "penitentials"—written documents prescribing penances for sins in various circumstances. The pursuit of perfection entailed an entire life of penitence.

O'Loughlin has written extensively on the penitentials. He describes *The Penitential of Finnian*, written probably in the late sixth century, as:

> A deliberately short handbook for pastoral use in dealing with the sins of repentant Christians. . . . The fifty or more situations envisaged as requiring penance cover the whole range of sins, and it assumes that the one judging the required penance—and there is no hint as to his status in terms of Holy Orders—will meet people from the whole of society, lay, monastic, clerical, men and women.[4]

Penances were specifically tailored to help the penitent to overcome their own particular weakness that led to the sin. And Finnian's Penitential seems to leave open the possibility that there was no necessity for the one who heard the confession and adjudged the penance to be in holy orders. In other words, to hear confessions it may not have been necessary to be an ordained deacon or an ordained priest. Furthermore, the monastic practice of frequent confession had spread to those outside the monastery.

In the following quotation, Henri Marrou identifies the Celtic system of penance as it developed in the monasteries with what would later become known as the "Chapter of Faults."

> Frequent, even daily confession of sins was part of the usual ascetical way of life. It was not only what monks even today know as the "Chapter of Faults" and "manifestation of conscience" to the Superior, but the association of the Superior in the sacrament of penance in the true sense. That is the innovation which became widespread; it even affected lay people, who came to ask the abbot or priests how to expiate their sins.[5]

The inclusion of ordinary people in penitential practices resulted not through compulsion, but from a genuine desire to strive toward the life of perfection, which prompted ordinary people to approach the "abbot or priests." Marrou typically omits any mention of the abbess as the one to be approached, and indeed abbesses were gradually excluded from hearing confessions. Yet we know that in the early seventh century, there was no difference between the roles and responsibilities of the abbot and the abbess.[6]

CONFESSION TO THE ABBESS

There are two good reasons to believe that Hild heard confessions and set penances. First, there is good evidence that this was common practice among abbesses at the time. Secondly, once the actual mechanics of the practice are understood, a careful reading of Bede seems to suggest that Hild too must have been active as a confessor.

Gary Macy provides much information regarding abbesses who heard confessions. He tells, for example, of St. Bertila, who, according to her hagiographer, heard confessions for the entire surrounding area. "[Bertila] drew the family of the monastery or the surrounding neighbors through holy communion, so that, hearing their confessions, they would do penance for their sins."[7]

One of the best known female confessors for whom we have reliable records is Saint Ita (or Ite), who lived in Ireland from around 475 to 570. There are numerous stories recorded in her *Life* that tell of her dealings with various sinners and the penances she set. One such example tells of a certain sister (*sanctimonialis*) who confessed to fornication, and who was restored having done penance given to her by the blessed Ita (*Et sanata est, agens penitentiam secundum iussionem sancte Yte*).[8] From Ita's *Life*, we learn that Brendan of Clonfert both sought her counsel[9] and obeyed her on matters involving third parties.[10] Stephanie Hollis points to the earliest *Life* of Brendan to show that Brendan made his own confession to Ita.[11]

The *Vita Prima Sancti Brendani* has yet to be translated from Latin into English. According to my own translation, chapter 71, to which Hollis refers, says that after five years away, Brendan returned and went first to Bishop Erc, and then to Ita, his foster-mother (*nutrix*). It then records how the truly saintly Ita received Brendan and his disciples, behaving "just like the Christ behaved with the apostles" (*quasi Christum cum apostolis*). Ita speaks to Brendan, asking why he was planning to undertake very difficult tasks without seeking her counsel [*absque consilio meo*]. She then advises him, and having taken her advice to heart [*Cuius consilio committens se*], Brendan continues to the region of Connacht where all works out well.[12]

This chapter is replete with biblical allusions. Furthermore, certain Latin words carry a whole depth of meaning that escape straight translation. The word *nutrix*, for example, can simply mean "nurse," or it may be translated as "foster-mother." Ita was in fact foster-mother to Brendan for the first five years of his life. *Nutrix*, however, is a strong word in this context. The *nutrix* is the one who gives life to the disciple. It is clear from this chapter that Ita acts in the person of Christ (*in persona Christi*) in relation to Brendan.[13]

HILD AND THE NEW SYSTEM

By the seventh century, Irish penitential practices had reached Northumbria. It would seem unlikely that Hild, having been instructed by Aidan, did not take on the responsibilities of confessor, and a careful reading finds what might well be regarded as supporting evidence for this in Bede. Bede praises Hild for her wisdom, her *prudentia*, a word that also implies discretion. Hild's wisdom, her discretion, was such that not only ordinary people in need, but even kings and princes sometimes, would seek her counsel. Furthermore, they would follow the counsel she gave (*Tantae autem erat ipsa prudentiae, ut non solum mediocres quique in necessitatibus suis, sed etiam reges ac principes nonnumquam ab ea consilium quaererent, et inuenirent*).[14] With Hild as with Ita in relation to Brendan, counsel [*consilium*] is given and followed. *Consilium* here would seem to imply judgment, as well as advice, a plan, or counsel. And in each case, the recipient acts on the judgment immediately and to good effect. Bede tells us that princes and ordinary folk, as well as the vowed religious of Hild's community, were drawn to her to discuss their difficulties.[15] They related to her the obstacles that hindered them from leading a fully Christian life. One interpretation would be to say that they confessed to her. She recommended the specific good works and, where appropriate, the reading they should undertake. One interpretation would be to say that she gave penances. Whether she had access to the penitentials we cannot tell, but on the whole, given their prevalence, it would seem likely that she did.

Thus, we are entitled to argue that Hild, as prominent monastic head, played an indispensable part in the spread of Celtic/Irish spirituality with its distinctive penitential practices. These penitential practices were to become fully part of the sacrament of penance as it developed over the centuries, and the innovations that Hild surely helped to consolidate remain part of the sacramental process to this day.

Without Hild and women like her, things might have turned out very differently. The Celtic practice of frequent private confession linked to spiritual counseling would eventually win out over the Roman practice of once-only public confession. But this was far from a foregone conclusion during the period when the Roman and the Irish systems operated concurrently. This is clearly illustrated by what happened in Spain. In 589 the Spanish Church, which had been Arian up to that point,[16] embraced Catholicism at the third Council of Toledo. Canon 11 of this council condemned private penance and demanded a return to Roman practices:

> It came to our knowledge that in some Churches in Spain people go through the discipline of penance for their sins, not according to the canons but in a most shameful manner, viz., as often as they happen to fall into sin they ask

> for reconciliation from the priest. To eradicate this execrable presumption this holy Council commands that penance be granted according to the old canons, which means that (the priest) first suspends from the communion the man who repents of his deed, that he lets him come frequently to the imposition of hands along with the other penitents, that after he has completed the time of satisfaction with the approval of the priest, the priest restores him to communion. But those who fall back into their former vices, either during the time of penance or after reconciliation, should be condemned in accordance with the severity of the earlier canons.[17]

In the end, it was the Celtic system of frequent confession with spiritual direction that prevailed and became the standard Roman rite of the western Church that still operates today.

WAS THIS THE SACRAMENT OF CONFESSION?

I have claimed that Hild and others responded to those who sought spiritual direction to overcome those lapses that prevented them from living a fully Christian life, by giving counsel, or making judgment. Furthermore, the judgment that was made, the counsel given, when followed, proved efficacious. This raises the question: When Hild and the other monastic heads responded to those who approached them in this way, were they engaged in what the Catholic Church today understands by the sacrament of confession?

One answer to this question is to be found in the online *Catholic Encyclopedia*. A paragraph titled "Confession to the abbess" begins,

> When the older monastic rules prescribe confession to the superior, they do not refer to sacramental confession, but to the "chapter of faults" or the *culpa*, at which the religious accuse themselves of ordinary external fault patent to all, and of minor infractions of the rule. This "confession" may be made either privately to the superior or publicly in the chapter-house; no absolution is given and the penance assigned is merely disciplinary.[18]

What the *Catholic Encyclopedia* says here might well apply to the monastic rules of the late Middle Ages, after the sacramental practices of earlier centuries had been removed from the agency of women. It is through this type of argument that the Magisterium (the teaching authority of the Catholic Church) is able to maintain that the exclusion of women from the administration of the sacrament of confession has been the constant tradition of the Church.[19] Such an argument, however, cannot be upheld with regard to Hild's own century, the seventh; thus, it cannot be said to constitute the constant tradition of the church *from the beginning*.

In claiming that confession to a monastic superior was not sacramental confession, the clinching argument in the quotation is that when confession was made to an abbess, no absolution was given. If we examine the Celtic system of confession as it developed in the fifth, sixth, and seventh centuries, no absolution was given by anyone, whether it be priest, deacon, abbot, or abbess. Absolution is the declaration that the priest makes acting on Christ's authority and in his name (*in persona Christi*) to the effect that the penitent's sins are forgiven. The words are spoken: "I absolve you from your sins, in the name of the Father and of the Son and of the Holy Spirit." In the centuries under consideration, forgiveness was not enacted with these words, and this is true of both the Celtic and Roman practices. Absolution in this sense was simply not part of the penitential process. Forgiveness was not located in a declarative statement. Furthermore, as O'Loughlin states in relation to the Penitential of Cummean, "forgiveness" for Cummean and those in the Irish tradition was "a process rather than an event."[20]

The remission of sins, according to Cummean, takes place in twelve different ways, which may overlap. O'Loughlin lists as follows: baptism with water; the disposition of the individual (*affectus*); almsgiving; the presence of tears (the attitude of sorrow); the acknowledgment of crimes; the affliction of heart (first) and body (penitential practices); the amendment of one's ways; the intercession of the saints; mercy and faith; helping another to convert from sin; offering forgiveness to another; and the baptism of blood (martyrdom). It was not until well into the second millennium that absolution by a priest came to be seen as essential to the sacramental forgiveness of sins.[21]

The other problem with the quotation from the *Catholic Encyclopedia* is that the very distinction that is being made between confession, which is sacramental, and confession, which is merely disciplinary, is anachronistic when applied to the first millennium. It was only centuries later, as canon lawyers sought to set out the rights and responsibilities of the various offices of the church, that they came to identify seven actions as "sacraments" and to define in legalistic detail what was meant by the term "sacrament" itself.

As Richard McBrien puts it "the Church lived through its entire first millennium and then some without ever having settled upon even a final definition of *sacrament*, let alone their precise number."[22] Before that, there were numerous sacred rites, using blessed ashes, holy oils, baptismal water, and so on, all of which were believed to mediate God's grace.

By the end of the eleventh century, there was a trend in Western Europe toward standardization and categorization in all aspects of life. In this more legalistic environment, a standard definition for "sacrament" was required, and clarification was needed regarding their exact number. In the first half of the twelfth century in Paris, Hugh of St. Victor set out a definition of a sacrament that seemed to call into question whether confession was a sacrament because confession seemed to lack a physical sign that resembled the grace that was bestowed—an essential element in Hugh's definition. Peter Lombard, in the middle of the same century, again in Paris, provided a definition that overcame this difficulty, and so the sacraments were set at seven. And their administration was very much the preserve of the ordained ministry.

As the legal mind-set associated with the Norman invasion of England began to sweep Europe in the eleventh century, the canon lawyers applied their legal minds to sacramental practices. The sacramental process of confession became as it were split off from other sacramental acts. Confession came to be seen as efficacious in itself, with its own power to reconcile the sinner. O'Loughlin discerns in the Irish spirituality that produced the penitentials a "unity" of the sacraments "wherein the individual encounters the mercy of God in Christ in the midst of his people." He describes this unity as having been "split up into boxes"[23] once the canon lawyers had imposed their neat legal structure.

To return to the original question: Were Hild and the other monastic heads engaged in what the Catholic Church today understands by the sacrament of confession? Looking again at the quotation from Marrou, we seem to find an answer different from that put forward by the *Catholic Encyclopedia*. Marrou considers that in the early period when people went to the abbeys to confess their sins and seek direction, the Superior, that is to say the head of the abbey, was associated with "the sacrament of penance in the true sense."[24] This must indeed be the case. If "confession" is not "sacramental confession" unless absolution is given, then there was no sacramental confession in the early medieval period. Furthermore, to argue a distinction between sacramental confession and disciplinary confession is to argue for a distinction that would not have been understood during this period and which simply did not exist.

THE PROCESS OF EXCLUSION

As the centuries wore on and the canon lawyers got down to work, this distinction, between the confession of sins, which is sacramental, and that which is not, did, of course, come to be made. It coincided with a move to ordain the male heads of monasteries and set them on a higher plane than their female equivalents. Such a move required the exclusion of the abbess from the role of confessor, an exclusion that took place in stages. So successful was the move that the twentieth-century *Catholic Encyclopedia* is able to assert correctly that "abbesses have no spiritual jurisdiction, and can exercise no authority that is in any way connected with the power of the keys or of orders." However, the way in which the *Encyclopedia* continues might well be construed as misleading:

> During the Middle Ages, however, attempts were not infrequently made to usurp this spiritual power of the priesthood, and we read of Abbesses who besides being guilty of many minor encroachments on the functions of the sacerdotal [priestly] office, presumed to interfere even in the administration of the sacrament of penance and confessed their nuns.[25]

The *Encyclopedia* says that abbesses would often in small ways take on things that only priests were allowed to do. It does not mention that in times past, the early seventh century, for example, these things, which at a later date only priests would be allowed to do, were in fact things that abbesses were allowed to do. They were actually part of the job description of the abbess.

Doubtless the *Catholic Encyclopedia* would argue that there is evidence from rulings of medieval councils and synods that expressly forbade abbesses from participating in confessional practice and castigating those who did so. What this points to, however, is not that the abbess had never had responsibility for hearing confessions, but rather that the responsibility that she had once had was being taken away. From the late seventh century, there was a determined attempt to wrest all spiritual power from everyone except ordained men, and so enhance the standing of the ordained by moving them onto an altogether higher plane. This maneuver was ultimately successful, but it took effect in a piecemeal fashion. Those abbesses who retained their powers for longer were those "presumed to interfere even in the administration of the sacrament of penance."[26]

It was during the period of transition, as the abbess gradually had her authority taken away, that Theodore became Archbishop of Canterbury in 669. Theodore's *Penitential* was compiled either during his lifetime of within half a century or so after his death in 690. Although it did not preclude women from acting as spiritual directors, it did rule that women should not formally adjudge penances. The fact that it was felt necessary to make this ruling indicates both that women were in fact setting penances and that tighter regulation of sacramental practices served as a means of excluding women from the "formal" side of this ministry.

It has already been demonstrated that it is anachronistic to talk of absolution in this context, and here it is evident that the matter at issue in the *Penitential* was the authority to adjudge penances rather than the authority to grant absolution. Stephanie Hollis comments:

> The exclusive concern with the lawfulness of women prescribing penance in *Theodore's Penitential* suggests that their exercise of the confessional did not

> entail absolution. But in this respect, their [women's] administration of confession is unlikely to have differed from prevailing practice, since confession was not generally held to be a sacrament until the 12th century, and in the early Roman church absolution was intimated by the laying on of hands, or by a prayer, but not by declarative statement.[27]

From the twelfth century to the present day, the authority to hear confessions hinges on the power to grant absolution in the name of Jesus who entrusted this power to the Church. The priest acts *in persona Christi.* The power to forgive sins became invested in the words of absolution "I absolve you from your sins . . ." rather than the adjudication of penance, as the Church moved into an increasingly legalistic world. In the Roman Catholic Church, women are currently excluded from administering the sacrament of penance on the grounds of the Church's constant tradition. Yet as I have shown, for centuries, women did administer sacramental confession. To argue against this on the grounds that women never had the power to grant absolution as a declarative statement would not only be anachronistic, but it would also mean that there was no constant tradition because in the early Church and in the early medieval period no one was granting absolution in this way.

NOTES

1. For evidence that the development in question is affirmed as belonging to the history of the Catholic tradition, see *Catechism of the Catholic Church* (Geoffrey Chapman 1994), 325 §1447: "Over the centuries the concrete form in which the Church has exercised this power received from the Lord has varied considerably. . . . During the seventh century Irish missionaries, inspired by the Eastern monastic tradition, took to continental Europe the 'private' practice of penance. . . . From that time on, the sacrament has been performed in secret between penitent and priest. In its main lines this is the form of penance that the church has practised to this day."
2. *The Didache*, ed. Mark Nash, based on the Roberts-Donaldson translation (London: WRCDT, 2009), ch. 4.
3. O'Loughlin, *Celtic Theology*, 61.
4. O'Loughlin, *Celtic Theology*, 52.
5. Marrou, "The Conversion of Northern Europe," 455.
6. In Anglo-Saxon England the legislation of church councils draws no distinction between what was expected of the leader of a religious community on grounds of sex; all had the same general responsibilities. See Yorke, *Nunneries and the Anglo-Saxon Royal Houses*, 123. Yorke (140 n161) refers to Catherine Cubitt's *Anglo-Saxon Church Councils c. 650–c.850* (London: Leicester, 1995), *passim*.
7. Macy, *A Hidden History of Women's Ordination*, 83. Then, Macy (p. 198 n162): "*Familiam quoque monasterii sive vicinos propinquos per sanctam communionem attrahebat, ut, datis confessionibus, paenitentiam pro peccatis suis agerent; ex quibus*

plurimis emendatis et sibi praemium adquisivit et illorum animabus lucrum fecit" (c. 6 of *Vita Bertilae Abbatissae Calensis*, in *Passiones vitaeque sanctorum aevi merovingici*, ed. B. Krusch and W. Levison, MGH, Scriptorum rerum Merovingicarum 6 [Hannover: Hahn, 1913], 106.

8. "*Quedam sanctimonialis, que fuerat sub cura sancte Yte, occulte fornicauit; et in crastina die beata Yta uocauit eam ad se, et ait ei: 'Cur tu, soror, non curasti custodire uirginitatem tuam?' Illa uero negans quod fecit, dixit ei sancta Yta: 'Nonne heri in illo loco fornicasti, et ita tibi contigit?' Statimque sciens illa beatam Ytam prophetissam esse de preteritis et de futuris, confessa est ueritatem rei. Et sanata est, agens penitentiam secundum iussionem sancte Yte*" in C. Plummer, ed., "*Vita Sancte Ite Virginis*," in *Vitae Sanctorum Hiberniae* (Oxford: Oxford University Press, 1910), Book II §16

9. "*Interrogans sanctus Brendanus quodam tempore beatam Ytam de tribus operibus que satis Deo placent, et de tribus que satis displicent. . . .*" in '*Vita Sancte Ite Virginis*,' Book II §22.

10. '*Vita Sancte Ite Virginis*," Book II §34

11. Hollis, *Anglo-Saxon Women*, 135

12. C. Plummer, ed., "*Vita Prima Sancti Brendani*," in *Vitae Sanctorum Hiberniae* (Oxford: Oxford University Press, 1910), Book I, 98–151, ch. 71 reads: "*Post quinque annos reuersus est homo Dei ad propriam regionem. Et audientes uicini et cognati aduentum eius, conuenerunt ad eum, interrogantes eum de suis magnis laboribus. Et audientes doctrinam eius, multi, relictis mundi vanitatibus, Christum secuti sunt. Et fecit ibi multas uirtutes et sanitates; inter quas uirtutes patrem suum conuertit ad Christum. Post hec uisitauit sanctum episcopum Ercum, et deinde sanctam Itam nutricem suam. Sancta uero Ita, quasi Christum cum apostolis, recepit eum cum discipulis suis. Et ait ei: 'Fili mi, quare absque consilio meo opus illud arduum attemptare uoluisti? Terram enim a Domino tibi ostensam non inuenies in pellibus mortuorum animalium; quia terra sancta est ualde, in qua sanguis humanus non est effusus. Applica ergo artifices qui sciant facere tibi uas ligneum. Forsitan sic explorabis terram illam.' Cuius consilio committens se Brandanus, in regionem Connacteorum perrexit; quia ibi magis apta ligna esse pro hoc opere credidit. Illic quoque parauit cum ingenio artificum nauem contra maris pericula satis tutam. Cumque artifices et fabri pro laboribus hanc mercedem quererent a iuro Dei, ut secum ire eos permitteret, hoc eis pro munere concessit. Et cum parati essent omnes ad intrandum nauim, tunc uenit quidam preconis in populo gerens officium, qui, genibus flexis suppliciter rogauit, ut uir Dei secum ire permitteret. Tunc pius pater precibus supplicantis inclinatus, vna cum ceteris admisit. Et totondit eum uir Dei, ut silicet signum religionis in capite deferret. Et nauigantes in nomine Domini primo uenerunt ad insulam Ayrne, vbi sanctos Dei Endeum et Pupeum et Nochatum inuenerunt, cum quibus in caritate non ficta per mensem unum comorati sunt.*"

13. For much of the twentieth century it was argued that a woman could not become a priest because she could not act *in persona Christi.*

14. Beda, *Historia Ecclesiastica Gentis Anglorum, Liber Quartus*, 21 [23] CLII. See Bede, *Ecclesiastical History*, IV.23.245–46.

15. *Tantae autem erat ipsa prudentiae, ut non solum mediocres quique in necessitatibus suis, sed etiam reges ac principes nonnumquam ab ea consilium quaererent, et inuenirent.* Beda, *Historia Ecclesiastica, Liber Quartus*, 21 [23], CLII.

16. Arianism rejected the full divinity of Christ and was considered heretical by Catholic Christians.

17. J. Neuner and J. Dupuis, eds., *The Christian Faith, in the Doctrinal Documents of the Catholic Church* (New York: Collins, 1986), §1607. The original text is to be found in J. D., *Sacrorum Conciliorum nova et amplissima* collectio (Florence: Mansi, 1759), IX 995.

18. "Absess," New Advent *Catholic Encyclopedia* at http://www.newadvent.org/cathen/01007e.htm. Accessed November 7, 2017.

19. See *Ordinatio Sacerdotalis*, 1994, §1 (https://w2.vatican.va/content/john-paul-ii/en/apost_letters/1994/documents/hf_jp-ii_apl_19940522_ordinatio-sacerdotalis.html; accessed September 19, 2018), the apostolic Letter of John Paul II to the Bishops of the Catholic Church on reserving priestly ordination to men. This document states that "priestly ordination, which hands on the office entrusted by Christ to his Apostles of teaching, sanctifying and governing the faithful, has in the Catholic church from the beginning always been reserved to men alone."

20. O'Loughlin, *Celtic Theology*, 63.

21. O'Loughlin, *Celtic Theology*, 63–64.

22. Richard McBrien, *Catholicism: New Study Edition* (New York: HarperCollins, 1994), 800.

23. O'Loughlin, *Celtic Theology*, 64.

24. Marrou, "The Conversion of Northern Europe," 455. The fuller quotation is above.

25. "Absess," New Advent *Catholic Encyclopedia*.

26. Hollis, *Anglo-Saxon Women*, 136.

27. Hollis, *Anglo-Saxon Women*, 136.

Chapter Eight

A Window onto Ancient Liturgies

When examining female monasticism in the first millennium, it is common to speculate on the work likely to have been undertaken by the men in the houses in which women religious lived. It is plausibly suggested that men would have been needed for their physical strength and so for protection and for a certain amount of heavy lifting. In addition, it is assumed that religious women would have had the ministrations of a preferably resident male priest to celebrate Mass and to hear confessions. In fact, as we saw in the last chapter, it fell to the abbess to hear confessions in her own community. And it was not simply the case that the abbess could hear the confessions of her nuns; this was her duty. Furthermore, there was no obligation for any nun to confess to anyone other than her abbess or someone delegated by the abbess.[1]

It remains to consider what weight was actually given in seventh-century England to the necessity for the weekly celebration of the Eucharist.

THE PLACE OF THE MASS

Church historians have implicitly assumed that in the hidden period that culminated in the seventh century ordained men were required in women's monasteries to celebrate Mass on a regular basis and to administer the sacraments. What has become clear is that attributing to this period the paramount importance of weekly Mass is anachronistic.

The requirement to be present at the weekly breaking of bread, that is to say, the Eucharist, forms the backdrop to the story of Christianization. Its origins lie in the command of Jesus to "Do this in remembrance of me" (Lk. 22:19), as he broke bread in an upper room at the Last Supper. Christians then "remained faithful . . . to the breaking of the bread" (Acts 2:42). The "breaking of bread" in the Jewish tradition referred to a Jewish meal at which the person presiding pronounces a blessing before dividing the bread. The Last Supper was, of course, a Jewish meal. After it, Christians came use the term "breaking of bread" to refer to the Eucharistic service, the memorial of the Last Supper, when, according to Christian belief, Jesus gave himself to his followers as food and drink.

The way in which the focus of a sincere prayer life moved away from the weekly celebration of the Eucharist has been well documented. Before the conversion of the Roman Empire, to be present at the Eucharist and receive communion had been the central defining characteristic of the prayer shared in common by the baptized. As the fourth century wore on, however, and official Christian worship gradually replaced official pagan worship, conversion on a huge scale diluted the sincerity of much of the now-public Christian worship. The reception of communion began to wane when the Eucharist became an act of public worship for a population that in many cases was only nominally Christian. Simultaneously for the fervent minority, stringent conditions were placed on those who were permitted to receive communion.

Participation in the Eucharist in that period from the fourth to the end of the seventh century does not seem to have been at the forefront of concern in the writings that have come down to us. To some extent, attendance at Mass had become more to do with asserting one's status as a full member of the Roman Empire, than journeying on the pilgrimage of faith. For many, it may have had little to do with seeking communion with God in Jesus Christ and been more about making a public statement of fidelity to the empire.

Looking back to the late Roman Empire, there appears to be evidence that the requirement to attend Church was bolstered by various prohibitions against certain types of work to free the general population for Sunday worship. The rationale for this prohibition can be found in the first story of creation in the Book of Genesis. After the creation of the world, God "rested on the seventh day" (Gen 2:2). Yet these oft-repeated prohibitions may have been more politically than religiously inspired.

It was Constantine in 321 who first legislated for rest on Sunday—the Day of the Sun—ostensibly to allow for Christian worship. Yet Constantine's need above all else was to keep the empire together. According to Dorothy Haines, there is little evidence that Sunday rest was a requirement of Church rulings at this time. It may have been that Sunday rest was designed more to placate members of the cult of Mithras, which enjoined sun worship, than to comply with the wishes of Christian leaders.[2]

It is not at all clear, therefore, that attendance at Sunday Mass was always the touchstone of sincere devotion that it has since come to be. The most telling evidence comes down to us from the monastic movements of the fourth, fifth, and even sixth centuries. Revisiting the founding of monasticism, covered already in chapter 2, it is plain that those involved in the extraordinary exodus from the city to the desert were to a large extent abandoning Sunday worship as it was practiced in the city.

Although little is written regarding the lives of monastic women in the fourth century, and subsequently, there is a good deal of recorded evidence telling of the lives of their male counterparts. Much is known, for example, about the life of St. Anthony, not least from his *Life* written by his friend St. Athanasius. Commenting on that *Life*, W. H. C. Frend says, "For most of his [Anthony's] life he could never have received the Eucharist, and his monks were laymen."[3] It is pretty clear that for Anthony and for thousands in the desert like him, it was simply the case that the Eucharist was not regularly celebrated.

Thus, it happened that once Christian worship had moved out of the home and into the public sphere, those passionate Christian men and women who sought a truly deep relationship with their Lord no longer found it in the experience of the weekly, now-public Eucharistic worship. As a result, there was an extended period in Christian history when the intense prayer life of its most saintly personages was not centered on the weekly celebration of the Eucharist.

In the desert, individual hermits began to cluster their cells so as to be near to each other. For the most part, they remained alone in their cell but would come together for worship on Sundays and feast days. It is not always entirely clear what form this worship took. Looking back through the lens of later teachings, it would be natural to think that they came together to celebrate the Eucharist, but that is perhaps unlikely, given what we know of the reticence of these early fathers with regard to ordination.

According to Sarah Foot, "Early monastic rules expressed some ambivalence about the place of priests within monastic communities,"[4] It is apparent that the great Benedict of Nursia exhibited a certain reticence. He was not ordained himself, and although he accepted into his community those already ordained, he did not encourage ordination for the rest. Foot, in a detailed study of monastic life, concludes: "It is far from apparent that a conventual mass was celebrated in his [Benedict's] monastery on Sundays and major feasts."[5]

All the evidence seems to support the view that the weekly gathering for the breaking of the bread, reported in Acts[6] and so central to Christian life in the very early Church and subsequently, was not at the heart of the monastic movement at its inception. Furthermore, this continued to be the case over centuries, even when figures like Benedict could have chosen ordination for himself and even as male communities included priests among their number.

If we now fast-forward to even the eighth century, the situation had changed. From the eighth century onward, there was a concerted effort backed up by laws of the Church to return to the weekly celebration of the Eucharist as the defining characteristic of Christian worship for every Christian. For much of the Church's history, the requirement has been expressed in terms of "attendance at Mass," particularly during those centuries when it was unusual for ordinary Christians to receive the Eucharist (Holy Communion) when attending.

THE EROSION OF WOMEN'S ROLES

With Theodore as Archbishop of Canterbury, we see strenuous efforts to bolster the ranks of the ordained. Hild herself had played an important part in the initial phase of this recruitment drive, educating, or at least overseeing the education of, many priests for ordination, including five who would become bishops. In the centuries that followed, there were efforts made to encourage frequent, even daily, reception of the Eucharist. With the English Church now far more tightly answerable to Rome, the offices that the abbess would perform in the celebration of the Eucharist were gradually taken away from her, as were many other sacramental roles as they came to be viewed as too sacred or too important to be undertaken by women.

Attendance at Sunday Mass would become what it is today in the Catholic Church, a touchstone of orthodoxy. Furthermore, confession and the imposition of penances would be removed from the duties of the abbess and reserved exclusively to the male priesthood. The imposition of a great many penances would act as a bar to the reception of the Eucharist and would be used by a male clergy to enforce discipline on women religious and to punish those who stepped out of line.

The installation of Theodore as Archbishop of Canterbury in 669 turned out to be one of those defining moments in the Church's history that would incrementally squeeze out opportunities for women. It marked one step of many that would combine to secure the obliteration of women's participation in the governance of the Church and their exclusion from sacramental roles.

Although it is not clear just how effective Theodore's rulings were in actually clamping down on women's activities in his own time, or indeed some years later, which is perhaps when his *Penitentials* were published, they did represent an inexorable move in that direction. The process was begun that would eventually lead to diversity of practice giving way to a uniformity in which the status of women was much reduced. The aim was to establish clear degrees of hierarchy and to create an unbridgeable gap between those who were ordained and those who were not. The ordained would be invested with a power and authority not available to any others of the faithful, and over the centuries ,the memory of women's sacramental roles would be obliterated. This trend would eventually relegate women to second-order status from which, as far as the Roman Catholic Church is concerned, they have yet to recover. Only by revealing those practices which Theodore's Penitential served to close down, is it possible to recover what were likely to have been Hild's liturgical responsibilities.

Hild exercised her ministry at the end of that period when abbot and abbess exercised the same responsibilities according to the legislation of church councils. It is something of a hidden period wedged between the fourth century, when the activities of the desert fathers (if not the desert mothers) were well documented, and the eighth century when the "reforms" of Theodore of Canterbury began to take effect and to be well documented by the Roman machine.

THE HIDDEN AGE OF HILD

And so to seventh-century Anglo-Saxon England! It would seem that the hidden age during which Hild lived was wedged between two ages that are more transparent. Before Hild came, the monastic flight to the desert and away from the weekly gathering of ordinary Christians for the Mass. After Hild came, the routine ordination of sufficient numbers of male monastics aimed at providing Mass, increasingly on a daily basis, for their own communities, for women's communities, and for ordinary Christians at large. Yet during many of the thirty-three years that Hild was abbess of her various monasteries, it is difficult to see how weekly attendance at Mass could even have been a practical possibility because of the lack of priests.

Before considering what we know about the priests that there were, we should remind ourselves that our main source, Bede, excludes the British bishops from his account of the evangelization of Northumbria. Max Adams argues that there were almost certainly British Christians in Northumbria during the lifetime of King Oswald.[7] One of the most frustrating gaps in our knowledge is that we do not know how these British Christians related to the Irish and Roman Christians—if at all. It seems most unlikely however, that they were providing weekly Mass for the Roman/Irish mission to which Hild belonged.

Setting aside the question of the British Christians, it is difficult to see how weekly Mass could have been at the center of life in Hild's monasteries, at least in the early years. When Paulinus, after Edwin's death went south with

Queen Ethelburga, he left the Deacon James in charge of the Church at York. A deacon would not have been able to say Mass. Yet York was the main church for the whole of Northumbria; the main bishopric was at York. The fact that Paulinus left a deacon in charge would seem to point to Paulinus having been the only priest in an extremely wide area. There is no record of further bishops at York until Chad in 644, where he remained until 669.

When Hild set up her first community with just a few companions, Aidan was Hild's counselor and teacher. No doubt when he visited, Aidan celebrated the Eucharist with Hild and her companions. Apart from that, however, it seems unlikely that a resident priest would have been available to provide the sacraments for her community. By the time Hild had built up a flourishing community at Whitby, one of her most important tasks was to educate men for the priesthood, some of whom presumably served the Whitby community and its outlying farms, workshops, and homes. By then, but perhaps not much before then, it is easy to envisage weekly Mass at the monastery Church.

Referring to the period in the late seventh and early eighth centuries, Mayr-Harting says that "there were people all over Northumbria lacking the sacraments."[8] This lack is no doubt understood by Mayr-Harting first and foremost as the lack of weekly Mass because of an insufficient number of priests to celebrate weekly Mass. Pretty well all the commentators I have come across understand the lack in this way. Yet the assumption that the sacramental life of the Anglo-Saxon population of the seventh century was seen primarily in terms of the weekly celebration of the Eucharist is to my mind questionable. All the evidence seems to point to the weekly celebration of the Eucharist being a later concern, connected to an elevated notion of priesthood and the push to impose Roman practices, Roman structures, and Roman patriarchy on a Celtic Church.

The Eucharist was, of course, celebrated throughout the seventh century, if somewhat irregularly, and a priest would have been required for this. Yet even then, it would seem that communion was rarely received. Dom Gregory Dix's classic account of the development Eucharistic practice points to the seventh century as the low point for the reception of communion in the West.[9] Furthermore, although a priest was needed for the celebration of the Eucharist to take place, it would seem that an abbess like Hild would have taken an active part in the Liturgy.

Theodore's Penitential throws shafts of light onto these long-forgotten Eucharistic liturgies when the Abbess Hild quite probably stood among the priests in the celebration of the Mass. According to Stephanie Hollis,

> *Theodore's Penitential* reveals that monastic women . . . took part in the liturgical celebration and the administration of the mass; most versions of the *Penitential* declare that it is permissible for them to "read the Lections and to

> perform the ministries which pertain to the sacred altar, except those which are the special function of priests and deacons.[10]

A later version of this canon is especially interesting because it is no doubt an attempt to reduce women's participation by excluding them from specific actions—a prohibition that would have been superfluous had it not been that these were actions which women commonly undertook. It reads:

> Women shall not cover the altar with the corporal nor place on the altar the offerings, nor the cup, nor stand among the ordained men in the church, nor sit at a feast among priests.[11]

The inference is that in Anglo-Saxon England it was customary for women to cover the altar with the corporal, place the offerings and the cup on the altar, stand among the ordained men in the church, and sit at feasts among priests. As the status of the priest was enhanced and that of women lessened, women were no longer even to stand alongside the priests. Yet looking back to that hidden world when Hild was abbess, it is surely possible to glimpse Hild, lost in adoration, standing there among the ordained.

THE LAST RITES

In addition to Hild's role in the celebration of the Mass itself, she would also have been responsible for distributing communion to the sick and the dying. When communion was received, it was often from the reserved sacrament. Some of the consecrated bread would be kept after the Mass and given to the communicant when it was deemed appropriate, most notably at the point of death. It would have been Hild's responsibility to arrange for the sacrament to be reserved in the house and to take communion to the dying. Communion received at the point of death is called viaticum, or food for the journey. As Bede recounts the last hours of the poet Caedmon, he gives a picture of what might have been the rites for the dying as he envisages how Caedmon's deathbed scene might have played out.

When Caedmon of Whitby Abbey knew he was about to die, he asked to be taken to the infirmary. After midnight, to the surprise of those around him, he asked whether the Eucharist was in the house. Because he was cheerful, as if in good health, he was questioned about why he was asking for the Eucharist, but he insisted that the Eucharist should be brought to him. With the Eucharist in his hand [*Qua accepta in manu*], he then asked those around him whether they were at peace with him, or whether they had any complaint or any grudge against him, [*interrogauit, si omnes placidum erga se animum, et sine querela controuersiae ac rancoris haberent*]. They all replied that they were at peace with him [*Respondebant omnes placidissimam se mentem ad illum, et ab omni ira remotam habere*]. They then asked him to remove from his heart any bitterness he might have toward them [*eumque uicissim rogabant placidam erga ipsos mentem habere*], to which he replied immediately that his heart was at peace with all the servants of God [*Qui confestim respondit: "Placidam ego mentem, filioli, erga omnes Dei famulos gero."*] He then consumed the communion host [*Sicque se caelesti muniens uiatico, uitae alterius ingressui parauit*]. After that, when told that it would not be long until the Night Office, he said that they should wait until then. He then made the sign of the cross and died peacefully in his sleep.[12]

Here we have from Bede an account of the last rites that must provide genuine insight into how these rites took place. Contrition and reconciliation were integrated into the reception of viaticum and concluded with liturgical prayer. Bede gives us so little to go on, but I like to think that Hild was still alive on Caedmon's death, that it was her responsibility to take the reserved host to the dying, and that she presided over these deathbed liturgies for Caedmon. Yet even if this is a leap of the imagination too far, given that Hild served as abbess at three monasteries of varying sizes over decades, not to mention the high death rate during those decades, there must surely have been occasions when Hild presided over similar bedside liturgies.

What are we to think of these scenarios? Was this "sacramental" confession? Did Caedmon receive the last rites from whoever brought him viaticum? These questions are anachronistic. Yet, as we will see in the next chapter, they are important questions nonetheless, if the claim is to be made that only men can administer the sacraments of the church and that this has been the case from the beginning.

HILD AND AN ANCIENT ORDER

Having established that in Hild's time, the frequent celebration of Mass was not—could not have been—at the center of the devout life, we need to ask, what were the liturgical practices that fed the undoubted, deep devotion of Hild and her followers?

It is well documented that communal prayer has been very much at the heart of monastic life since the fourth century. Since then, and for the following two to three centuries, it was pretty universally the case that the person responsible for leading this communal prayer was not an ordained priest but the head of the monastery. In many cases, when talking in general terms, the head of the monastery was assumed by later writers to be male, obscuring the role of the abbess as the liturgical leader. Yet it would have been Hild who took the lead in the celebration of the Liturgy in her monasteries.

That period of history when Hild and other abbesses like her presided over the monastery and its Liturgy was coming to an end. Heads of male monastic orders would be encouraged to seek ordination, whereas heads of female monastic orders, hitherto among the main driving forces behind the evangelization of England, would have their responsibilities reduced. This change would mean that in male religious orders, the high point of worship, the celebration of the Eucharist, could now be celebrated by the head of the order, introducing a disparity between abbot and abbess, which in Anglo-Saxon England had not previously existed. Hild did not belong to that changed situation.

THE CORPORATE PRAYER OF THE MONASTERY

The heart of the monastic life, its very core, was the communal round of prayer. Then as today, it was the daily round of prayer, which marked the monastery out as the place where the soul could commune with God.

The round of prayer consisted principally of the singing of the psalms according to a fixed order, together with the readings from passages of Scripture. It was common for monks and nuns in double monasteries to sing the divine office, the Liturgy of the Hours, together. Where the abbess was in charge, as was most often the case, it would have been she who presided at this Liturgy. We know that there were both male and female lectors; that is to say both men and women would read aloud from the Bible.

The divine office, as this round of prayer was also called, took place at set times of the day and the night, providing the structure into which all other activities fit. Times for solitary prayer, for sleeping, for reading, for ablutions, for eating, for working, and for leisure activities, all would be allotted to accommodate the fixed hours of the round of prayer.

The composition of the prayer would take account of the liturgical cycle. In other words, as well as celebrating Sundays and Feast Days with a special intensity, the periods leading up to the major feasts; thus, the six weeks of Lent before Easter and the four weeks of Advent before Christmas would be marked according to their specific nature. So, for example, Lent was marked by an attitude of penitence, and Advent by expectation. Different days of the week, such as Friday when the Lord was crucified, were marked according to their significance, and other months or seasons were treated according to their own associations.

We know that in seventh-century Britain there was considerable variation between one religious house and another. In Hild's time, the structure of the divine office would have quite likely developed, varying from monastery to monastery, according to the circumstances of the place and size of the community. It is important for Bede that Hild imposed a regular way of life at her monasteries. As she moved from Hartlepool to Whitby, he seems keen to stress that it is the same rule that she imposed [*Nam eisdem, quibus prius monasterium, etiam hoc disciplinis uitae regularis instituit*].[13] Yet it would seem likely that with the divine office as with other liturgical activities, Hild developed its structure as she moved from one community to another and as the numbers of professed religious increased.

THE PROCESSION

High on the list of Hild's other liturgical responsibilities as a monastic leader would have been the procession. We get a description of ancient processions in progress by returning to Bede's account of Augustine's landing in Kent. First, there is the meeting between Ethelbert and Augustine on the island of Thanet.

The scene is set with the king, having arrived on the island, sitting in the open air, and summoning Augustine and the other monks into his presence. They approached the king with one of their number carrying a silver cross and another a board on which had been painted an image of the savior. The first thing they did was to offer a prayer to God by singing a litany, asking that they themselves and those for whom they had come would be granted eternal salvation.[14]

It was common practice to sing a litany in the course of a procession. In those days, the structure and the composition of the litany was varied and complex. At its most basic, it consisted of a series of short statements or intercessions spoken aloud by a single person, each statement being followed by the same response from the whole community. It would be set in the context of God's mighty deeds and could, for example, include a list of saints' names, followed by the response, "pray for us." Intercessions (prayers for help) would be made for a particular purpose. In the example, Augustine and his companions were praying for their own eternal salvation and the salvation of the Britons who were the target of Augustine's mission.

The next procession that Bede describes occurs when Ethelbert had given Augustine permission to preach in the town of Canterbury. Once again, the procession was led by a monk carrying a cross and an image of Christ painted on a board. (See figures 8.1 and 8.2 for images of the two processions.) As they approached Canterbury, they all sang a litany together: "We beseech thee, O Lord, for Thy great mercy, that Thy wrath and anger be turned away from this city, and from Thy holy house, for we have sinned. Hallelujah."[15]

Figure 8.1. Augustine arrives in Kent in procession, from a stain-glass window of St. Martin's Church.
Photograph by David Inman.

Figure 8.2. Augustine processes into Canterbury, from a stain-glass window of St. Martin's Church.
Photograph by David Inman.

Processions with the recitation of litanies were common; some, like Rogation Days (four days set aside to bless the fields and ask for God's mercy), were prescribed in the missal. There were processions with relics, processions to holy wells, and processions with bodies to the place of burial. Certain processions were given high prominence. Significantly O'Loughlin says that "if

. . . your community were making a great procession this impinged as much as, if not more than, the need to be present at the Sunday Eucharist."[16]

In the 1950s, I lived in a house that had formerly been a presbytery and that backed on to fairly extensive convent grounds. I well remember seeing a long line of nuns processing in twos through the woods and praying. It was an inspiring sight. Sometimes they would stop, and one or two nuns would break off to talk to my mother. We might do well to think of Hild with her handful of companions processing along the banks of the river Wear, reciting the Liturgy of the Hours or one of the litanies she had adapted for the locality; perhaps even adapting it as she went along, according to the needs she encountered. Essentially, Aidan had recruited Hild for evangelization, for preaching, and for providing pastoral care for those within and outside her community. We might think of her breaking away from her companions and stopping to talk to those she met, listening to their cares, and encouraging them with words from the Gospel.

Again we might do well to imagine Hild, some thirty years later, leading a much larger procession around the extensive Whitby estates. Again, the chanted liturgies would have been adapted to meet the cares and concerns of those she encountered. High on the list in this deeply penitential age would have been prayers for mercy and forgiveness. Then there would have been special prayers when sickness afflicted the population; prayers for the dead; prayers for the harvest; and prayers for protection in times of war.

We know that Aidan walked the lanes of Northumbria in preference to riding on horseback. Aidan wanted to meet people quite literally on an equal footing. Hild would undoubtedly have been inspired by Aidan's example. Yet there was more to the procession than getting from A to B, more to the procession than meeting people, and more even than using the journey to pray. The act of processing in community was itself sacramental. As O'Loughlin says, "the action of processing *was* the prayer; by actually walking one was entering into the mystery, and the words were an addition giving focus and expression to the act of processing."[17]

SEVENTH-CENTURY SACRAMENTS

O'Loughlin tells us that "the actual act of walking was a sanctifying activity." It was an act that made holy, an act that was a means of grace. The question then arises, was the procession sacramental?

By the action of walking in procession a person "entered into the mystery."[18] In the early Church, there was a strong connection between the word "mystery" and the word "sacrament." In certain circumstances, the Greek word "mysterion" was translated by the Latin word "sacramentum."[19] O'Loughlin plainly views the procession as a sacramental act, an act by which one enters into the mystery of God in Jesus Christ.

The community prayer at the heart of monastic life is sometimes described as "non-sacramental." A division has been set up between the liturgy of the hours, the processions, the litanies, and other forms of corporate prayer of the early medieval Church and the sacraments. Such a division would have been incomprehensible to the Church of the seventh century. As we have seen in chapter 5, it was not until the twelfth century that the Church settled on seven celebrations that were to be identified as "the sacraments." (And, of course, in the sixteenth century ,the Reformation Churches reduced this to two: Baptism and Communion.) In the first millennium, a far looser understanding of "sacrament" pertained.

Augustine of Hippo (not to be confused with Augustine of Canterbury) is generally credited with providing the most basic definition of a sacrament as "a visible form of invisible grace." Yet he himself regarded many things as "sacraments," such as the Creed and the Lord's Prayer,[20] the baptismal font, the giving of salt at baptism, and the ashes that signified penitence. From this perspective, of course, it is evident that the various elements of the communal prayer of the monastic life were sacraments.

When, from a modern perspective, various forms of prayer are described as non-sacramental, what is meant is that none of the (seven) sacraments were celebrated. Thus, the thinking is that unless an ordained priest was presiding, no one was baptized[21]; no subsequent sins were officially forgiven; the Eucharist was not celebrated; no one was confirmed, ordained, or sacramentally married; and no one received Extreme Unction (the last anointing) as it was called at the Council of Trent or the Anointing of the Sick as it was renamed at the Second Vatican Council. When Augustine's understanding is applied, however, a different judgment is reached. It was Augustine of Hippo, who above all others shaped early medieval understanding of sacramental theology. In the light of Augustine's teaching, among the many things regarded as sacraments would surely have been, for example, walking in procession.

There is another way of looking at the question of what was and what was not a sacrament in the seventh century, which has already been touched on in chapter five. If the question is to be determined by the way in which sacraments are defined today, then in the seventh century, not all of the seven sacraments existed. As demonstrated in the last chapter, if the words of absolution need to have been spoken for a confession to have been a sacrament, there was no sacrament of confession in the seventh century. The same logic has to be applied to the sacrament reserved for the end of life, the Anointing of the Sick as it is now called.

In Bede's account of Caedmon's death, we have a moving account of Caedmon being reconciled to his community and receiving his last communion—viaticum. The reconciliation (confession) is wedged between his taking the communion host into his hands—by a stretch of the imagination from the hand of Hild—and his consuming the host. Here we have from Bede an authentic portrayal of the last rites of the Church. To dissect this deathbed scene to discern whether Caedmon did or did not receive the seventh sacrament for those in danger of death seems hardly appropriate. If what is now called the Anointing of the Sick is the culmination of a tradition that stretches back to Christ himself, then Caedmon's deathbed scene is how that tradition played out in the seventh century. Even if Hild was not at Caedmon's bedside, to deny that women as well as men were the ministers of this sacrament is to contradict the evidence.

The seventh sacrament, the Anointing of the Sick, is an especially interesting one because the way in which it has been practiced and the way in which it has been understood has changed significantly in the course of history. It exemplifies the folly of taking what pertains in one's own time and applying it directly to another. (The sacrament of Marriage is similarly pertinent but will not be dealt with here.) As recently as 1963, the *Constitution on the Sacred Liturgy* § 73 declared: "Extreme Unction," which may also and more fittingly be called "Anointing of the Sick," is not a sacrament intended only for those who are at the point of death." Rather it should be given as soon as a person "begins to be in danger of death from sickness or old age." Up to that point, it had certainly been regarded in practice as a sacrament for those at the point of death. A sure indication that a person was about to die was the priest being called to give the last anointing or Extreme Unction.

As currently understood, the defining characteristic of the Anointing of the Sick is presumably an anointing. From the evidence available, it does not appear that Hild anointed the dying, but then no one else did either. It was not until the beginning of the ninth century that anointing became established among the last rites. According to Richard McBrien, "Nowhere in the early tradition does one find mention of the Anointing as a sacrament of *preparation for death*. Where mention *is* made of a 'sacrament of the dying,' the reference is always to the Eucharist, administered as Viaticum."[22] It was Hild's specific task as abbess to administer Viaticum to those at the point of death.

When what constitutes a sacrament is determined by current standards, it is not merely that Hild did not administer the sacrament of the dying. In the seventh century, no one did. This is because at this period of history there was no anointing with holy oil connected to the last rites. Current sacramental theology would collapse if there was no continuity between the seven sacraments as they are currently celebrated and as they have been celebrated in the Church since the beginning. When the sacraments were defined as seven, they were understood as the culmination of sacramental practice as it had developed from the beginning up to that time. A practice in which Hild played a full part!

NOTES

1. Macy points out that in the early medieval period the abbess had a duty to hear her nuns' confessions (Macy, *A Hidden History of Women's Ordination*, 82; 198 n159 he refers to Muschiol, *Famulia Dei* 41). He also says that "there is no provision in either monastic rules or canonical legislation for nuns to confess to anyone other than their abbess or her delegate. For all intents and purposes, abbesses played the same role for their communities in hearing confession and in absolving from sin as did bishops or priests for their communities. The abbesses' power to remove nuns from either table or the divine office or both is regularly termed 'excommunication' and parallels within the community of nuns the power of bishops to excommunicate within the larger community of the church." (Macy, *A Hidden History of Women's Ordination*, 82–83; to learn more, Macy 198 n161refers to cc. 18–20, in Waldebert of Luxeuil, *Regula ad virgines, PL* 88: 1067B–1068C, and cc. 69–71, in Donatus, *Regula ad virgines*, de Vogüé, "La Regle," 304–5).

2. Dorothy Haines, *Sunday Observance and the Sunday Letter in Anglo-Saxon England* (Cambridge: D S Brewer, 2010), 5 n20

3. Frend, *The Early Church*, 191

4. Foot, *Monastic Life*, 176

5. Foot *Monastic Life*, 205

6. In addition to Acts 2:42 already mentioned, there is Acts 20:7 "On the first day of the week we met for the breaking of bread."

7. Adams, *King of the North*, 246.

8. Mayr-Harting, *The Coming of Christianity*, 247.

9. Gregory Dix, *The Shape of the Liturgy* (London: A & C Black, 1986), 18.

10. Hollis, *Anglo-Saxon Women*, 137 refers to *Theodore's Penitential*, II.vii.I.

11. Hollis, *Anglo-Saxon Women*, 137.

12. Bede, *Ecclesiastical History*, IV.24 250. Beda, *Historia Ecclesiastica, Liber Quartus*, 22 [24] CLVI.

13. Beda, *Historia Ecclesiastica, Liber Quartus*, 21 [23] CLII.

14. Bede, *Ecclesiastical History*, I.25 75; Beda, *Historia Ecclesiastica, Liber Primus*, 25, XXVI.

15. Bede, *The Ecclesiastical History of the English People in Latin and English* (SPQR Study Guides Book 20) I. 25, Location 5111 in Kindle

16. O'Loughlin, *Celtic Theology*, 155

17. O'Loughlin, *Celtic Theology*, 152

18. O'Loughlin, *Celtic Theology*, 151

19. *Handbook of Catholic Theology*, eds. W. Beinert and Francis Schüssler Fiorenza (New York: Crossroads, 1995), 605.

20. Alister E. McGrath, *Christian Theology: An Introduction* (Oxford: Blackwell, 1997), 497.

21. Though, if no priest was available, any person could baptize someone who was in danger of death.

22. McBrien, *Catholicism*, 844.

Chapter Nine

Hild the Overseer

In 1973, a book by Joan Morris was published under the title *Against Nature and God*. The title alludes to a claim made in a pamphlet by John Knox that claimed, to the displeasure of Queen Elizabeth I, that it was "against Nature and God" for a woman to rule over men.[1] Yet in relation to Hild's story, the subtitle of Morris' book—*The history of women with the jurisdiction of bishops*—is even more interesting. Morris points out that neither Saint Benedict nor (later) Saint Francis were ordained priests, or ordained bishops, yet as superiors of religious orders they were "overseers" of their own districts and had what were later termed "quasi-episcopal" prerogatives. Following in this tradition, for a considerable period in the history of the Church, those who ruled the monasteries, whether women or men, had rights and privileges "as if a bishop."

To illustrate the independence of the abbess in relation to the bishop, Laura Swan tells the story of Caesaria, Abbess of Saint John of Arles in Gaul. Around the beginning of the sixth century, Caesaria had moved to secure premises after her first monastery was destroyed by invading Franks and Burgundians. In this safe enclosure, Caesaria held the keys to the lock, which would have been on the inside of the door. This fact is significant in itself because in later medieval times, the lock would be located outside, and the local bishop or abbot would have the keys. More significantly, however, Bishop Caesarius, who had written the Rule for Caesaria, considered the authority of the abbess so important that his Rule forbade any abbess ever to transfer the authority of her office to a bishop. The Pope himself confirmed this injunction in writing.[2] Morris names the pope as Hormisdas (514–26)[3] and gives a reference as to where this written confirmation is to be found.[4] She also gives a sense of the tussles that went on over the competing jurisdictions of abbess and bishop.

A century after Pope Hormisdas had made this ruling regarding Arles, Pope Gregory the Great had made Benedictine monasteries exempt from episcopal jurisdiction, answerable only to the Pope. We know that the royal abbey of Notre-Dame de Jouarre in Gaul was exempt from episcopal oversight. Jouarre was founded in the seventh century through the efforts of Saint Balde. Balde, who became the third abbess of Jouarre following on from two of her nieces, was a close contemporary of Hild. She died "at a very advanced age" in 680, the same year as Hild.[5]

Morris demonstrates that a great many monasteries, whether headed by an abbess or an abbot, were exempt from the jurisdiction (the legal rule) of bishops. Thus, in their own monasteries, responsibilities normally associated with a bishop fell to the monastic head. In other words, the monastic head, whether female or male, enjoyed the same jurisdiction as the bishops of their day. Top of her list as Morris expounds this argument is Hild's monastery at Whitby.[6]

In this chapter, I will look at three specific ways in which Hild exercised rights and duties "as if a bishop," three ways in which she acted as "overseer," a word often taken as a synonym for Bishop. The first concerns her overall jurisdiction as abbess, including the setting and gathering of taxes; the second concerns her responsibility for the selection and appointment of bishops; and the third concerns her role as "teacher," a role that is identified from the earliest Christian times as one of the primary functions of a bishop.

HILD'S JURISDICTION

Crucially, monasteries did not come under the jurisdiction of either civil or ecclesiastical authorities in the matter of taxes or tithes. Rather it came within the jurisdiction of the monasteries to raise taxes in their own domains. Morris points out that, although there had been some wrangling between bishops and monastic heads with regard to tithes, "the right of abbesses to this form of jurisdiction was not questioned until about the time of the Council of Trent,"[7] when the status of abbess was undermined. But for Hild, financial independence secured the ability to act independently across a whole range of other matters.

Morris records that in parts of the Celtic Church preeminence was given to abbots and to abbesses over bishops. Here, among other places, she cites Iona,[8] with a reference to Bede. According to Bede, in the case of Iona, it was the abbot, an ordained priest, who exercised authority over the bishop.[9] The bishop was thus subject to the abbot, and Morris infers that in a monastery headed by an abbess, the bishop would be similarly subject, as was in fact the case.

Hild's jurisdiction over her monastery was grounded in her ordination as abbess. In chapter 5, I discussed various ordination ceremonies that may have been used when Hild was installed as abbess at Hartlepool. Yet we can be fairly certain that Hild was ordained abbess in the sense that she went through some sort of ceremony on taking up her new role and that the word that would have been used was "ordained."

The word "ordained" in relation to women has been translated as "blessed," by later writers influenced by a theology that seeks to elevate the male priesthood onto an altogether higher plane than any form of "order" or ministry exercised by women. These later theologians have sought to impose a later understanding of what was meant by ordination on an earlier period, rather than look at the way in which ordination was understood at the time. Yet if we take seriously the theology of ministry as it stood in the seventh century, it is plain that women were ordained.

Specifically, as we have seen in chapter 5, there is considerable evidence from ancient documents that the abbess, once elected, was ordained by the bishop and that the ceremonies themselves were freighted with symbolism indicating that she was to exercise certain offices "as if a bishop." Gary Macy, who has extensively researched the hidden history of women's ordination, and especially female clergy in the medieval west, writes:

> Abbesses were described as ordained in several books of ritual in the early medieval period. This is not surprising given the definition of ordination as the ceremony celebrating and effecting entry to a new ministry in the church. Abbesses were an important and influential ministry throughout the Middle Ages. As in the case of *episcopae*, *presbyterae*, and deaconesses, they performed functions that were later reserved to the male offices of bishop, priest, and deacon. These functions, in themselves, did not constitute them as ordained. They were ordained because of their new role as head of a monastic community, just as an abbot was ordained when he took up such a role.

The early medieval church, however, did think of abbesses as ordained as any other clergy in this period.[10]

That women were ordained in the early medieval period is incontrovertible. If one were to add the caveat, "whatever ordination might mean," it would also be necessary to add the same caveat with regard to men's ordination. Men and women were ordained to a whole complex of ministries, none of which equated exactly to the understanding of the canon (church) lawyers of later centuries.

What we do know, however, is that as church councils became established in Anglo-Saxon England, they drew up legislation to regulate what was expected of monastic life. Noticeably, when it came to what was expected of leaders of religious communities, no distinction was made on grounds of sex.[11] It is also incontrovertible that Hild exercised official public ministries and that she exercised jurisdiction in her own monastery in areas now reserved exclusively to bishops. Hild was in sole control, and in some sense, at least the ordained leader of her monastery.

THE MONASTERY AS THE BASIC ECCLESIAL STRUCTURE

Transposing the independence of monasteries to our own time, one might imagine a monastery as an independent area within the larger whole that is the diocese, rather like a foreign embassy in a capital city. However it was not like this in seventh-century England. As we saw in chapter 3, when Gregory the Great sent Augustine to convert the English, he had planned for a bishop in York and a bishop in London, each with authority over twelve further bishops strategically situated to cover the whole of Britain. These structures had simply not materialized. John Blair in his *The Church in Anglo-Saxon Society* reports that in 669, when archbishop Theodore of Tarsus arrived in Canterbury, "the English episcopate was reduced to three: Wine, bishop of London by simony; Chad, holding the Northumbrian see uncanonically; and Wilfrid, uncontrollable and currently without a see."[12]

There would have been Welsh/British bishops, some of whom had met with Augustine and had refused to submit to his authority because of his perceived arrogance. Yet five years after the synod of Whitby, of those bishops who owed allegiance to the Augustinian mission, Bishop Wine's bishopric had been bought, which of course made his position invalid, and Bishop Chad had been installed at York after Wilfrid, already appointed, had refused to be consecrated by the Welsh bishops. Having traveled to Compiègne for a decidedly more splendid consecration Wilfrid had returned to find his see already occupied by Chad. It was not until 735 that York became the prestigious center envisaged by Gregory I and Theodore.

The attempt by Augustine's mission to set up church structures along episcopal lines had initially proved a spectacular failure. Yet the seventh century is justifiably regarded as the Golden Age of Northumbria. Here was seen the most amazing flowering of Christian culture, and it was in the fertile ground of the monasteries that this amazing flowering took place. It was the monasteries that formed the basic ecclesial structure within which Christians lived out their life of faith.

Henri Marrou locates the origins of this phenomenon in Ireland and other Celtic countries. "Whereas in the rest of the Christian world the episcopal church was the basic unit of religious organization, in Ireland and also to a large extent in the other Celtic countries it was the monastery almost exclusively which filled this role. Its jurisdiction spread to the neighboring countryside."[13] In England, the Celtic influence combined with the virtual collapse of Rome-inspired episcopal system meant that what Marrou says of Ireland is equally true of Hild's Anglo-Saxon world.

Blair talks of "a para-monastic system" that prevailed in England as well as other parts of northwestern Europe over what he terms "more orthodox modes of Church organization."[14] The more orthodox arrangements to which Blair refers are of course the Roman system with its hierarchy of archbishop, bishop, priest, and deacon. Monasteries, says Blair, were not merely of "central and enduring importance. . . in local religious life," but also "the basis of the first English parochial system."[15] Thus, to a large extent, the monastery exercised the functions of a parish, and insofar as the monastic head had episcopal jurisdiction, a diocese.

It would, therefore, be anachronistic to think of Christian life in the Anglo-Saxon England of the seventh century in terms of a developed system of parishes served by parish priests, overseen by the bishop of the area. It was those who lived in monasteries who served the needs of the Christian population. Their lives in community were structured around their daily round of prayer combined with a real concern to serve those outside the monastery. They were well placed and well equipped to preach and to give spiritual direction to the local population, and as they attracted more members, to send some of their number to engage in missionary activities further afield. It was those who headed the monasteries who were at the forefront of the entire Christian endeavor. On the island of Lindisfarne, this would have been Aidan, who had the title of bishop; a few years after Aidan's death, on the headland of the Northumbrian coast at Streanaeshalch, also known as Whitby, this would have been the Abbess Hild, whom Aidan had trained up for that very purpose.

A BLURRING OF BOUNDARIES

It is evident that those boundaries that in later centuries would be set to mark off absolutely the roles of bishop from the roles of abbess were considerably blurred in Hild's time. To a large extent, the roles were interchangeable. The same blurring seems to have occurred regarding the status of those living on monastic lands. The demarcation between those who were simply workers on the monastic estates and those who were in religious orders may not have been that clear-cut. According to Blair, "monastic lifestyles could have impinged on people who were not so different from ordinary peasants."[16]

Blair comments on a story that is recounted in both accounts of the Life of St. Cuthbert. The story takes place at Osingadun, a dependent holding of Whitby, after Hild had died and been succeeded by Aelffled. While feasting with Aelffled, Cuthbert went into a trance and saw the soul of a holy man from Aelffled's household being carried up to heaven. Aelffled, having made enquiries, found that all the brothers at Whitby were still alive, only to discover later that "one of the brethren in the shepherds' dwellings" had died falling from a tree.[17] Cuthbert seems to be making no distinction between the brothers who lived in the monastery proper and had presumably taken orders and those who lived outside the monastery proper on monastic lands. It is evident that the strict categorization of people so favored by the Church in later centuries simply did not pertain.

When it comes to the extent to which Hild's responsibilities overlapped with those of seventh-century bishops, there is a frustrating void. Although Bede provides the bare facts of Hild's evident achievements, he tends to be silent on a number of issues that are of such interest to those who now try to recover a wider sense of the Catholic tradition before the sidelining of women's activities. Thus, for example, little is to be learnt from Bede regarding Hild's liturgical responsibilities, and her pastoral engagement is referred to in only the most general terms. Then there are the merest of glancing references, the slightest of clues, to her role in selecting and educating those destined for the priesthood and her role in appointing bishops to various sees. Both the latter roles were the prerogative of bishops or those who held episcopal responsibilities.

HILD THE BISHOP-MAKER

Bede tells us that five men from Hild's monastery were later to become bishops. Once Hild's jurisdiction as abbess is taken seriously, this fact brings with it further implications. It surely points the way to recognizing that Hild was responsible for the selection, education, and appointment of the clergy, including bishops. It would probably have been Hild, not some higher authority, who would have selected those to be educated for the priesthood or as potential bishops. In the first instance, at any rate, it would have been Hild herself who decided who should be admitted to her monastery.

As we will see in the case of Caedmon, she encouraged those in whom she recognized a particular gift for the spiritual life to enter. Bede reports that "having received him [Caedmon] into the monastery, she [Hild] and all her people admitted him to the company of the brethren."[18] Are we to assume that it was Hild who received his vows? Not a great deal is known regarding the ceremony involved on entrance into monastic life beyond what we saw in chapter 5: the relinquishing of all possessions; the reclothing; and the tonsure for men. It appears to have been a rite replete with dramatic symbolism in which it would seem that Hild played a leading part.

Having selected those who should enter the monastery, it seems most likely that it would also have been for Hild to select those to be prepared for ordination to various offices, including those of priest and bishop. Bede mentions by name five bishops educated during Hild's tenure, as well as a sixth, Tatfrith, who was destined for Hwicce but died before his consecration. The five are Bosa, Aetla, Oftor, John, and Wilfrid. Bosa, John, and Wilfrid were all appointed to York. Wilfrid, who was known as a man of outstanding holiness, should not be confused with his more famous predecessor, Wilfrid I (also known for his holiness since he was declared a saint by the Church, but with a decidedly more colorful past). Aetla became bishop of Dorchester, possibly Dorchester-on-Thames, rather than Dorchester in Dorset.[19] Oftor became bishop of Hwicce. A detail on the Saint Hilda Monument in Whitby shows Hild and her five bishops. (See figure 9.1.)

Figure 9.1. Hild and her five bishops on the Saint Hilda Monument in Whitby.
Photograph by Professor Mark A. Wilson.

As these men were educated for future service in the Church, Hild would presumably have had in mind where and in what capacity they might most usefully serve once ordained. The ability to appoint bishops to a particular see brought with it the ability to influence greatly the future shape and direction of the Church. The most prestigious among the appointments here were those of Bosa, John, and Wilfrid II, all of whom at one time or another served as bishop of York. Though in decline during Hild's lifetime, York was intended to be (and would become) the primary see in the north of England, and second only to Canterbury in the whole of Britain.[20]

Hild's influence in the appointment of bishops is evident in the complicated history of the bishops of York in the period after Wilfrid I was appointed in 664. After a disagreement with Theodore, Archbishop of Canterbury, who wanted to divide his extensive diocese, Wilfrid vacated York in 677. He was subsequently dismissed from the bishopric and made an appeal to Rome against his dismissal. Hild wrote to the Pope, arguing that Wilfrid should not be reinstated. Patrick Wormald points to this incident as demonstrating just how much weight was attached to Hild's voice when it came to the appointment of bishops:

> When. . . the aggressively eloquent young St Wilfrid, was. . . appealing at the papal court against dismissal from his bishopric (678/80), Hilda was singled out alongside the archbishop of Canterbury as one of his two accusers. She had taken the opposite view from Wilfrid's about Easter, and was evidently among the first in the long line of English people who have found Wilfrid rather more than they could take. More to the point, her hostility really counted.'[21]

Wilfrid's successor, Bosa, would have been Hild's appointment, and it is likely that she was supported by Theodore in effecting the departure of Wilfrid I and his replacement by Bosa.

Hild's role in the appointment of Bosa is pretty clear. It seems likely that she took on the same role with regard to the appointment of the other bishops to their various sees. If this task did not fall directly to Hild, it is surely inconceivable, given the high regard in which she was held and her role in their formation, that her opinion was not given considerable weight with regard to the appointments that were made during her lifetime.

HILD THE TEACHER

Among the responsibilities that Hild may have shared with bishops was that of teacher. When it comes to Bede's account, the nearest he arrives at calling Hild a teacher is when he says that she taught the virtues mercy, purity, and so on, and especially peace and charity. It needs to be borne in mind that a distinction is made by Bede between the teaching of virtue, which is open to any virtuous Christian, and the study of Scripture and its interpretation, which in time would become the preserve of men in holy orders. When it comes to the latter, Bede stops short of attributing the title "teacher" to Hild.[22] It would therefore be possible to argue that, having determined who in the monastery should study Scripture and ensured that they did so, Hild's responsibility ended; Hild herself did not teach those men who were destined for holy orders.

Stephanie Hollis lists modern authors who think along these lines, having "generally taken their cue from Bede." Among those she mentions are Christine Fell, Peter Hunter Blair, and John Godfrey.[23] Yet I would argue with Hollis that the fact that Bede fails to identify Hild as a teacher should not be given that much weight. It is true that Bede does refer to Aelffled, who succeeded Hild as Abbess of Whitby, as a devoted teacher (*deuota Deo doctrix*),[24] though the more usual term, used, for instance, of West Country abbesses such as the teacher of Leoba, is *Magistra*. Yet as with Hild, Bede is similarly silent with regard to teaching when he writes about Abbess Hildilid of Barking, "effusively hailed [by Aldhelm] as a learned monastic teacher . . . in *De Virginitate*."[25] Bede makes no mention of Hildilid's teaching. Rather in a manner similar to his description of Hild, he applauds her devotion and her energy and that she promoted the observance of regular discipline, while making provisions for the needs of the community. The virtues that he attributes to Hildilid and to Hild are similar, and importantly from Bede's point of view, he tells us that they were both committed to the regular observance of the Rule.[26]

As with Hild, we can see here that Bede's account of Hildilid is colored by his desire to see a uniform (Benedictine) Rule for all monastic houses in England. As with Hild, he avoids any suggestion that women monastics like Hildilid might have had any serious role in scholarly or missionary work or anything that would have extended their activities or influence beyond the walls of the monastery.

Bede was part of the movement that sought to demarcate male ordained priests and bishops from those not so ordained, especially women. The bishop is regarded as the teacher par excellence, and it is his sacred task to ensure orthodoxy or right teaching. Bede was not about to identify Hildilid or Hild as teachers because that would push them over the line, blurring the distinction between abbess and bishop. Just as Bede's account avoided the interpretation that Hild had selected priests and bishops, so now he avoids the interpretation that Hild was their teacher.

Minimally, we should assume a reticence on the part of Bede directly to identify Hild as teacher because it would sit uncomfortably with the place of women in his Romanizing agenda. Furthermore, Bede does not deny outright that it was Hild who did the teaching, and in all likelihood, Hild did indeed take on this quasi-episcopal role. For one thing, if Hild did not teach, it is difficult to see who did the teaching that undoubtedly took place. As Hollis says, "there is no discernible means by which Whitby could have produced men equipped for holy orders unless Hild herself taught them."[27]

The idea that Hild was not herself scholarly is belied on several counts. First there is the time she spent at her first monastery by the River Wear being instructed by Aidan. Aidan had called Hild north to head the evangelization drive, and it must have been in his mind as he instructed her that there was a need to educate priests. Then there is the fact that Aelffled, who had been with Hild since infancy, was a renowned Latin scholar. Where did this scholarship come from? Did it come from Hild, or was she taught by someone else? If by someone else, would Hild have been content not to have taken the opportunity to learn herself? Then there is the great importance that Hild attached to the study of Scripture.

Then the high level of scholarship among women monastics generally should be taken into account. Aldhelm's treatise on virginity, *De Virginitate*, written for Cuthberga and the nuns at Barking Abbey about six years after Hild's death, offers precious insights into the scholarly world of seventh-century Anglo-Saxon monastic women and gives a glimpse of the sort of books that they owned and read. Aldhelm specifically recommends that the nuns at Barking should read Cassian's *Collationes Patrum* (*The Conferences*) and Gregory's *Moralia in Job* (*Morals on the Book of Job*). Aldhelm plainly believed that these works were among the books in the nuns' library at Barking.[28]

De Virginitate comes in two versions, one prose and one metric, and was written in deliberately complicated Latin. Henry Mayr-Harting describes the treatise's introduction as, "an elaborate comparison between virginity and athletic or scholarly exercises, the Latin of which, like the rest of the treatise, must have been more than exercise for the minds of most of the ladies to whom it was directed."[29]

Aldhelm, of course was renowned for his skillful, not to say complicated, use of Latin, which he saw as in many ways more important than the writing's actual content. Doubtless it was a difficult read for anyone other than Aldhelm himself. Yet rather than acknowledge the fact that in sending *De Virginitate* to the women religious at Barking, Aldhelm must have had a high regard for their Latin scholarship, Mayr-Harting, doubtless inadvertently, takes the usual route of belittling the scholarly accomplishments of religious women. This last criticism may be a little harsh; it will be up to the individual reader to decide. Aldhelm, in fact, speaks of the remarkable intellects of religious women,

> roaming widely through the flowering fields of scripture . . . now scrutinising with careful application the hidden mysteries of the ancient laws. . . . Now exploring wisely the fourfold text (of the Gospels). . . now duly rummaging through the old stories of the historians and the entries of chroniclers. . . now sagaciously inquiring into the rules of the grammarians and the teachers of experts on. . . the rules of metrics.[30]

Another figure whose writings give us an insight into the educational achievements of monastic women around this time was Boniface, born in Devon, Wessex, around 675. Boniface was at the forefront of that powerful missionary drive at the heart of Celtic Christianity, which continued to penetrate into continental Europe despite the fact that the Synod of Whitby of 664 had favored Roman over Celtic ways. Boniface was a scholar of some distinction. It was he who compiled the first-ever Latin grammar written in England.[31] And Boniface worked closely with women missionaries, most notably Leoba. It should not be forgotten that Hild was initiated into the religious life by the Irish missionary, Aidan. The Irish took education seriously and there were many learned women in the Irish Church.

Boniface's missionary activities took him to Germany, from where he corresponded with many religious women back in Wessex, whom he urged to join him. Discernible in these letters is the high degree of learning of his correspondents. Of Leoba, who was to join him and work closely with him, it was said by later hagiographies that "the Scriptures were never out of her hand."[32]

Against this background and with constant travel between monasteries, it is possible to conclude that the level of scholarship at Whitby could well have been high. For more able students, the education on offer at Whitby would have gone well beyond the ability to read a minimum of basic Latin texts. It is clear that there was some exchange of scholars between Whitby and Canterbury. Oftor, bishop of Hwicce, had studied at both Hartlepool and Whitby under Hild, before moving to continue his education at Canterbury under Archbishop Theodore, who was a renowned scholar. John, bishop of Hexham and then York, on the other hand, made the reverse move, going from Canterbury to Whitby. After studying in Canterbury under the celebrated abbot Adrian and learning medicine under Theodore, John went on to further his education at Whitby Abbey. It was John who ordained Bede as deacon and priest.

For more able students, the education on offer at Whitby went well beyond the ability to read a minimum of basic Latin texts. For this, books would have been needed. It seems probable that Hild would have begun to build up her library as soon as she returned to Northumbria, possibly from texts received from Aidan. Books were hugely precious items, given the laborious nature of their production; yet we know that books were widely circulated to various monasteries. Books arrived in the west from the Near East and were transported across the Christian world from one monastery to another. Hild would likely have received books from her many visitors, and later on, from her own missionaries returning to the abbey from their journeys and probably from journeys that she herself made.

Over in the monastery at Chelles, where Hild at one time had intended to go to join her sister Hereswith, there was a substantial library. At the time when Hild was Abbess of Whitby, Abbess Bertila headed its famous monastic school. From the *Life of Bertila*, we learn that English royalty asked her to send over to England men and women whom she had taught so that they could found monasteries and crucially so that they could teach. The *Life* tells us that the teachers she sent brought with them many books.[33]

If there is reasonably strong evidence that Hild was a scholar and a teacher, the question arises as to whether she circulated any of her own writings. The unspoken assumption was that Hild herself wrote nothing or nothing of note. Yet the fact that no writings of hers survive tells us very little.

That unwarranted assumption that women wrote nothing of note has been so reinforced through the centuries that it remains virtually unquestioned in theological circles. Bertram Colgrave's text and translation of the life of Gregory the Great, which came out in paperback in 1985, has the confident title, *The Earliest Life of Gregory the Great: By an Anonymous Monk of Whitby*.[34] Women's contribution to early medieval scholarship has been so effectively blotted out that it would hardly occur to a reader of this *Life* to ask why, in this double monastery (according to some authorities now a single-sex monastery for women) headed by an abbess, it should be taken for granted that the author of this celebrated *Life* was a man.

Given how important she deemed scriptural study to be, it is hard to believe that Hild did not engage in it herself. The reading of sacred texts as a means of growth in the spiritual life was an integral part of the daily round of monastic life. Hild was plainly a highly intelligent woman and the head of the most important center of learning in Anglo-Saxon England before the arrival of Theodore at Canterbury.[35] It would seem inconceivable that she did not engage in learning herself, especially if we take account of the high level of learning among women monastics generally during this period in history. Given her probable ordination to the clerical state when she became abbess, it would seem unlikely that she was not also a teacher and in that respect on a par with bishops.

NOTES

1. The title of the pamphlet, *The First Blast of the Trumpet against the Monstrous Regiment of Women*, can hardly have endeared him to the Queen.
2. Swan, *The Forgotten Desert Mothers*, 147–48.
3. Morris, *Against Nature and God*, 19.
4. Morris, *Against Nature and God*, 162 n9 gives the reference: Caesarius, "Regula Virginum," *Codex Regularum Monasticarum*, ed. Holsten and Brockie (Augsburg: 1759), vol. 2.
5. Morris, *Against Nature and God*, 33.
6. Morris, *Against Nature and God*, 24.
7. Morris, *Against Nature and God*, 17.
8. Morris, *Against Nature and God*, 19.
9. Bede, *Ecclesiastical History*, III.4 149; Beda, *Historia Ecclesiastica, Liber Tertius*, 4, LXXXI.
10. Macy, *The Hidden History of Women's Ordination*, 80–81.
11. See Yorke, *Nunneries and the Anglo-Saxon Royal Houses*, 123, who refers to Cubitt's *Anglo-Saxon Church Councils c. 650–c. 850, passim*.
12. Blair, *The Church in Anglo-Saxon Society*, 79.
13. Marrou, "The Conversion of Northern Europe," 453.
14. Blair, *The Church in Anglo-Saxon Society*, 1.
15. Blair, *The Church in Anglo-Saxon Society*, 5.
16. Blair, *The Church in Anglo-Saxon Society*, 213.
17. Blair, *The Church in Anglo-Saxon Society*, 213.
18. Bede, *The Ecclesiastical History of the English People*, IV. 24, Location 28962 in Kindle.
19. Hunter Blair "Whitby as a Centre of Learning in the Seventh Century," 27.
20. London failed to become the metropolitan centre envisaged by Gregory, and Canterbury became the primary see in Britain. As far as the Anglican Church is concerned, Canterbury continues to this day to be the primary see. For the Catholic Church, the primary see is that of Westminster.
21. Patrick Wormald, *The Times of Bede*, edited by Stephen Baxter (Oxford: Blackwell 2006), 267–68.
22. Bede, *Ecclesiastical History*, IV.23; Beda *Historia Ecclesiastica Liber Quartus*, 21.
23. Hollis, *Anglo-Saxon Women* (258) refers to Fell, "Hild, Abbess of Streonaeshalch," 95; Christine Fell, *Women in Anglo-Saxon England and the Impact of 1066* (Oxford: Oxford University Press, 1986), 109–28; Blair, "Whitby as a Centre of Learning in the Seventh Century," 29–30. J. Godfrey, "The Place of the Double Monastery in the Anglo-Saxon Minster System," in *Famulus Christi: Essays in Commemoration of the Thirteenth Centenary of the Birth of the Venerable Bede*, edited by G. Bonner (London: SPCK, 1976), 345.
24. Beda, *Historia Ecclesiastica: Liber Quartus*, 24 [26].
25. Hollis, *Anglo-Saxon Women*, 258.

26. Regarding Hildilid, he says: *Successit autem Aedilburgi in officio abbatissae deuota Deo famula, nomine Hildilid, multisque annis, id est usque ad ultimam senectutem, eidem monasterio strenuissime, et in obseruantia disciplinae regularis, et in earum, quae ad communes usus pertinent, rerum prouidentia praefuit.* Beda, *Historia Ecclesiastica, Liber Quartos*, 10 CXXXIV. Regarding Hild, he says: *Cum ergo aliquot annos huic monasterio regularis uitae institutioni multum intenta praeesset, contigit eam suscipere etiam construendum siue ordinandum monasterium in loco, qui uocatur Streaneshalch, quod opus sibi iniunctum non segniter inpleuit. Nam eisdem, quibus prius monasterium, etiam hoc disciplinis uitae regularis instituit; et quidem multam ibi quoque iustitiae, pietatis, et castimoniae, ceterarumque uirtutum, sed maxime pacis et caritatis custodiam docuit.* Beda, *Historia Ecclesiastica, Liber Quartos*, 21 [23] CLII.

27. Hollis, *Anglo-Saxon Women*, 262.

28. Hollis, *Anglo-Saxon Women*, 79.

29. Mayr-Harting, *The Coming of Christianity*, 194.

30. Simpson, *Hilda of Whitby*, 109–110 quotes from Fell, *Women in Anglo-Saxon England and the Impact of 1066*, 110–11.

31. Peter Stanford, *The She-Pope* (London: Arrow, 1998), 47.

32. Stanford (*The She-Pope*, 47) refers to Talbot's *The Anglo-Saxon Missionaries in Germany* (London 1954).

33. Hollis, *Anglo-Saxon Women*, refers to *Vita Bertilae* Ch. 6.

34. Colgrave, ed., *The Earliest Life of Gregory the Great.*

35. See chapter 6, which also references Hunter Blair, "Whitby as a Centre of Learning in the Seventh Century," 30. "During the middle years of the seventh century, Whitby was unquestionably the pre-eminent center of learning in Anglo-Saxon England."

Chapter Ten

Whitby: At the Origins of English Poetry

In previous chapters, we have seen Hild engaged in the administrative responsibilities of overseeing the most prestigious institution in the whole of northern England. There has been the suggestion that she was probably a teacher; we have imagined her ministering to the sick, caring for the poor, presiding at liturgy, and celebrating certain sacraments. In this chapter, as a different window is opened onto her life, we catch a glimpse of her creative immersion in the developing culture of her time. It was Hild who "discovered" the person who was arguably the first English poet, Caedmon.[1] From this vantage point, we look on Hild playing a foundational role in the tradition of Christian poetry in English, a tradition that was to shape English culture for the centuries to come.

Bede devotes the whole of chapter 24 (22) of his *Ecclesiastical History* (*Historia Ecclesiastica*) to Caedmon's story. What distinguished Caedmon's poetry from other compositions of the time was that it narrated history in Anglo-Saxon English from an explicitly Christian perspective. And thanks to Hild, Caedmon was among the first poets, if not *the* first, whose Anglo-Saxon compositions were set down in writing. (See figure 10.1 for an artist's impression of Caedmon.)

CAEDMON'S FEAST

Bede tells us how unlikely a prospect Caedmon was to become any sort of poet at all. We first hear of him as a shy, elderly, unlettered cowherd tending his animals on the Whitby estate. His story begins as he attends a feast. We know that feasts were commonplace and that people from all walks of

Figure 10.1. Caedmon the poet
By artist Eileen Harrisson.

life would have participated in feasts of some sort. Using our imagination to picture the feast that Caedmon attended, there are various possibilities.

We have already encountered in chapter 1 a description of a feast. The story told to Edwin by one of his chief advisors, encouraging Edwin to adopt Christianity, describes the king sitting at dinner in his banqueting hall on a winter's day with his thegns and counselors. The warmth of the fire inside the hall is evoked in contrast to the raging winter storms of rain and snow outside. Hild would no doubt have remembered such gatherings with her great-uncle, and it seems likely that as Abbess of Whitby she held similar gatherings for eating and drinking, singing and storytelling.

We know that hospitality was central to the character of religious life at Whitby. Furthermore, we know that Hild was extremely well connected, and we can be pretty sure that she hosted gatherings for nobility and high-ranking clergy. What we do not know is whether servants, peasants, farm workers, and so on were also huddled into the outer reaches of the hall, enjoying some of the bounty from the feast, sheltering in the warm, and imbibing the festive atmosphere.

It was customary for poets or bards to sing their compositions during feasts, playing the harp for accompaniment. To be a singing bard was a high-status profession, but at the feast that Caedmon attended, the harp would be passed round from hand to hand so that everyone could take a turn in singing. As the harp made its slow progress toward Caedmon, he would shrink from the prospect of having to sing in front of the others; he would get up, leave the feast, and go to his bed.

Sarah Foot considers that it was not in the monastic hall that Caedmon shrank from his turn to entertain the gathering. Because he was still living the secular life, she believes that he would have been feasting in the company of peasants like himself. Here the storytelling was likely to have consisted of "entertaining rather than edifying tales." Foot suggests that "It is this type of '*convivium*' that rendered Caedmon despondent, and caused him to leave."[2] Caedmon is depicted as both serious and shy and the last person to compose anything superficial or irreverent.

Frustratingly we can only guess at whether Foot is correct, or whether Hild might have hosted feasts that would have included both royalty and her peasant workers. Yet it is still possible to recreate in our imagination something of the liveliness and sociability of the convivium from which a shy soul such as Caedmon might readily shrink.

We know something more of monastic feasting from a letter dated 797, written by the scholar Alcuin of York to Higbald, bishop of Lindisfarne. Alcuin complained that the monks would rather sing about fictitious heroes than sing about the one true Christ. More than a century after Caedmon's feasting days, the situation in the country was different. The golden age inherited from Hild was being shaken by terrifying Viking raids. It is understandable that Alcuin condemned the recitation of Anglo-Saxon sagas as he no doubt thrashed around in his mind to explain the terrifying attacks on the monasteries by the Danish invaders. Alcuin saw the Viking onslaughts on the monasteries of the eighth century as divine retribution for the lax monastic life.

Singing was an indispensable element of any feast. The bards would sing of their heroic ancestors in compositions like *Widsith*, an Anglo-Saxon poem from the sixth or seventh century, "perhaps the oldest of all English poems."[3] These epic sagas told of the bravery of the great warriors, who were the ancestors of the Anglo-Saxons, and whose lineage, it was thought, could be traced right back to the pagan gods. Most famous of all the sagas that accompanied the feasting was the great epic poem *Beowulf*, with its hero prince, the handsome Ingeld.

In the monastery, however, the singing of great epic poems should have been replaced by the singing of biblical stories, with the hero Christ. In his letter, Alcuin reprimanded Higbald, the bishop of Lindisfarne, and his monks for preferring to enjoy barbarian rather than Christian songs.

> The words of God should be read at the monks' feasts. There the reader should be heard not a harpist, the discourses of the Fathers not the songs of the heathens. What has Ingeld to do with Christ? The house is narrow, it cannot contain both. The king of the heavens will have nothing to do with heathen and damned so-called kings. For the eternal king rules in the heavens, and the lost heathen repines in hell. The voices of readers should be heard in your houses, not the cackling of the crowd in the street.[4]

Mayr-Harting reminds us that a century before Alcuin, the saintly Cuthbert had warned his fellow monks of Lindisfarne against storytelling (*fabulis*).[5] Cuthbert, who had moved to the island of Farne in search of greater solitude, had been joined by other monks for the purpose of celebrating the feast of Christmas. Cuthbert had a sense of foreboding and repeatedly warned that they should take care.

> And a little time after, while we were indulging in feasting, rejoicing and storytelling, I again began to warn them that we should earnestly engage in prayers and vigils and be ready for the approach of any temptation. They said: "You give us good, yea excellent, instruction, but nevertheless, because the days of fastings, prayer and vigils abound, today let us rejoice in the Lord. For the angel, when the Lord was born, gave the shepherds glad tidings of great joy which was to be observed by all the people." I answered: "Well, so be it." But when, while we were feasting and spending the day joyfully, I repeated these words of

admonition for a third time, they understood that it was not in vain that I made the suggestion so anxiously.[6]

Cunque post haec aliquandiu epulis exultationi, ac fabulis indulgeremus, rursus admonere coepi ut solliciti existeremus in orationibus et uigiliis, atque ad omnes temptationum incursus parati. Et illi, Bene inquiunt et optime doces, sed tamen quia abundant dies ieiuniorum, orationis et uigiliarum, hodie gaudeamus in Domino, nam et angelus nascente Domino evangeliz*abat pastoribus* gaudium magnum, quod *esset* omni populo *caelebrandum. Et ego, Bene inquam faciamus sic. Sed cum epulantibus nobis et diem laetum ducentibus tercio eiusdem ammonitionis uerba repeterem, intellexere illi quia non frustra haec tam studiose suggererem.*[7]

Mayr-Harting tells us that "the word '*fabulae*' implies secular rather than religious talk, even pagan tales."[8] Foot suggests that, by Alcuin's time, the inclusion of lay guests from the aristocracy at the monastic dinner table was causing problems for the monastic way of life. The nobility expected to be entertained while they ate, with traditional stories of battles and heroic deeds, sung to the accompaniment of the lyre.[9]

At any rate, Caedmon, whether reticent because of the nature of the songs that were being sung or through simple shyness, left the feast he was attending, unwilling to take his turn at singing. Following his early departure, he had a dream, in which he was asked to sing a song. His protestations that he could not sing were of no avail. He was told by the voice in the dream that he would sing to him. When Caedmon asked what he should sing about, the reply came back that he should sing about the creation. At this point Caedmon was at once inspired to sing in praise of God, using original words which simply came to him in the dream.

When he woke the next morning, Caedmon remembered what he had sung in the dream and went straight to the reeve to tell him what had happened. The reeve in turn took him straight to Hild, who asked about the dream and listened to the verses that had come to him. At this point in the story, Bede, perhaps to make the point that Hild was reliant on her male contemporaries, introduces to the scene a number of learned men, whereupon all the men agreed that Caedmon's gift was divinely inspired and came direct from the Lord.

Bede tells us that these learned men explained to Caedmon a passage from scripture and asked him to turn it into verse. By the following morning Caedmon had composed excellent verse. It was then Hild, who, delighted that Caedmon had received such grace from God, advised him to enter the monastery.

At a distance of some half a century from the actual events, during which time women were being steadily written out of history, Bede no doubt saw the presence of the scholarly men as necessary to give the story credence. Yet Bede is clear that it was Hild who recognized God's grace working within Caedmon (*abbatissa amplexata gratiam Dei in uiro*), it was she who recognized his calling and urged him to leave the secular world and enter religious life (*saecularem illum habitum relinquere, et monachicum suscipere propositum docuit*), and it was she who received him into the community and ordered that he should be instructed in the scriptures (*susceptumque in monasterium cum ombibus suis fratrum cohorti adsociauit, iussitque illum seriem sacrae historiae doceri*).[10]

It says much for the high-born Hild that she was able to recognize both holiness and genius—the workings of the Holy Spirit—in a cowherd. More than that, it perhaps tells us something about her evangelizing ministry. Hild may well have had the insight to see that through Caedmon's verses in English, the English peasantry, who knew no Latin, would be drawn to the love of Jesus in a way that would not otherwise have been possible.

THE SANCTIFICATION OF THE SAGAS

A century after Caedmon, Alcuin certainly regarded the entertainments at Lindisfarne as a sign of lax living. He deplored the practice of reciting traditional narrative poems like *Widsith* and *Beowulf*. Yet there was a strong tradition that would have been familiar to monastics coming from the great Augustine of Hippo (not to be confused with Augustine of Canterbury who has figured so prominently in our discussions of Hild). Augustine had said of the Platonists (pagan Greek philosophers) "if [they] have said things by chance that are truthful and conformable to our faith, we must not only have no fear of them, but even appropriate them for our own use from those who are, in a sense, their illegal possessors."[11] Using the writings of ancient Greek or Roman thinkers to explain Christian teachings was a practice that was widely accepted, and indeed we find Bede himself quoting from Virgil.[12] Making use of the traditional sagas of the Germanic invaders would have been a similarly accepted practice.

The traditional epic poems, therefore, were not entirely disconnected from Caedmon's poetry. Caedmon's gift for poetic composition was recognized as a gift, coming directly from divine inspiration, but that is not to say that the compositions themselves came out of nowhere. Rather there was a grafting of Christian concepts onto the hugely rich Germanic tradition of pagan mythology. Facilitating this cross-fertilization was the way in which these sagas from an oral tradition were first written down. It was in the monasteries that the English poetry of the heathen age was first written down, and as Frank Stenton points out, "most of it only survives in texts which are affected by Christian ideas and imagery."[13]

When we look at that most famous of all epic poem of Anglo-Saxon literature, *Beowulf*, we find that this saga was itself imbibing something of the Christian tradition as it developed. Many strands of the *Beowulf* poem had been handed down orally for centuries, but the poem as we have it now is regarded as the creative work of a single poet. It is not at all clear when this masterly reworking was achieved. It may have been as early as Hild's own period, the seventh century, or as late as the Danish invasions of the ninth or tenth centuries. We have a copy that dates from around the year 1000.

It is interesting to see how the author of *Beowulf* treats of creation. In this extract, the "obdurate being" represents the forces of evil. *Beowulf* records how:

> that obdurate being—that one which waited in places of darkness—suffered tormentedly for a time because each single day he heard the loud noise of happiness in the hall: the lyre's music was there, and the clear singing of the poet. He who was skilled in recounting the creation of men in time distant declared that the Almighty made the earth, a plain radiant to look upon which water encircles; he, taking delight in his achievement, established the sun and the moon, those luminaries, as light for those living in the world; he embellished the earth's surfaces with branches and with leaves; life too he created in each of those species which go their vital ways.[14]

The "obdurate being," the forces of evil personified, is unable to bear the happiness of those who rejoice in the goodness of God's creation. The account of creation itself is reminiscent of Genesis 1 and many of the psalms. The pagan myth itself has assimilated into its telling aspects of the Christian story.

Perhaps part of the genius of Hild as she nurtured Caedmon's gift was to realize that the pagan myths could be reimagined in such a way as to draw the Anglo-Saxon peoples into the Christian story. Tales of heroism in warfare against enemy armies could be retold in terms of spiritual warfare against the devil, and all the various manifestations of evil that confronted the beleaguered soul.

Specialist in Anglo-Saxon poetry S. A. J. Bradley writes:

> Not inconceivably, the very dynamic of Caedmon's poetic revolution may have been the realization that the traditional heroic mode was in fact little compromised by the constraints of Christian action and sentiment—that, indeed, the heroic idiom may prove a didactic tool in mediating a whole host of Christian concepts, such as that of spiritual warfare.[15]

It was perhaps Hild who realized that the heroic idiom of the epic sagas and the use of the Anglo-Saxon language could become a tool for the spread of the Gospel. It was Hild who recognized Caedmon's gift, she who nurtured his education in Christian spirituality. While the language of the Church continued to be Latin, perhaps Hild had an inkling that Caedmon's poetry, composed in Anglo-Saxon, would become an instrument of evangelization for the ordinary people, the unlettered population of England in the early Middle Ages.

As he adapted the structure of the traditional heroic sagas, Caedmon translated the most important Christian teachings into popular songs. As Bede lists the subject matter treated in Caedmon's compositions—the creation of the world, the origin of the human race, the events recorded in Genesis, and so on—it is difficult to think of what other Christian teachings he might have included.[16]

The list suggests that Caedmon's output was considerable, way beyond the one fragment of verse that remains extant. Bede would have known this. Caedmon composed his initial verses no earlier than 657, and possibly as late as the 670s. (Hild died in 680.) Bede was born in 672 or 673, living his entire life in Northumbria where he wrote *Ecclesiastical History* in 731. He was exceedingly well informed about the state of the Christian Church both in England and abroad, and he made every attempt to record history accurately. He would have been aware of Caedmon's compositions as the popular songs of his day.

Although we can take Bede's list as reliable evidence for the multiplicity of Caedmon's themes, it should not be taken as accurate in every detail. It seems unlikely that Bede had come across Caedmon's compositions exactly as he includes them. More likely, wanting to underline Caedmon's influence and even his sanctity, he attributes to him writings covering the entire syllabus of Christian teachings.

Paul Cavill, a specialist in Old English, thinks that the list of Caedmon's compositions was intended to demonstrate that at Whitby Caedmon had followed the same program of learning as had been set out by the great Augustine of Hippo.

> And the programme of education which Caedmon undergoes in the monastery, and which he uses for his verse, closely matches the educational programme laid out by St. Augustine of Hippo in his educational treatise, *De Catechizandis Rudibus*. In other words, Bede is interpreting Caedmon for his audience: Caedmon was close to being a saint, and he followed in the footsteps of those who taught the faith.[17]

There can be no doubt that Bede intended to impress on his reader the magnitude of the contribution made by Caedmon to the evangelization of England.

CAEDMON'S SANCTITY

As well as attributing to Caedmon the whole gamut of Christian teachings there is further evidence that Bede intended to portray Caedmon as an exceptionally holy man. As with Hild, it is in the manner of his death.

We have already noted with Hild that a specific stylized manner of reporting a person's death was intended as a pointer toward holiness or sainthood. Bede records Hild's illness during the last six years of her life, then her reception of viaticum to strengthen her for the journey (*via*) from this life to the next. Finally, she summoned her sisters, and after words of encouragement to them, she joyfully welcomed death.

We see similarities in Bede's telling of Caedmon's death, though the illness that preceded it lasted only fourteen days. On Caedmon's last day, his attendant was surprised when Caedmon asked to be accommodated in the house for the sick and the dying because he did not seem near to death. Similarly there was surprise when he asked for viaticum. Caedmon gave no sign of even being unwell; he was talking normally and seemed to be in cheerful spirits. Nonetheless, Caedmon repeated his request that the Eucharist should be brought to him. When this request had been granted, he talked to his fellow monks gathered around him, ensuring that they were charitably disposed toward him, and he to them, before passing away quietly in his sleep.

Exploring the theme of conversion, Cavill again finds evidence of Bede's desire to underline Caedmon's saintly credentials:

> Caedmon himself is converted progressively. For someone who left parties in case he had to sing, he becomes someone whose verses convert many. He is converted first to be able to sing. Then he is converted to monasticism. And finally he is converted into a saint. We ought to note that Bede quotes Galatians 1:1, in relation to Caedmon's gift. St Paul writes of his apostolic vocation, given to him by God, "not from man, nor by human means," and Bede makes a similar claim for Caedmon's gift. It means upheaval in his life, just as it did for St. Paul, a complete break with what went before. . . . Through Caedmon's gift, he became a kind of apostle to the English.[18]

The illness, the viaticum, the deathbed conversations, and finally, the knowledge and joyful acceptance of immanent death—these characteristics represent the perfect death of an exceptionally holy person.

THE HANDING DOWN OF CAEDMON'S VERSE

Although Caedmon wrote many poems, the several lines recorded by Bede are the only lines directly attributed to Caedmon that we now have, albeit in several versions. In *Ecclesiastical History*, Bede gives what he understands to be the "theme" of Caedmon's hymn because he is writing in Latin, explaining that a straight translation could not do justice to the original beauty and dignity of the verses. Sherley-Price translates Bede's rendering as follows:

> Praise we the Fashioner now of Heaven's fabric,
> The majesty of his might and his mind's wisdom,
> Work of the world-warden, worker of all wonders,
> How he the Lord of Glory everlasting,
> Wrought first for the race of men Heaven as a rooftree,
> Then made the Middle Earth to be their mansion[19]

Bede does not give a version of the hymn in the vernacular. Even his Latin version is intended as a paraphrase of Caedmon's poem, rather than an exact translation. As Cavill says, "Bede's concern was to give a correct Latin paraphrase of the verse, not to translate the poem."[20]

Yet we have access to the Old English versions through the scribes, who copied Bede's *Ecclesiastical History* and who added to it an Old English version of Caedmon's poem. We know that Caedmon's poems had been copied into various Saxon dialects and that they formed part of the oral tradition. These scribes wrote into their manuscripts the hymn, which was familiar to them.

Cavill translates the main West Saxon version of the poem as follows:

> Now we ought to praise the Guardian of the kingdom of heaven,
> the might of the Creator and his understanding,
> the works of the Father of glory, how he, of each wonder,
> the eternal Lord, established a beginning.
> He first created for the sons of the earth
> heaven as a roof, the holy Creator;
> then the world, the Guardian of humankind,
> the eternal Lord, afterwards created
> the land for the people, the almighty Lord.[21]

Cavill tells us that there are something like 125 complete or partial manuscripts of Bede's *Ecclesiastical History* from the medieval period. Some of these are in Latin and some Old English. Under King Alfred (849–899), there was a push toward having important educational works available for those ignorant of Latin, and the English translation of Bede's *Ecclesiastical History* was completed around the end of the tenth century. Only 25 of these 125 manuscripts contain an Old English version of *Hymn*, with the earlier Latin copies providing the English version of Caedmon's poem as an addition.

So in the earliest manuscript containing the *Hymn* in Northumbrian Old English, the Moore manuscript of about 737, the poem appears at the end of the book, complete, along with some glosses and other notes.

Cavill recognizes significant differences between the earliest manuscripts and the later Alfredian ones:

> When the Alfredian translator came to Caedmon's Hymn he missed out Bede's passage about the difficulty of rendering poetry in another language, and simply gave the Old English text of the *Hymn* substantially as we find it in the earliest manuscript.

Then Cavil points to a slightly different phraseology between earlier Northumbrian Anglo-Saxon version and the later West Saxon version.

> There is one significant difference between the earliest manuscripts and the Alfredian ones. The Alfredian versions have the phrase "he first created *for the sons of earth* heaven as a roof," and the italicized phrase in Bede and the Northumbrian versions is "for the sons of men." In other words, the Alfredian translator knew the *Hymn* in an English form. He was not translating Bede's Latin. All the evidence from the manuscripts confirms the view that Caedmon's *Hymn* was widely known in a strong oral tradition.[22]

The Alfredian translator obviously knew the *Hymn* from contemporary use, thus indicating that Caedmon's verse was widely known for at least two or three centuries after its original composition.

ALDHELM: ANOTHER CHRISTIAN POET

From a literary point of view, Caedmon's significance lies in the fact that the surviving fragments of his poetry represent the first writings we have handed down to us in the Old English or Anglo-Saxon tongue. A somewhat later contemporary of Caedmon was Aldhelm (640–709), abbot of Malmesbury, in present-day Wiltshire, who later became bishop of Sherborne from about 705. We have already come across Aldhelm and his writings to the nuns of Barking. He is chiefly remembered for being the first Anglo-Saxon to write extensively in Latin. Many of his works have been handed down to us and particularly significant are his writings on metrical verse. Aldhelm's Latin writings consisted of extravagant vocabulary in a complex artificial style.

Yet it is also recorded that he wrote in the vernacular. Bradley tells us that a life of Aldhelm, written in the twelfth century by William of Malmesbury records Aldhelm, like Caedmon "winning congregations by similarly singing of Christ in the language and poetry of the Anglo-Saxons."[23] Bradley reckons that Aldhelm "vies with Caedmon for the title of first Christian poet in the English vernacular."[24]

For several reasons, it seems likely that the title of first English poet should go to Caedmon, rather than Aldhelm. To begin with, though it is not possible to give exact dates for the compositions of each, it seems likely that chronologically Caedmon's compositions came first. Aldhelm was born (640) and died (709) somewhat later than Caedmon. Caedmon was elderly when Hild took him in to the monastery, where he stayed for some time under Hild's supervision, and Hild died in 680.

Then it is necessary to take into account the stretch of time between Aldhelm's compositions in the late seventh early eighth century and the account of his life by William of Malmesbury in the twelfth century.

Centuries earlier Bede himself had mentioned Aldhelm and devoted some space to his writings. Bede specifies an important work that criticizes the British who still refuse to conform to Roman authority regarding various matters, particularly with regard to the correct date for the celebration of Easter. He also mentions Aldhelm's *On Virginity*, which Bede praises for the excellence of its Latin composition. Yet Bede makes no mention of Aldhelm writing anything in Anglo-Saxon. Finally Bede certainly implies that it was Caedmon who was the first to write Christian verse in the vernacular.

Whether Caedmon or Aldhelm should be regarded as the first English poet—and in my view, it is Caedmon—I am nonetheless firmly with Bradley on the following point:

> Wherever the innovatory credit is to be placed, the achievement is a momentous one in English literary annals. The ancient vernacular poetry, which might well have been abandoned on account of its unredeemed worldliness or paganism, was successfully sanctified.[25]

It seems to me that the innovatory credit belongs firmly with Caedmon and Hild, who sponsored him.

THE FIRST SCHOOL FOR ENGLISH POETS

Hild's drive to promote scholarship plainly extended beyond Scripture and Latin. As well as running what we today would call a seminary with Latin as the working language, it would seem that she was remarkable for her time in appreciating the evangelizing potential of original composition in the vernacular, the language of the ordinary people. It seems entirely possible that it was Hild who set up the first-ever school of English poetry. If Caedmon's poetry was widely used as a tool of evangelization, and if it spread abroad beyond Whitby, it would seem likely that it was not only learned by heart but also much copied in the scriptorium at Whitby.

Once in the monastery, Caedmon's compositions delighted those who taught him. As he slowly but steadily worked on what he learned in the monastery, he was no doubt captivated by the words of Scripture. Bede tells us that he was like an animal chewing the cud, combining learning with inspiration to produce such delightful poetry that his teachers, in their turn, were captivated by his delightful (divinely inspired) words (*doctores suos uicissim auditores sui faciebat*).[26] His teachers became the ones who listened. The likelihood is that it was those teachers who heard Caedmon, wrote down his compositions, and then copied and circulated them outside the monastery of Whitby.

We know that there were others, following on from Caedmon's success, who began to compose religious verse in English. Interestingly one of these was Bede himself. Cuthbert's "Letter on the Death of Bede" contains a death song that is generally accepted to be the work of Bede himself. Translated by D. H. Farmer it reads:

> Before that enforced journey no one becomes
> Wiser in thought than he may need be,
> For considering before his going hence
> What for his spirit of good and evil
> After his death day might be judged.[27]

Others like Aldhelm of Malmesbury might have written Christian poems in Anglo-Saxon, but presumably there must have been some at Whitby itself trying to follow Caedmon's example and compose Christian poems in English.

Hild ensured that Caedmon's compositions in Anglo-Saxon, that is to say, Old English, were disseminated as an evangelizing tool for the ordinary people. Her decision to bring Caedmon into the abbey, to have him educated in Scripture, to encourage him in his gift for composition, was to initiate a new tradition of Christian songs—a tradition that would be responsible for converting the English imagination. Up until the seventh century it had been left to the singing bards with their narrative poems in the vernacular to develop Anglo-Saxon culture and a sense of English history in the context of its pagan past. In the centuries following Caedmon, as his poetry was disseminated and emulated, passing into different dialects, England produced in its own native tongue a powerful tradition of Christian poetry, unquestionably superior to that of any other European country of the same period.

We might well conclude that it was Hild who was responsible for setting in train the great tradition of English poetry which continues to this day.

NOTES

1. Later in this chapter I discuss whether Caedmon or Aldhelm can best lay claim to this title.
2. Foot, *Monastic Life*, 240.
3. Frank Stenton, *Anglo-Saxon England* (Oxford: Oxford University Press, 1971), 193.
4. Alcuin's Latin, *Letter 124*. Written to Higbald of Lindisfarne in 797, translated by Paul Cavill, in Paul Cavill, *Anglo-Saxon Christianity: Exploring the Earliest Roots of Christian Spirituality in England* (London: HarperCollins, 1999), 167–68.
5. Mayr-Harting, *The Coming of Christianity*, 316 n15, gives the following reference: *Two Lives of St. Cuthbert*, ed. B. Colgrave, Bede, c.27, 246.
6. Colgrave, *Two Lives of Saint Cuthbert*, Chapter XXVII, 246.
7. Colgrave, *Two Lives of Saint Cuthbert*, Chapter XXVII, 246.
8. Mayr-Harting, *The Coming of Christianity*, 225–26
9. Foot, *Monastic Life*, 240.
10. Beda, *Historia Ecclesiastica, Liber Quartus*, 22 [24]. CLVI.
11. S. A. J. Bradley, trans. and ed., *Anglo-Saxon Poetry* (London: Everyman, 2003), xvi. Quotes from *Saint Augustine: Christian Instruction*, tr. J. J. Gavigan (New York, 1950). Vol. II in *The Fathers of the Church: A New Translation* Bk. II, ch.40, 112–13.
12. For example, *Ecclesiastical History*, IV.25, 253–54; *Historia Ecclesiastic, Liber Quartus*, 23, CLIX; Bede quotes from the *Aeneid*.
13. Stenton, *Anglo-Saxon England*, 192
14. Bradley, *Anglo-Saxon Poetry*, 413–14; quotes from *Beowulf* (London: British Library, Cotton Vitellius A), xv, fol. 132a–201b §86.
15. Bradley, *Anglo-Saxon Poetry*, xvii.
16. Bede, *Ecclesiastic History*, IV.24 249–50; Beda *Historia Ecclesiastica, Liber Quarto*, 22, CLVI.
17. Cavill, *Anglo-Saxon Christianity*, 92.
18. Cavill, *Anglo-Saxon Christianity*, 93.
19. Bede, *Ecclesiastical History*, 24; 248–49.
20. Cavill, *Anglo-Saxon Christianity*, 103.
21. Cavill, *Anglo-Saxon Christianity*, 96.
22. Cavill, *Anglo-Saxon Christianity*, 104.
23. Bradley, *Anglo-Saxon Poetry*, 3.
24. Bradley, *Anglo-Saxon Poetry*, 367.
25. Bradley, *Anglo-Saxon Poetry*, 3–4.
26. Beda, *Historia Ecclesiastica, Liber Quartus*, 22 [24] CLVI.
27. Bede's Death Song in "Cuthbert's Letter on the Death of Bede" translated by D. H. Farmer, in Bede, *Ecclesiastical History*, 358.

Chapter Eleven

Underlying Tensions Come to a Head

When he sent Augustine to cross the Channel and convert the English, Pope Gregory had little knowledge of the state of the country. Nonetheless he drew up quite specific plans for the structures that Augustine should set up to govern the English Church. Gregory imagined the various parts of Britain still to be structured as they had been under the Roman Empire, and he planned for Augustine to govern the Church along similar lines. The system of archbishops and bishops would run along the same lines as the structures that operated in Rome.

RELATIVE HARMONY IN NORTHUMBRIA

Just as Patrick before him had found the Irish Christians unwelcoming, so Augustine had been unable to work with the Welsh/British bishops who represented the remnants of Christianity from Roman times.[1] After a first meeting with him they had discussed whether to accept Augustine's authority. They called a second bigger meeting where they would make their decision according to Augustine's demeanor. As we saw in chapter 4, they found him haughty and unbending, rather than meek and lowly in heart and decided that if he showed so little respect for them when they were not under his authority, he would hardly respect them if they allowed him authority over them. The rift between the British and those aligned to Augustine would continue, so that in 664 Wilfrid, the great Romanizer, refusing to acknowledge the authority of the British bishops, traveled to Compiègne in Gaul to be ordained Archbishop of York.

While Augustine failed to win over those British Christians who had perpetuated the faith since the Roman occupation, he received a warm reception from the Christians in Kent who owed their faith to Queen Bertha. We saw how Bertha welcomed Augustine and enabled him to make Canterbury his base. Paulinus, sent by Gregory, was then able to join Augustine, traveling subsequently to Northumbria as chaplain to Ethelburga, who was to marry Edwin. It was in Northumbria that Paulinus converted Edwin and his great-niece, Hild.

Paulinus was forced to leave Northumbria when Edwin was defeated and killed in battle in the winter of 632–633, and the Church in Northumbria fell into decline. The revival of the Northumbrian Church would come under King Oswald, who in 635 invited Aidan to come out from Iona and make his base at Lindisfarne. In 647, Hild joined Aidan's mission.

From 635 until 664, when the Synod of Whitby took place, there were in Northumbria Christians who owed their faith to the Augustinian or Roman mission and those who followed Aidan and the Ionian or Irish practices. What is striking is that Augustinian mission worked alongside the Irish/Ionian mission in relative harmony. That is not to say that fierce debates, which were argued with some passion, did not sometimes arise.

Notably there was an ardent campaigner for the Roman method in calculating the date of Easter in the person of a certain Irishman named Ronan. Ronan appears to have disputed openly and forcefully with Finan, who had succeeded Aidan at Lindisfarne on Aidan's death. Finan apparently gave as good as he got. Yet whatever discord there may have been between the likes of Ronan and Finan, in the general scheme of things in Northumbria, divergence of practice did not cause undue concern. Many influential figures, like Hild herself, saw no contradiction in owing allegiance to aspects of both traditions.

Henry Mayr-Harting, in his classic work *The Coming of Christianity to Anglo-Saxon England*, endorses the view that relations between the Celtic- and the Roman-leaning monastics were generally harmonious. Those "who lived in the generation before the Synod of Whitby were not so sensitive to the 'basic conflict' between Romans and Celts as modern historians have sometimes been." Mayr-Harting then goes on to discuss the situation in a monastery at Gilling in Deira. This monastery probably observed the Roman Easter in its early years because it was founded on land granted to the Roman-leaning Eanfled. Yet the first abbot of Gilling, Trumhere, had apparently been educated by the Irish, and when he was appointed bishop of the Mercians, he accepted consecration from the Irish "without demur." Furthermore, his successor Tunbert subsequently resigned the abbacy to devote himself to prayer and study in Ireland. Mayr-Harting concludes: "It is not easy to say whether we would call Gilling a Roman or a Celtic institution; and contemporaries felt no need to label it in these terms."[2]

Benedicta Ward, who has made a detailed study of the Synod of Whitby, is likewise at pains to reject the notion that there was any kind of "clash between two kinds of Christianity". The Synod of Whitby "was in no way an anti-Irish, pro-Roman tussle. . . . [It] was not seen by the participants as a quarrel between different styles of Christianity." She insists that "there was no deep-seated antagonism between the two sides."[3] The mutually held belief in the supreme importance of the Resurrection meant that each side had far more in common than what divided them. All were agreed on the supreme importance of the Resurrection. All were agreed that the day of the week when the Resurrection was most appropriately celebrated above all others was Sunday. The complicated matter of working out exactly on which day of the year it should be celebrated as *the* climactic feast of the entire Christian calendar was not an issue of overriding importance.

Mayr-Harting says that it was even hard work to engender enough interest to make a debate of it. Referring to the actual composition of the Whitby Synod, he has this to say:

> The established figures of the Northumbrian church at the synod—Colman of Lindisfarne, Cedd, Hilda of Whitby—were all on the Celtic side. The Roman side had to be packed, packed first of all with people who wouldn't have dreamt of stirring up the debate themselves, like the chaplain who had come from Kent with Eanfled, or the peaceful and now elderly James the deacon; and secondly with outsiders like Agilbert, the Frankish bishop of the West Saxons, and his priest Agatho, who were friends of Alfrith and Wilfrid. Nothing shows more clearly than the composition of the Roman party at Whitby what hard work was needed to make a debate of it.[4]

So what was the main impetus behind the synod? Who was actually pushing for it? Mayr-Harting thinks that the answer lies with Alfrith and not solely because of his love of the truth about the date of Easter. As we will see in the next chapter, Alfrith was engaged in a power-struggle with his father, King Oswy, who had succeeded his brother Oswald as king of Bernicia and eventually the whole of Northumbria. Alfrith hoped that in alliance with Wilfrid that he would be able to weaken his father's position by discrediting Celtic religious practices.

Thus, rather than being a make or break issue for the Northumbrian Church, the question of when to celebrate Easter was more a niggling difference that would eventually need to be resolved. Another matter of difference between the Celtic and the Roman monks was the fact that each set of monks had a different style of tonsure or haircut.

THE TONSURE

When a man became a monk, in a deeply symbolic act he allowed his head to be shaved and adopted a specific haircut or tonsure as a sign of his dedication to God. The style of tonsure was further a sign of the tradition to which he belonged. D. H. Farmer explains:

> Differing styles of tonsure, itself a sign of dedication to God, became concrete symbols of party loyalties. Roman clergy shaved the crown of the head but left a circle of hair all round the head above the temples, in memory of Christ's crown of thorns. The Celtic clergy however shaved the front of the head, but allowed the hair to grow in flowing locks behind. Allegiance could be discerned at a glance.[5]

It was possible to tell at a glance to which party the monk belonged. When there was friction between them, each would defend their style of tonsure with claims that had no basis in historical reality. The Romans attributed their own style to Saint Peter and claimed that the Celtic style derived from Simon Magus.[6] This was the Simon who had offered money to Peter if he would give him the power to bring down the Holy Spirit on those who had been baptized (Acts 8:1–9). Simon was considered to have been the first heretic, and it is from him that we get the word "simony," meaning the sin of attempting to buy an office in the Church or to buy God's grace. The implication, therefore, was that the Celtic monks were in some sense heretical.

The Irish themselves attributed their style of tonsure to St. John.[7] In the Eastern part of the Church, the whole head was shaved in the manner, so it was thought, of St. Paul. None of these claims or counterclaims was in any way historical, but of course no one at the time had any way of verifying the matter one way or another. Nor would they have been particularly interested in doing so. They simply did not have the modern notion that historical reality should be the arbiter of truth. If anyone might think this strange, they might consider as just one example the unwillingness of the Catholic Magisterium over many recent decades to engage in scholarship that calls into question the dearly held "truth" that women in the early Church were not "ordained" as deacons.[8]

As a measure of just how important the "correct" form of tonsure had become, when Theodore was appointed Archbishop of Canterbury, he delayed for four months before beginning the journey from Rome to Canterbury. He had to wait for his hair to grow sufficiently so that he could receive a circular tonsure. Despite this, it does not appear that the difference between the Roman and the Celtic tonsure was a matter of any great friction in the Northumbrian Church.

THE DATING OF EASTER

Although the Northumbrian Church generally appears to have been relatively relaxed regarding the correct date for Easter, for those who had the responsibility of working out the liturgical calendar, the matter was of some importance. And its long and complicated history meant that the best of brains were needed for the task.

From the beginning, there had been controversy in the Church with regard to when Easter should be celebrated. In the early days of the Church, there had been a clash between Judaists, those Christians who continued with Jewish practices, and anti-Semites, Christians who saw the future of their new religion outside Judaism. Early Christians had originally celebrated Christ's Resurrection on the day of the Jewish Passover, the fourteenth day of Nisan; Nisan is the first lunar month of the Jewish year. The view then took hold that Easter ought to be on a Sunday and that the Nisan 14, the day of the Jewish festival, should be avoided. This was the ruling decided on at the Council of Nicea in 325, and those who failed to go along with it were condemned as heretics, known as "Quartodecimans." It was not entirely clear, however whether Easter was to be celebrated on Nisan 14 if it fell on a Sunday.

The tradition that came down to the Irish monks was based on an earlier practice, one that preceded the Council of Nicea. They followed an earlier history, which derived from Anatolius, Bishop of Laodicea. The Ionan monks were not, therefore Quartodecimans, and there practices were not from the Roman point of view "heretical." Yet whenever Nisan 14 fell on a Sunday, they celebrated Easter a week earlier than the Roman church.

The second and more complicated problem with regard to the dating of Easter was to do with the fact that Easter was based on lunar months (calculated by the phases of the moon) and on the timing of the vernal equinox (the day in the spring when the hours of darkness and the hours of light are equal). Because the lunar month differed from the calendar month, some complex calculations were necessary. The calendar month or solar month (based on the movement of the sun) was common throughout the empire. It required specialist skills in computistics to calculate the date of Easter over a cycle of years. Thus, for example, an Easter table with a nineteen-year cycle was produced by professional computists in Alexandria. Tables multiplied. Confusion was rife. The tables used by the Irish differed from those of the Alexandrians and both differed from those of the Roman church.

In Anglo-Saxon England, the matter was further complicated by the fact that some Irish missionaries, having discovered on travels that their calendar differed from the Dionysian calendar used in Rome and Gaul, had early adjusted their dating of Easter accordingly in the seventh century. Thus, it was not a clear-cut case that those of Irish heritage used the Ionan calculation and those who had been converted by Augustine's mission used the Roman. Thus, the use of the Dionysian calendar spread throughout many parts of Ireland in the seventh century, but was not adopted by many British churches or by the Dalriadan center of Iona.

THE TRIGGER

To situate the story, it will help to go over again in brief outline the history of the Northumbrian royalty from the time of Edwin and Ethelburga to the reign of Oswy and Eanfled. At the time of Hild's birth, Edwin had fled Deira when Ethelfrith the king of Bernicia attempted to add Deira to his territory. Subsequently Edwin had returned to Northumbria and killed Ethelfrith, whereupon his sons, Oswald and Oswy, fled to Dalriada, the Irish kingdom centered on what is now southwest Scotland. Here, both sons were converted to Irish Christianity.

When Edwin was killed in battle by the pagan Penda in 662–663, there followed a period of confusion with no recognized king until Northumbria split again along traditional lines into the subkingdoms of Bernicia in the north and Deira in the South. Oswald reunited Northumbria in 634. When Oswald was killed by Penda's Mercian forces, he was succeeded by his brother Oswy, who finally defeated Penda at the Battle of Winwaed in 655.

For Eanfled's ancestry, we again begin with Edwin and Ethelburga, because she was their daughter. Her maternal grandmother had been Bertha, the Frankish princess. Eanfled had been baptized in Northumbria by Paulinus, Ethelburga's chaplain, even before Edwin's own baptism, but had been brought up in Kent after her father's death, where she had learned and followed Roman customs. Her chaplain was a priest from Kent named Romanus.

As Bede recounts the matter, one year, Oswy and Eanfled found themselves celebrating Easter at different times: Oswy following the Irish calendar, and Eanfled celebrated the Roman date for Easter.

The actual trigger to the Synod of Whitby involves a story about King Oswy and Queen Eanfled of Northumbria. Before Bede embarks on the story, he tells us that Aidan had died and had been succeeded as bishop of Lindisfarne by Finan, who had been ordained bishop by the Irish.

> *Interea Aidano episcopo de hac uita sublato, Finan pro illo gradum episcopatus a Scottis ordinatus ac missus acceperat. . .*
>
> *His temporibus quaestio facta est frequens et magna de obseruatione paschae, confirmantibus eis, qui de Cantia uel de Galliis aduenerant, quod Scotti dominicum paschae diem contra uniuersalis ecclesiae morem celebrarent.*[9]

Roughly translated:

> Meanwhile, bishop Aidan having been taken up from this life, Finan, who had been ordained and sent by the Irish, took up the bishopric. . . . Around this time there was a persistent large-scale questioning regarding the observance of Easter, by those who had come from Kent or Gaul, who affirmed that the Scots [Irish] were celebrating Easter Sunday on a day contrary to the custom of the universal church.

"About this time" (*His temporibus*) is significant here. The controversy regarding the observance of Easter seems to have erupted when it happened that Queen Eanfled and her court were still fasting and keeping Palm Sunday when King Oswy had completed his Lenten observance and was celebrating Easter. "About this time" refers to the period after Finan, who argued so violently with Ronan, had been installed as bishop of Lindisfarne. We know that Bede considered Finan's views to be stubbornly heretical, which may in part account for his negative assessment of Finan. Nonetheless, it is interesting to see how favorably Aidan is presented both in relation to his successor and to his predecessor. Aidan was not the first missionary to have been sent out from Iona to found a monastery on Lindisfarne. The first had received a hostile reception from the Northumbrians and had gone back.

Aidan's predecessor had been unable to work with the local population, and it seems that his successor was equally unsuited to the task. Aidan must have been an exceptional man, able to win over and work alongside people of strongly held views that differed from his own. During his tenure of something like sixteen years, the harmony between the Irish missionaries, the Roman missionaries, and as far as we know the remnant of British Christians from the Roman occupation was quite remarkable. The harmony that Aidan established continued right up to the Whitby Synod, when trouble was stirred initially for political rather than theological reasons.

THE BEST OF VARIOUS CUSTOMS

Thus, for nearly three decades, Roman and Irish ways operated side by side and in communion with each other. Some people might be tempted to think that such cooperation between those whose practices differed was some sort of aberration, operating outside the mainstream of the Church, which would not have been tolerated by Pope Gregory in Rome. This is far from the truth.

Despite his Roman mind-set, with its propensity for regimentation, Pope Gregory was not necessarily wedded to the idea of uniformity in the way that later figures like for example Wilfrid would be. This is evident from Gregory's continuing correspondence with Augustine. Once Augustine had crossed the Channel, he continued to seek and receive advice from Gregory. In one of his questions, Augustine asked why customs varied in different churches, when all hold the same faith. Augustine wanted to know why Mass was not the same in the churches of Gaul as it was in the Church of Rome.

Gregory replies to Augustine that he is obviously familiar with the Roman custom because he grew up with it, but that if he should find practices more pleasing to God, whether they comes from Rome or the churches of Gaul or any other churches, he should make a careful selection of them for use by the English, who are still new to the faith.

> *Sed mihi placet ut, siue in Romana, siue in Galliarum, seu in qualibet ecclesia aliquid inuenisti, quod plus omnipotenti Deo possit placere, sollicite eligas, et in Anglorum ecclesia, quae adhuc ad fidem noua est, institutione praecipua, quae de multis ecclesiis colligere potuisti, infundas.*[10]

It is evident from this reply that Gregory did not see uniformity of custom as a necessary prerequisite for communion with Rome. Augustine specifically asks Gregory about differing practices that were to be found in Gaul. In reply, Gregory extends what is permissible to the customs that might be more acceptable to God whether they are the customs to be found in the Church of Rome, Gaul, *or any other Church.* Augustine is quite definitely to regiment the English Church, determining what is and what is not devout, but diversity of practice was to be no obstacle to unity; indeed the best of various customs were to be taught to the English.

The point that must be stressed here is that differing practices did not put their adherents outside communion with Rome. Thus, when Hild, as we will see in later chapters, engaged in various ministries from which women are now excluded, it was not the case that she was outside the Catholic tradition. In a manner that was completely orthodox in the seventh century, men and women worked alongside each other in the mission of the Church, sharing both sacramental and leadership offices.

There are, therefore, no grounds for any suggestion that the ministries undertaken by Hild in the seventh century lay somehow outside the Roman Catholic tradition. It was the eighth-century reforms, rather than the unswerving tradition of the Church, that relegated women monastics to second-class status.

NOTES

1. At this point in the history, "British" and "Welsh" are used interchangeably to differentiate them from the Anglo-Saxons, the Irish, and the Scots.

2. Mayr-Harting, *The Coming of Christianity*, 106.
3. Benedicta Ward, *A True Easter*, 4–5.
4. Mayr-Harting, *The Coming of Christianity*, 108. In a footnote Mayr-Harting refers to J. Meissner, *The Church in England after the Synod of Whitby* (1929, 13–14), which makes this point.
5. Farmer, "Notes," in Bede, *Ecclesiastical History*, n192, 371.
6. Farmer, "Notes," n192, 371.
7. Foot, *Monastic Life*, 159.
8. Pope Francis has recently set up a commission to investigate this matter, admitting to ignorance of the relevant scholarship. Such ignorance stems from a refusal to engage in the scholarship of women theologians and a ban on the discussion of women's ordination for decades. For ordination rites for women deacons, see Macy, *The Hidden History of Women's Ordination*, Appendix I, 133–42.
9. Beda, *Historia Ecclesiastica, Liber Tertius*, 25, CVIII.
10. Beda, *Historia Ecclesiastica, Liber Primus*, 27, XXIX.

Chapter Twelve

The Synod of Whitby

From the beginning of Christianity, the leaders of the Church have met together to decide on various questions that have arisen with regard to the tenets and the practices of their faith. They have ruled on matters of morality and on the way in which the institutions of the Church should be regulated. The very earliest of such meetings, as recorded in the New Testament, was the Council of Jerusalem. It was called to settle a dispute between Peter and Paul regarding whether non-Jewish male converts to Christianity needed to be circumcised (Acts 15).

The decisions of Church councils have always been treated with great seriousness and considered binding on the wider community, either locally or worldwide depending on the makeup of the participants. The synod that took place at Whitby was one such decision-making meeting or council. The word "synod" comes from the Greek *synodus* where it simply means an assembly. It corresponds to the Latin word *concilium*, or council.

COUNCILS AND SYNODS UP TO THE SEVENTH CENTURY

The practice of settling questions through collective debate continued from the beginning to the present day. As Norman Tanner writes with regard to the five great ecumenical councils held between the fifth and eighth centuries, "theological statements of the highest quality, and of lasting significance, were forged through collective debate."[1] Ecumenical councils were those councils whose teachings were determined by the whole Church, that is to say the Latin-speaking western Church centered on Rome, and the Greek-speaking eastern Church centered on Constantinople.

Tanner also mentions "the importance of local councils," selecting for special mention "the third council of Toledo in 589 . . . the councils in France convoked by Boniface in the eighth century," and significantly from our point of view, "the synod of Whitby in 664."[2] The council that Hild hosted and in which she and her community participated was up there in importance with Toledo, which saw Spain reject Arianism and embrace Catholicism and with the influential councils presided over by Boniface in France in the 740s.

One of the most important Church councils of all time preceded the five ecumenical councils mentioned by Tanner. Indeed the teachings of these five might be considered as simply expansions on those of the first Council of Nicea in 325. The principle question under discussion could not have been more central to the Christian faith: Was Jesus fully God? Was he (to use the Greek word) *homoousios*, that is to say, was he "of one being," with the Father?

Despite the undeniably theological nature of the dispute, it was not the bishop theologians who brought about the Council, but the Roman Emperor Constantine. After the Christianization of the Roman Empire in the fourth century, it was Constantine who exercised the highest legal authority in the Church as well as in the state. The question of Jesus's full divinity was causing divisions within the empire, and Constantine wanted to maintain unity. It was not the case that secular rulers were simply observers or were acting in advisory capacity only. The Emperor was the highest authority in the Church. The contentious word "homoousios" was inserted into the Nicene Creed at the express wish of Constantine.[3]

Juridical authority continued to rest with secular rulers for a number of centuries. In Carolingian times, juridical primacy belonged to the Frankish rulers, and Frankish rulers saw themselves and behaved as the Church's divine right rulers.[4] There was, therefore, an undeniable and important precedent for the active and influential involvement of secular rulers in Church councils. That same practice of secular rulers doubling as Christian authorities operated in early Anglo-Saxon Britain. Barbara Yorke, in her detailed study of the conversion of Britain from 600 to 800, says that "Kings continued to regard themselves as leaders of the church once the initial period of conversion was past."[5] The Whitby Council, like the Nicene Council, is a prime example. It was called at the instigation of a secular ruler, King Oswy. According to Bede's detailed account, it was Oswy who opened the council and gave the inaugural address, Oswy who determined who should speak and when, and Oswy who put questions to the various parties. Finally, it was Oswy who determined the clinching argument and made the final decision.

WHITBY: A "PROPER CHURCH COUNCIL"

Given the significant roles taken by King Oswy and by Hild at the synod of Whitby, some scholars have questioned the status of the Whitby council. Among them is Peter Hunter Blair, who thinks that Bede's use of the term "synod" for Whitby is something of an anachronism. Hunter Blair regards the Council of Hertford in 672–673 as the first formal ecclesiastical gathering.[6] I have argued elsewhere that what is anachronistic is to judge Whitby by later standards.[7]

The Synod of Whitby, which Hild hosted, does not belong in the new phase of Church history inaugurated in Britain by Theodore. Rather it belongs in that perhaps deliberately forgotten period when women and men worked alongside each other as equals, when secular leaders saw themselves as leaders of the Church as well, and when women had an authoritative voice in the Church's decision making.

The turning point came with the Council of Hertford, called by Archbishop Theodore, recently arrived in Canterbury, rather than King Oswy, recently deceased. The list of participants given by Bede would seem to suggest that it was confined to bishops and priests.[8] The exclusion of others from formal Church councils would be enforced gradually over the coming centuries. Yet the first chapter or canon of the Council of Hertford, to which all present had to swear, was the incorporation of the teaching of the Council of Whitby with regard to the calculation for the date of Easter.

In a similar vein to Hunter Blair, Benedicta Ward, in a brief but knowledgeable study of the Whitby synod, questions whether it was a "church council" at all. Ward suggests rather that it was merely a meeting between the king and his thanes and the local bishop to decide on a number of matters.

> The meeting was called by Bede "*synodus*" that is a meeting for consultation, but it was not necessarily a "church council.". . . As with early church councils, such as Nicea, the difference between a church council and a secular meeting should not be pushed too far; but this was the seventh and not the fourth century, and bishops were perfectly capable of calling their own councils for church affairs. Here there was no archbishop present.[9]

The argument that no archbishop was present carries little weight. There was only one functional archbishopric in England at the time of the synod, and it is not clear whether the post holder, Deusdedit, had but months to live or was in fact already dead. Scholarly opinion is divided as to the exact date of Deusdedit's death, which is calculated according to various pieces of information given by Bede, not all of which can be reconciled.[10] Furthermore, there is no consensus as to whether Bede's year ran from September or from January.

Nor do we know for certain in what month the synod itself took place. If we follow the account Max Adams, who cites historian Richard Abels as his source, Bede's year began on January 1, and Deusdedit succumbed to the plague on July 14, *before* the synod took place. Abels argues that Deusdedit's death was the trigger that gave urgency to the matters to be decided at the synod.[11]

Therefore, apart from Deusdedit, who may have just died, there was no other archbishop in Britain; archbishops were not so much absent as non-existent. There were, however, three bishops in attendance at the Whitby council in the persons of Agilbert, the Frankish bishop of the West Saxons, Colman of Lindisfarne, and Cedd, who had been ordained by the Irish, worked among the East Saxons, but had no fixed see. Following what Hunter Blair has to say about the state of the episcopacy in England in the 660s, I reckon that the only two absentees were the bishop of a vast Midland area and the bishop of East Anglia.[12]

No mention is made of the Welsh bishops encountered by Augustine, and indeed they seem to have dropped out of the official narrative after their refusal to submit to Augustine's authority. Similarly ignored are any British bishops there may have been in the north of England. It is quite possible that some of this latter group even attended the synod. Overall, it is impressive that half the episcopacy of Britain belonging to the Irish and Roman traditions was present, all the more so when the plague that swept Britain at the time is taken into account.

With regard to her argument that Whitby was merely a meeting among the king, his thanes, and the local bishop, Ward concedes that Nicea was a Church council despite considerable imperial involvement. In making the argument that Whitby was a secular rather than a Church council, she places it within the context of later Church councils, such as Hatfield, rather than the earlier ones such as Nicea. Yet it is precisely the case that, up until the mid-seventh century and a decade or so beyond that, Church councils in Anglo-Saxon England did in fact belong to the era that began with Nicea, rather than the era that included both Hertford and Hatfield, and followed the arrival of Theodore in Canterbury.

The synod or council of Hatfield, which probably took place in Hatfield, Hertfordshire, was called by Theodore, Archbishop of Canterbury in 680, the year of Hild's death.[13] Theodore was, in fact, one of the key figures, ushering in what was essentially a new phase of Church history. With Theodore and the reforms he initiated, there was a concerted drive to insist that ordination to the priesthood elevated men onto an altogether higher plane than the rest of the baptized. At the same time bishops like Wilfrid of York were insisting on the rich trappings of office to make visible their own, even more exalted status. It was then that the routine ordination of abbots to the priesthood started to become commonplace, thus maintaining their status on Church councils. Abbesses, meanwhile, were to be excluded from priestly ordination and relegated to a lower status.

The exclusion of women from formal Church councils did not take place immediately and everywhere. In a work on nunneries and the Anglo-Saxon royal houses, Yorke writes that at the local level, abbesses, like abbots, had taken their place at major Church councils until the middle of the eighth century. Subsequently they tended not to be present, though some abbots continued to attend.[14]

In happy ignorance of what was to come, it was Hild who hosted what is probably the most important synod to have been held in Britain. When it was determined that there should be a gathering to iron out differences between Roman and Irish practices, it naturally fell to Hild to host the synod. She was accustomed to receiving visitors of all ranks, and she was held in universally high esteem. And, of course, she had built up the Whitby monastery into the preeminent Christian center in the North of England.

THE PROPONENTS

Bede has it that it was King Oswy who opened the proceedings, and Bede puts into Oswy's mouth what is clearly his own thinking. First, they all served the same God; more than this, they were all hoping for the kingdom of heaven. Therefore, they should not differ in their celebration of the sacraments because these were the sacraments of heaven. Bede here expresses the view, which would have made a lively impression on the minds of the people of his day more so perhaps than of our own generation, that participation in the sacraments was participation in the very life of heaven. Oswy's own thinking is likely to have been less high-minded. Like Bede, he would have wanted uniformity, and he would have couched his speech in religious language, but his focus was more this-worldly and political than other-worldly and religious. In a rather pleasing turn of phrase, Mayr-Harting says of Oswy that "obsessive religiosity was the last weakness which anyone could impute to him."[15]

According to Bede, Oswy's son, Alfrith, was also present at the synod, and it is quite possible that Queen Eanfled was present herself. We know that Eanfled's chaplain, the priest, Romanus, was at the synod. Yet Romanus was not the principal advocate of the Roman cause; nor would he have had the slightest inclination to stir up a controversy with Irish missionaries.

Ronan, the zealous Irishman who had come up against Finan of Lindisfarne, and who had been the champion of the Roman cause up to that point, does not seem to have been at the synod, perhaps having died in the interim. It was Agilbert, the Gaulish bishop of the West Saxons, who was the main proponent of the Roman case. It would appear that there was no one closer to home who felt strongly enough about the matter to plead the Roman case with sufficient authority and conviction.

Agilbert was a friend of Alfrith, suggesting that it was Alfrith who had involved Agilbert. This would support the theory that Alfrith was trying to cause difficulty for his father. On the other hand, it may be that Oswy was willing to be swayed to his wife's side on account of the political advantage of cementing relations with Rome and the remnants of its empire. At any rate Agilbert stayed in Northumbria for some time, and it would seem that it was during the course of his stay that it was decided to hold the synod.

Reinforcing the argument that Agilbert was an outsider is the fact that he could not be understood in English. He, therefore, asked Wilfrid to argue in his place. This Wilfrid should not be confused with the Wilfrid whom Hild had educated and was, like the Wilfrid in question, later to become a bishop of York. Rather the Wilfrid of the synod was a friend of both Alfrith and Agilbert. He was accompanied at the synod by a priest named Agatho.

Wilfrid was the abbot of Ripon, in what is now Yorkshire. He had been born in Northumbria, and he had entered the monastery at Lindisfarne before going to Canterbury and then Rome, returning to Northumbria after a three-year stay in Lyons. It was Alfrith who gave him the monastery at Ripon; it was Agilbert who ordained him priest.

Wilfrid was an obdurate man, rigid in his views on matters of discipline and precedent. One might say that it was Wilfrid's life work to eliminate Irish practices from the Church and replace them with Roman observance. Wilfrid's stormy character seems to have been in strong contrast to the generally peaceable demeanor other church officials on the Roman side. It is unlikely that Romanus or the elderly musician,[16] James, the deacon who had served at York with Paulinus, were spoiling for a fight.

On the side of retaining Irish customs was bishop Colman, who had replaced Finan at Lindisfarne upon his death. Colman was accompanied by members of the Irish clergy. How many clergy there were and indeed what exactly is meant by "clergy" it is difficult to know. That they were priests seems unlikely given the lack of priests in that part of the world at the time, and the fact that they are not named. They may have been in minor orders. As we saw in chapter 5, ordained abbesses were considered members of the clergy, though it is unlikely that Bede had abbesses in mind.

It can safely be assumed that Hild was also for retaining the Irish customs. Like Colman, she was accompanied by her community. Again their number is not given, nor any of their names. Naturally Bede does not refer to them as "clergy." Nonetheless as I argue in chapter 9, they too could have been in lower orders. That women were "ordained" to a whole complex of ministries in the early medieval period is incontrovertible. Faced with the evidence, those who hold the view that women have never been ordained merely argue that what was meant by ordination for men and what was meant by ordination for women is entirely different, an argument that owes more to much later theology than to historical evidence.

Finally on the side for retaining Irish customs was another bishop. This was Cedd, who had long ago been ordained by the Irish. Cedd acted as a most careful interpreter for both parties. Cedd was an Anglo-Saxon. It was he who had founded Lastingham. He was made bishop on Iona to serve the East Saxons, but he acted as a careful and impartial observer at Whitby.

THE SYNOD AS A WHOLE

We have established that there were many parties active at the synod, including of course Hild and, I would argue, her sisters. In Bede's detailed account, we hear mainly of how the Easter question was argued, with the focus on the exchange between Wilfrid and Colman. Yet as Catherine Cubitt remarks, "The narrative shape given to the council by Bede and Stephanus probably reflects their perception of how a council should be conducted rather than its actual proceedings."[17] Thus, although Bede presents Wilfrid and Colman as the main protagonists, it would seem inconceivable that Hild did not contribute to the debate, given the high esteem in which she was held by all parties, royal and ecclesial, and on both sides of the argument.

Although Hild had been baptized by the Roman Paulinus, she had been initiated into the religious life by Aidan, and it is most probable that her inclination was to back Colman. Yet it would seem that she accepted the decision of the synod to go with Wilfrid and Rome. It is generally thought that she exerted her influence to bring about a peaceful conclusion, and she is known as a "peace-weaver." Certainly Bede saw her as such. As he lists her many virtues, such as mercy and purity, he lays special emphasis on her peace and charity.

Apart from the Easter question, there were other matters to be discussed. The last chapter explained how the difference between the Roman and the Irish tonsure had become an issue. The Romans claimed that their tonsure gained its authority through Saint Peter and accused the Irish of following the practices of the heretic, Simon the Magician, of Acts chapter 8. The Irish themselves claimed to be following practices derived from Saint John. In the following section, the same pattern with regard to the Easter question is detected. Wilfrid claims authority from the apostle Peter, Colman from John the evangelist, and Wilfrid accuses Colman of heresy.

THE EASTER QUESTION

Today, we have largely lost touch with the way in which the liturgical year used to underpin the entirety of daily life. In 2006, the Catholic bishops of England and Wales decided to move the celebration of certain major Feasts to the Sunday nearest to the date on which they had been traditionally celebrated. Presumably, they were responding to low numbers at weekday celebrations. The biggest outcry came from communities of vowed religious, who retain a much stronger link with the liturgical year than the secular world. In fact, such was the outcry that in 2017, the Feasts of the Epiphany and of the Ascension of the Lord were returned to their original dates: January 6 and the Thursday after the sixth Sunday of Easter, respectively. In medieval times, it was not only vowed religious and the ordained whose lives were regulated by the liturgical calendar. For the whole population, daily life, the passing of the seasons, and times for work and times for leisure and creativity were all integrated into and dependent on the liturgical year.

In the last chapter, we began to see some of the complexity of the issues involved in the dating of Easter. It was much bigger than a simple choice between two dates. Hunter Blair lists three cyclical tables operating in the western church. One was based on an eighty-four-year table, and two based on nineteen-year cycles, each with different calculations for the phases of the moon. The first was obscure in origin and dated possibly from the third century.[18] And this was just the western church. Determining which tables to use had been a vexed question for the whole of Christendom for centuries. Working out these tables was the preserve of the best mathematical minds available.

Wilfrid was a clever man, well versed in the history and what was thought to be the provenance of the various tables. Colman, on the other hand, was little interested in mathematical calculations and complex tables, relying rather on his devotion to Columba, the original founder of the monastery on Iona, Colman's spiritual father, and one of the great saints of the age. Colman defended the traditions handed down by Columba with a claim that they had their origins in the practice of John the Apostle.

When Agilbert was asked to respond, instead of doing so, he asked that Wilfrid might take his place. Agilbert did not speak English, and he said that rather than using an interpreter—presumably Cedd—he would prefer Wilfrid to put the case on his behalf. Agilbert was doubtless familiar with not only

Wilfrid's intricate knowledge of and strong feelings about the Easter question but also with Wilfrid's aggressive debating tactics.

Oswy gave his permission for Wilfrid to speak on behalf of Agilbert and Colman was subjected to Wilfrid's counterargument, in which he employed the same kind of mocking point scoring that people in the United Kingdom are so accustomed to hearing at Prime Minister's Question Time.

Wilfrid said that the Easter customs that should be followed were those used in Rome, where the Apostles Peter and Paul had been martyred and were buried. He then went on to claim that those same customs were observed in every other part of the world—Africa, Asia, Egypt, Greece, and so on. There were only two peoples, obstinate enough and stupid enough to contradict everyone else: the Picts and the Britons.

Wilfrid's words echo the sentiments of a letter that survives, written by Cummian of Clonfert to Ségéne, Abbot of Iona and teacher of the young Oswald, "Can anything be more absurd than to say of our mother the church—Rome errs, Jerusalem errs, Antioch errs, and the whole world errs, the Irish and Britons alone are in the right?"[19] Since Augustine's rebuff by the Welsh bishops, there had been relentless pressure on the Irish Church to go over to the Roman method for calculating the date of Easter, and from the 630s onward, many southern Irish Churches had submitted, but Iona had refused to budge.

In response to Wilfrid, Colman said that it was strange that he should be called stupid when he followed the customs of the Apostle John. In an extended answer calculated to show off his superior learning, Wilfrid began by denying that he would call John stupid. John followed the traditions he did because he observed the Law of Moses, at a time when many Christians were also Jews. But all the successors of John, claimed Wilfrid, followed Peter, whom Colman was deliberately contradicting. And for good measure Wilfrid claimed that Colman was not even following John correctly because Colman did not follow exactly the decrees of Moses.

As well as Bede, Eddius Stephanus, Wilfrid's biographer, gives an account of the synod of Whitby. Stephanus seems to show Wilfrid accusing the Irish of being Quartodecimans, though it is obvious from both Stephanus and from Bede's account that they were not.[20] Quartodecimans, who kept Easter on any day of the week, provided it was the fourteenth of Nisan, had been condemned as heretics at the Council of Nicea. As Ward states, "The Irish calculated Easter in a perfectly orthodox manner; the problem was that they were using lunar tables which had reached them from Rome but had been replaced elsewhere."[21] Thus, in Stephanus's account we detect a willingness on Wilfrid's part to move what was essentially a long-standing difference in the interpretation of lunar tables onto the level of heresy.

After his appeal to the Apostle John was trumped by Wilfrid's appeal to the Apostle Peter, Colman tried another tack. He cited in his defense the holy man Anatolius and the most reverend father Columba himself. Could they have been acting contrary to Holy Scripture? Wilfrid dealt first with Anatolius, detailing his calculations, and then claimed once again that Colman did not follow the calculations correctly.

Wilfrid's words with regard to the customs of Columba demonstrated just how little respect he had for any traditions other than his own. His was a hard-line approach in stark contrast to the generally harmonious relations between the Irish and the Roman parties that had existed up to that point. He began this part of his answer cordially enough. He was not going to condemn Colman's fathers, whom he did not know. He was willing to grant that they could well have kept the rules and customs they did in primitive simplicity (*simplicitate rustica*). Their ignorance meant that the way they kept Easter was not seriously harmful. According to Wilfrid, however, if Colman's fathers had been approached by a Catholic scholar, they would readily have gone along with what he told them. By "Catholic," Wilfrid meant "universal." Wilfrid accuses Colman of being prepared to follow a few people on a far-off island cut off from the universal church, even though learned men have made him aware of the decrees of the Apostolic See, even though he has been informed of the teachings of the universal Church, which are endorsed by Scripture.[22]

It was an unequal contest rather along the lines of Luther's humiliation at the hands of Cardinal Cajetan.[23] Skillfully Wilfrid belittled the tradition that Colman held so dear and boxed Colman into a corner. Either he accepted the Roman calculations for the celebration of Easter, or he was a heretic.

For Wilfrid, Colman's sin lay not in following the practices of his fathers, but in continuing to follow them when those with greater knowledge had pointed out their error. The clinching argument came from Wilfrid when he said that however much of a powerful saint Columba may have been, he could surely not take precedence over Saint Peter, to whom the Lord had given the keys of the kingdom of heaven. Oswy asked if this was true about the keys of the kingdom and both Wilfrid and Colman said that it was. The matter was then decided by Oswy, who declared that he would not contradict Peter because Peter guarded the gates of heaven, and when he himself reached the gates he feared to be turned away.

Wilfrid clearly did not want to make enemies of the whole Irish Church by saying that Columba himself was at fault. Yet he made it plain that in his view Colman would be committing a grave sin if he were to continue with Irish practices. Bede records Wilfrid quoting to Colman the words of Jesus in Matthew 7:22. "When the day comes many will say to me 'Lord, Lord, did we not prophesy in your name, drive out demons in your name, work many miracles in your name?' Then I shall tell them to their faces, 'I have never known you.'"[24]

On all sides the matter of performing the Easter liturgies on the correct date was a serious matter. To refuse to celebrate them on whatever was held to be the correct date would have been a sin. It would have been to go against the traditions that had been handed down and to go against Scripture. Wilfrid actually goes further than this in what he says to Colman. He accuses them of being guilty of sin for rejecting the decrees of the Apostolic See. If Colman refused to accept Roman practices, now that it had been shown to him that they accorded with Scripture and the tradition of the Church going back to Peter, according to Wilfrid, he would be willfully rejecting the true celebration of Easter. He would be going against the determinations of the Apostolic See and damning his eternal soul.

Yet for Colman at least, it was not a question of the acceptance or rejection of papal authority.

NOVELTY AND CREEPING EXCLUSION

Wilfrid, and perhaps Ronan before him, were introducing something new into the Northumbrian Church. It was not merely the case that it would make practical sense for there to be a common practice. Nor even that streamlining would strengthen the underlying unity of the Church. The novelty lay in the notion that the Irish practices were heretical. The novelty lay in the notion that Irish practices were not simply different, but wrong, and ultimately not for any theological or scriptural reason, but because they went against the decrees of the Apostolic See, which are confirmed by scripture.

A see is a geographical area over which a particular bishop has jurisdiction. The "Apostolic See" was of course the see of Rome, where Peter had been martyred, and the bishop of Rome, the Pope, was Peter's successor. Because Jesus had given Peter the keys of the kingdom of heaven (Matthew 16:19), the Pope, through what is known as the "Petrine office," claimed authority over the whole church—a claim rejected by the Eastern Orthodox Churches to this day. The extent of this authority was being newly interpreted by Wilfrid.

Hans Küng tells us,

> In Carolingian times . . . there was still no trace, even in the West, of any generally recognized juridical primacy enjoyed by the popes. Juridical primacy belongs to the Frankish rulers, as it had previously belonged to the Byzantine emperor, and the Frankish rulers saw themselves and behaved as the Church's divine right rulers. Scarcely half a century after Charlemagne, however, Pope Nicholas I (c. 800–867) appeared on the scene with a full-blown "Petrine"

> understanding of the importance of his office. Boldly, he attempted to put an end to the age-old autonomy of the national churches and to bring them under the central authority of Rome.[25]

Thus, while all in the West, during Wilfrid's lifetime, would have accepted the Pope's authority at some level in matters of doctrine, they would still have thought it appropriate to challenge papal teachings if, for example, they seemed to be at odds with other authorities, like the great Jerome.[26] In the Christian world of the seventh century, there was nothing like the notion of papal infallibility as it developed in the Catholic Church, reaching a high point in the nineteenth century. And when it came to matters of custom or discipline, there was no obligation to conform to Roman or any other customs that differed from one's own tradition.

The unity of the Christian Church manifested itself in a common Scripture, a common tradition as expounded by various authorities from both the eastern and the western Church, a general acknowledgement that the bishop of Rome had a special place among the bishops, and somehow held everything together. I have already dwelt at some length on the fact that up until the 664 synod, diversity of practice was not seen as a bar to Church unity. Gregory himself had urged Augustine to teach to the English the best of the practices he had encountered, no matter where he had found them.

Wifrid introduced something new into the mix, when he argued not only that Colman was celebrating Easter on the wrong date, but that he was wrong to put himself at odds with the whole of the rest of Christian Church. It was not simply that Wilfrid was blind to the reality (it was not the case that throughout the whole Church only the Irish refused to accept the Roman calculations), it was that Wilfrid was introducing a new understanding of what it meant to be an authentic part of the Christian Church that acknowledged the headship of the bishop of Rome. For Wilfrid, the true Church consisted precisely of those who accepted Roman ways when they were explained to them. And that explaining was to be Wilfrid's life work. Wilfrid saw the Easter controversy in terms of rejection or acceptance of the Petrine office.

It is striking that Bede's account of the Synod of Whitby, hosted by Hild, makes so little mention of her. Bede is quite clear that her counsel, above all others, was sought out by royalty and by clergy. There can be no question that she played a pivotal role in the debates. Yet despite Bede's obvious admiration for her, Bede was already of the mind-set that discounted the active participation of women in the debating process. None of the debate as it unfolded is put into Hild's mouth.

Eddius simply notes that "the abbots and priests and men of all ranks in the orders of the Church gathered together in a monastery called Whitby, in the presence of the holy mother and most pious nun Hild, as well as of the kings and two bishops, namely Colman and Agilbert."[27] In fact, this is less dismissive of Hild's importance than it might at first sight appear. Hild sits with the kings and bishops into whose presence the priests and others are brought, and she is named first. Perhaps even more significant is Eddius's description of Hild as "holy mother and most pious nun." Eddius acknowledges her holiness and status as mother despite the fact that, as we will see in the next chapter, she had actively opposed Wilfrid in one of his major controversies.

Nonetheless it cannot be denied that Hild's active part in the synod has been a written out of history in both accounts that come down to us. Yet the synod itself remains hugely significant for the telling of Hild's story. The seeds sown by Wilfrid would eventually result in a much narrower definition of what would count as an authentic part of the Christian tradition under the primacy of the bishop of Rome.

NOTES

1. These were the councils of Ephesus in 431, Chalcedon in 451, Constantinople II in 553, Constantinople II in 680–681, and Nicea II in 787. Tanner, *New Short History*, 55.
2. Tanner, *New Short History*, 65.
3. J. N. D. Kelly, *Early Christian Doctrines* (London: A & C Black, 1977), 233.
4. See Chapter 2, "The Roman System," in Küng, *We Can Save the Catholic Church!* for a full discussion of how it was the emperor, rather than the pope, who for centuries exercised the highest legal authority in the Church.
5. Yorke, *The Conversion of Britain*, 127.
6. Hunter Blair, "Whitby as a Centre of Learning in the Seventh Century," 7n90.
7. Anne Inman, "Women Deacons in Anglo-Saxon England," *The Pastoral Review* 13, no.1 (Jan/Feb 2017): 42–46.
8. Bede, *Ecclesiastical History*, IV. 5. 213; *Beda, Historia Ecclesiastica, Liber Quartus*, 5, CXXIX.
9. Ward, *A True Easter*, 7.
10. Stenton, *Anglo-Saxon England*, 129.
11. Adams, *The King of the North* (316–17) cites Richard P. Abels, "The Council of Whitby: A Study in Early Anglo-Saxon Politics," *Journal of British Studies*, 23.I: I-25.
12. Hunter Blair, "Whitby as a Centre of Learning in the Seventh Century," 15.
13. This council was called by Theodore to condemn the heresy of Eutyches and to ensure that all the British bishops were orthodox on the matter. Eutyches (378–454) was the main proponent of Monophysitism, the teaching that Jesus Christ had only one (divine) nature. The Council of Chalcedon 451 affirmed the personal unity of Christ in two natures: human and divine. The Council of Hatfield, likewise, ensured that all British bishops affirmed another crucial teaching of Chalcedon, the full divinity of the Holy Spirit.

14. See Yorke, *Nunneries and the Anglo-Saxon Royal Houses*, 123, who refers to Cubitt's *Anglo-Saxon Church Councils c. 650–c. 850*

15. Mayr-Harting, *The Coming of Christianity*, 108.

16. See Foot, *Monastic Life*, 203.

17. Cubitt, *Anglo-Saxon Church Councils*, 90.

18. Hunter Blair, "Whitby as a Centre of Learning in the Seventh Century," 19.

19. Adams, *The King of the North*, 310, quotes from Cummian, *De Controversia Paschali*; Cotton Vitell. A. xii Healy J., 'Insula sanctorum et doctorum: or Ireland's ancient schools and scholars', Dublin: Sealy, Bryers and Walker 1912.

20. Bertram Colgrave, trans., *The Life of Bishop Wilfrid by Eddius Stephanus* (Cambridge: Cambridge University Press, 1985), X 21; XI 25; Bede, *Ecclesiastical History*, III 25. Beda, *Historia Ecclesiastica, Liber Tertius*, 25.

21. Ward, *A True Easter*, 15.

22. Bede, *Ecclesiastical History*, III. 25 191, Beda, *Historia Ecclesiastica, Liber Tertius*, 25, CXII–CXIII.

23. For a development of this comparison, see Anne Inman, "Lessons from the Reformation: When Papal Power Trumps Legitimate Debate," *The Pastoral Review* 13, no. 6 (November/December 2017): 20–27.

24. *The New Jerusalem Bible* (New York: Doubleday, 1985).

25. Kung, *Can We Save the Catholic Church*, 86. Küng goes on to say that Nicholas's claim was based on two earlier forgeries, the pseudo-Isidorian forgeries and the forged *Donation of Constantine*.

26. Columbanus accepted the primacy of the pope but had suggested in a letter to Gregory the Great that he might be guilty of heresy if he brought into question Jerome's authority. See Mayr-Harting, *The Coming of Christianity*, 111.

27. Colgrave, *Life of Bishop Wilfrid*, X 21.

Chapter Thirteen

The Aftermath

The reactions of the various parties to the decisions of the Whitby Synod showed a marked divergence between Colman, who was unwilling to adopt Roman traditions, and Wilfrid, who insisted on Roman traditions as the price of orthodoxy. Between these two extremes, those affected for the most part dutifully accepted the Whitby rulings, while respecting Colman's decision to leave Lindisfarne and return to Iona.

COLMAN'S STANDING AFTER WHITBY

Cedd, who was among those who accepted the decision to abide by Roman customs, returned to his own bishopric. Colman, however, unwilling to give up his allegiance to the traditions that came from Columba, returned to Iona. Apart from the requirement to change the date for the celebration of Easter, perhaps the thought of wearing a different style of tonsure, such a public and at the same time intimately personal break from his former life, was too much for him. He took with him those of his community who likewise wished to return. Nonetheless, he remained on good terms with the community that he left behind and with King Oswy. As Mayr-Harting puts it, when Colman left Lindisfarne, he was not "shaking the dust off his feet."[1]

Colman's departure left a vacant see in Northumbria, which was filled by Tuda, who had been trained in southern Ireland and already followed Roman customs. His episcopacy was to be short-lived as he died soon afterward. Meanwhile Eata, who was abbot of a monastery at Melrose, was appointed Abbot of Lindisfarne to rule those of the community who had elected to remain there when Colman and others withdrew. Eata had been taught by

Aidan, and it was at Colman's request that Oswy gave him the abbacy, demonstrating the high regard Oswy retained for Colman.[2] In Oswy's eyes, at least Colman was no a heretic.

Bede's attitude to Colman is also instructive. An acknowledged expert in computistics, Bede was absolutely convinced of the correctness of the Roman dating for Easter. Yet as we have already seen in chapter 6, he, like Oswy, had a high regard for Colman and the Irish. As he looked back on Colman's life, he chose the time of Colman's departure from Lindisfarne to hold up the community there as a model of good behavior. It was Wilfrid, and perhaps only Wilfrid, who seems to have regarded Colman's determination to keep up the Irish traditions as gravely sinful. It was Wilfrid, and perhaps only Wilfrid, who saw it as a matter of schism—a decisive break with the Roman church.

Paul Cavill, in his *Anglo-Saxon Christianity*, could be seen as a spokesperson for Wilfrid when he says that "at Whitby, the center of Celtic sentiment, the decision was taken to follow the path of catholicity rather than schism."[3] This certainly seems to be the way in which Wilfrid saw things. Yet even Bede, who embraced so much of the Romanizing agenda, did not retrospectively condemn Colman as a schismatic.

Mayr-Harting discusses how Colman himself might have seen his relationship to the Pope as he refused to adopt Roman practices.

> Colman is not reported to have specifically denied the authority of the papacy at Whitby, but as the question did not present itself to him primarily as one of acceptance or rejection of the petrine office, we may imagine that his attitude towards it was somewhat ambiguous.

Mayr-Harting then tells us of two letters that had been written to different Popes by Columbanus, an Irish missionary in Gaul in the late sixth century. He had come under pressure to adopt Roman customs. In the first letter, Columbanus sees the Easter question as a matter of doctrine. Citing Jerome as a precedent, he says that Gregory might be in danger of heresy. At the time of the second letter, Columbanus is being hounded by the Gaulish bishops to adopt the Roman Easter.

> Here, in contrast to the earlier letter, he seems to make the whole question less one of doctrine than one of custom and discipline in which there was no overriding obligation for particular churches to conform with Rome or with one another. This, perhaps was nearer to Colman's view, as against the browbeating implications of Wilfrid that the matter was one of Faith.[4]

Mayr-Harting hits the nail on the head when he says that for Colman there was no overriding obligation for particular churches to conform to Rome or one another. It is clear that this was the majority opinion of those at the

Whitby synod and subsequently Bede. Mayr-Harting is also correct to say that the question of uniformity of practice did not present itself to Colman as one of acceptance or rejection of the Petrine office. But Colman's attitude only seems ambiguous when analyzed from the perspective of later or different contexts.

Colman would not have dreamt of splitting matters of doctrine from matters of custom. The custom that had been handed down to him from Columba of celebrating Easter on a certain day was inextricably bound up with what he believed the Apostle John to have taught, that is to say, his doctrine, regarding the death and resurrection of the Lord. Regarding Colman's attitude toward the authority of the Pope, here again there is no ambiguity. Colman accepted the Pope's overarching status as head of the Church. That did not mean that everything coming from the Pope must be obeyed without question. Crucially, the unity of the seventh-century Church did not rest on either an unquestioning obedience to Rome or on uniformity of practice.[5]

The reason why it is so important to judge the seventh-century Christian Church in its own context is because whatever later judgements are made, they cannot be retrospectively applied to condemn those who in their own contexts were orthodox players in the Church's mission. As this applies to Colman, so it must apply to Hild. It must apply to countless women, forgotten or written out of history, who ministered sacramentally to the people of their day.

PROTOCOL AND THE ELEVATION OF BISHOP

Despite the goodwill exhibited by Colman and his successors at Lindisfarne, the Northumbrian Church was to suffer a period of extreme turbulence following the synod. The turmoil centered on Wilfrid, who was determined to stamp out what he saw as "Irish errors," Wilfrid proceeded to regard the Ionan clergy as heretics. His zeal was such that even for a community to remain in contact with Iona was sufficient to earn his distrust.[6] Indeed his abhorrence of non-Roman ways was such that when he was appointed to take up the see of York, he refused to be consecrated by any of the bishops in Britain.

Yet it is unlikely that the attraction for Wilfrid of Roman ways was confined to the calculations for the dating of Easter and the type of tonsure that should be worn by monks. Wilfrid was set to be a bishop and there was in Rome a markedly different understanding of the way in which it was appropriate for a bishop to behave. The Irish understanding of the episcopacy at its best is exemplified by Aidan's refusal to use a horse on his travels through Northumbria. It is not even always clear that Aidan was a bishop,[7] so little did he stand on ceremony or engage with the privileges of office. In marked contrast, the Roman view of the episcopacy was heavily focused on the dignity of the office and the corresponding respect it demanded. There was, as Thomas Noble writes, an increased emphasis on the elite status of the bishop:

> The seventh century was an important time in the elaboration of the protocol of the Roman church, in other words of the ceremonial definition of office and hierarchy. The clergy of the Roman church wore distinctive clothes and appeared in public ceremonies that were reserved to them alone. The seventh century was therefore a decisive moment in the making of the elite of medieval Rome.[8]

Wilfrid traveled to Compiègne in Paris for his episcopal consecration by the same bishop, Agilbert, who had only recently ordained him as priest. Agilbert had returned to Gaul, rather than his see in West Saxony, after the Whitby Synod. He had fallen out of favor among the West Saxons because of his inability to speak the Saxon language. Eleven other bishops were participants at Wilfrid's consecration. The bishops were thus said to have numbered twelve in all, symbolic of the twelve apostles gathered around Christ. The whole ceremony was a thoroughly splendid affair, with Wilfrid being carried into the sanctuary on a golden chair after the actual consecration.[9]

It would be possible to make too much of the contrast between Wilfrid on the one hand and Aidan and Colman on the other. Writing about Aidan and Colman, Bede no doubt idealizes their virtues as he rebukes the monks of his own day for their laxity. It is quite possible, for example, that Bede exaggerated in his description of the poverty of the Lindisfarne community under Colman's direction, as we saw in chapter 6. Only about five decades after Colman's departure, the Lindisfarne Gospels, one of the most celebrated illuminated books in the world, was already in production. Only a wealthy monastery could have produced such a work. Either when Colman left Lindisfarne, there was a marked change of ethos, or in Bede's portrayal of the poverty at the monastery, there was something of an exaggeration.

Similarly when we think of Hild, who embraced the humble lifestyle of the Irish, it is important to remember that Whitby itself, in Hild's time the greatest center of learning in the whole of the north of England, must have been a wealthy monastery. The tithes collected from its outlying farms would have been considerable. Hild was herself an Anglo-Saxon princess—a status she retained as a vowed religious. Furthermore, high-born women, who entered the monastery more for protection than out of religious zeal, would have expected a certain degree of comfort in their living arrangements. The rejection of worldly goods was symbolized by the giving over of all worldly possessions to the community as a whole, while the community itself increased in wealth.

Yet when all this has been said, it is nonetheless true that there was an underlying difference in attitude with regard to the episcopacy, which is best illustrated by contrasting Wilfrid with Aidan. Aidan, through his refusal to take a horse as he walked the byways of Northumbria, chose to be on the same level as the people he served. Wilfrid, on the other hand, chose to be lifted up above the people on a golden chair. Aidan's status as bishop is barely acknowledged, indicating that he barely acknowledged it himself, putting service at the heart of his ministry. Wilfrid, on the other hand, needed to ensure that the dignity of his elevation was marked by an elaborate ceremonial, even at the cost of leaving vacant for some time see to which he had been appointed.

Crucially, Aidan had been able to regard Hild as a coworker in a way that Wilfrid and others who saw themselves as an elite group elevated onto an altogether higher plane had not.

HILD'S ATTITUDE TO THE SYNOD

When it comes to the attitude of Hild and her community to the questions to be decided at the synod, their inclination would have been to retain Irish customs. Nonetheless, most commentators agree that they were prepared to accept the decision of the synod, whatever that might be. But it is not at all clear that those who were prepared to agree to a common dating process for Easter and a common style of tonsure realized how far-reaching the consequences of these agreements would be.

Most importantly, as the Irish party, and indeed many of those who followed Roman customs, had gone into the Whitby negotiations, it had not been a question of Roman practices *or* women as coworkers because the two had not previously been regarded as incompatible. It seems likely that most of the participants, as they entered the synod, had no inkling that they would be paving the way for the eventual total subordination of women in the mission of the Church.

Yet according to Wilfrid's ultimately successful agenda, there was to be a clean break with the relationships of the past—the phrase "hard Brexit" comes to mind. The work done by women would be downgraded, and women themselves would come to be regarded not as coworkers but as subordinates. It is difficult to tell to what extent this outcome could have been foreseen by the Northumbrian Church, accustomed as it was to the relatively harmonious relationship between the Irish and the Romanizing party.

At the time of the Whitby synod, Hild was the most influential Church leader in the north of England, and Whitby the leading Christian institution.[10]

The church that Paulinus had built at York, which, according to the Gregorian plan, should have been the main northern center, had failed to flourish. Meanwhile Hild had worked harmoniously with the bishops based at Lindisfarne.

The decision at Whitby meant that there would be a realignment of the Northumbrian Church away from the episcopal base at Lindisfarne backed up by Iona and toward the see of York backed up by Canterbury. Yet even the prospect of this realignment may not have alerted Hild to the profound changes that were to take place because she still retained considerable influence over the shape of the episcopacy. Her own monk, Bosa, would be appointed as one of the three bishops who were to cover Northumberland when Wilfrid began his first period of exile in 678.[11] On Wilfrid's return to the bishopric of York, Bosa remained a bishop in Northumbria for nine years, though Wilfrid refused to work with him and eventually had him removed. By this time Hild had died. Yet interestingly, in 691, when Wilfrid himself was expelled, it was Bosa who took over from him as Bishop of York.

In the event a strong pro-Roman see at York saw limitations placed on the ecclesial spaces that could be occupied by the women of Whitby. The adoption of Roman ways resulted in an increase in episcopal authority and corresponding diminution of the authority of the abbess. Yet until Wilfrid's uncompromising stance became evident, and until he eventually prevailed, this may not have been foreseen as the inevitable consequence of the new allegiance to certain Roman practices.

CONFUSION

The somewhat shambolic situation regarding the appointment of bishops began immediately on the conclusion of the Whitby synod. It was Oswy's son, Alfrith, who had sent Wilfrid to Gaul to be made bishop for the people of Northumbria—with his father's approval, according to Bede. When Wilfrid did not return for some time, Oswy took matters into his own hands and decided to appoint Chad in place of Wilfrid. Barbara Yorke thinks that Hild may well have been one of those who "intrigued to have Chad appointed to the See of York while Wilfrid was being consecrated in Francia."[12] Although she may not have foreseen the full consequences of the Whitby decision, Hild must surely have been alarmed by Wilfrid's uncompromising anti-Irish stance during the synod itself.

At any rate, Chad was sent by Oswy to Canterbury for consecration, only to find the see vacant. (This would suggest that it was not known at the time of the synod that Deusdedit had already died. We know elsewhere from Bede that Oswy conferred with King Egbert of Kent and together they sent their own choice of successor to Rome for consecration.[13] If Oswy had known that Deusdedit had died, he would have known that the see was still vacant and would not have sent Chad there for consecration.) When it transpired that there was no archbishop in Canterbury, Chad proceeded to West Saxony to be consecrated by Wini and some of the Welsh/British bishops.

This consecration sheds a frustratingly narrow shaft of light onto the co-operation that existed between the British/Welsh bishops and those ordained by Rome. Bede wants nothing to do with Welsh/British because they refused the authority of Augustine in 597. Yet here they are at some date after 664 coming together with Wini to consecrate Chad. The matter is complicated by the fact that Wini was later to be guilty of simony because having been ousted from West Saxony, he attempted to buy the bishopric of London. Nonetheless at the time of Chad's consecration Wini was a bishop of the Roman tradition, working together with Welsh/British bishops.

There would certainly have been British bishops in the north of England if Adams is correct. Adams argues that from the foundation date of Lindisfarne in 635, British, Irish, and Roman traditions existed side by side. Judging by the surviving number of inscriptions, long-cist cemeteries, and Eccles-type place names, Adams concludes that "in the north of the kingdom British churches and British traditions seem to have predominated."[14]

In the turmoil that followed the Whitby synod, there was a hardening of attitude regarding which bishops would be regarded as properly consecrated and which would not, and Wilfrid was at its heart. From 664, for all those bishops who could not trace their elevation back through the Augustinian mission to the Pope, the validity of their orders was being called into question.

OPPOSITION TO WILFRID

On his return to England after his episcopal ordination, finding Chad ensconced in the bishopric of Northumbria, Wilfrid lived at Ripon until 669. He would only be able to claim his see when Oswy died and was succeed by his son Ecgfrith as King of Northumbria. (It would seem that Alfrith had failed comprehensively in his struggle to oust his father.) Ecgfrith's succession coincided with the arrival in Canterbury of its new Archbishop Theodore, who deposed Chad to make way for Wilfrid.

The fact that Wilfrid did not have it all his own way is perhaps an indication of how alien to the Northumbrian Church were his views. He was certainly in for a bumpy episcopal ride, spending twenty-six out of his forty-six years as bishop in exile. Although secular rulers seem to have instigated his years of banishment, he also managed to fall out with Theodore, Archbishop of Canterbury, who initially ruled in Wilfrid's favor against Chad.

Wilfrid's first period of exile began in 678. By this time he had fallen out of favor with Ecgfrith. It is also likely that the king was affronted by Wilfrid's ostentatious lifestyle and large entourage. There seems to have been a particular concern about the size of Wilfrid's retinue of armed followers, which had the potential to rival that of the King. Eddius, in his biography of Wilfrid written shortly after Wilfrid's death, points the finger of blame at Queen Iurminburg.

> For Ecgfrith's queen, named Iurminburg, was at that time tortured with envy. . . . She eloquently described to him [Ecgfrith] all the temporal glories of St. Wilfrid, his riches, the number of his monasteries, the greatness of his buildings, his countless army of followers arrayed in royal vestments and arms.[15]

It may well be true that Wilfrid's expulsion was more the doing of Iurminburg than of Ecgfrith because Ecgfrith's mother Eanfled and sister Aelffled were both strong supporters of Wilfrid, and it would be more natural to think that initially at least he had shared their support. However Ecgfrith may also have been aggrieved because Wilfrid had advised his first wife, Etheldreda, to leave him and enter a monastery.

By this time, it was not only Ecgfrith and Iurminburh who were becoming concerned at the vast extent of the power base that Wilfrid had built up. Theodore was working to put in place a network of bishops to cover the whole country; each bishop having a definite seat. He wanted Wilfrid's huge diocese to be divided into smaller sees, but Wilfrid resisted, unwilling to give up any part of his jurisdiction. Things came to a head in 678, and Wilfrid was expelled from his diocese.

Upon his expulsion Wilfrid traveled to Rome to plead his cause with the Pope. This was the first time ever that an English churchman had appealed to Rome to settle a dispute within the English Church. In going over the head of the Archbishop of Canterbury and asking the Pope to settle the dispute, Wilfrid's action exemplified the many moves afoot in the latter part of the seventh century to increase the prestige of the papal office and draw the whole of the western Church ever more tightly under Roman control.

According to Eddius, Hild sent representatives of her own to Rome to put her side of the matter.[16] It seems likely that she was working together with Theodore, who also sent his own representatives to the Pope.

Pope Agatho, at a Roman synod in 679, did in fact judge that Wilfrid should be restored but agreed with Theodore that the Northumbrian see should retain several bishops. Wilfrid met with further resistance and was not restored until the Synod of Nidd in 706, after a second appeal to Rome in 704. At the Synod of Nidd, Aelffled, who had succeeded Hild as Abbess of Whitby, pleaded Wilfrid's cause. Thus, it would seem that Hild and Aelffled may have been on different sides of the argument when it came to Wilfrid. Whether this was in fact the case will be discussed in chapter 15.

WILFRID'S LEGACY

This first expulsion was merely the beginning of Wilfrid's difficulties. Because, however, our concern is with Hild, it will not be helpful here to detail the opposition he continued to face. Instead it will be useful to show how Wilfrid's Romanizing project is viewed in the traditional account of Catholic history. The *Catholic Encyclopedia* writes:

> Beyond all others of his time, St. Wilfrid stands out as the great defender of the rights of the Holy See.

When the historical context is taken into account, it would seem that Wilfrid in fact did more than "defend the rights of the Holy See." It would seem that he bolstered the rights already in place, building on what was already there to extend significantly the reach of papal power. The *Encyclopedia* continues:

> For that principle he fought all through his life, first against Colman and the Scottish monks from Iona, and then against Theodore and his successor in the See of Canterbury; and much of his life was spent in exile for this reason. But to him above all others is due the establishment of the authority of the Roman See in England, and for that reason he will always have a very high place among English saints.[17]

Wilfrid's legacy, his place among the saints, even, is down to the fact that he "established the authority of the Roman See in England," and that "he fought all through his life" against the Scottish—that is to say the Irish—monks, and against Theodore. Yet as we have seen, before Wilfrid's relentless drive to excommunicate those who adhered to Irish customs, the Anglo-Saxon Church had no problem in accepting the overall leadership of the Pope. The Irish-leaning elements of the Anglo-Saxon Church had worked in harmony with the Romanizing elements, to such an extent that the two could merge happily in one individual or one institution, as at Ripon. The overall precedence of the Pope as Bishop of Rome was never an issue. Wilfrid's contribution to the life of the Anglo-Saxon Church was to work for a solution to a problem that he provoked.

What Wilfrid actually achieved in Anglo-Saxon England, pretty well single-handedly it would seem, was to impose a new orthodoxy, whereby those who did not accept his new and specific vision of what constituted allegiance to Rome were damned as heretics. It is true to say that there were others who were working toward clericalism, but the elimination of all opposition seems to have been of Wilfrid's own invention.

Theodore's *Penitentials*, for example, were heading in this direction, though as has been said in chapter 8, it is not at all clear that his rulings were effective in clamping down on women's activities in his own lifetime or indeed some years later when his penitentials were published. And it would seem from this chapter that Theodore was content to cooperate with Hild in both representations to Rome and the appointment of bishops.

Much of the discussion has centered on Wilfrid's role as bishop of York, whether in possession of his see or excluded from it. However ,the strength of his position lay not only in his episcopacy but also in his increasingly powerful role as monastic head. His antipathy toward Irish customs combined with his tireless efforts to establish and to bolster the effectiveness of Benedictine monasteries sounded the death knell for the type of leadership by women that had been exercised by Hild. The Rule of Benedict, as we have seen, was not favorably disposed toward women's leadership except insofar as it was overseen by male clerics, in whose hands lay the greater authority. Eventually, in the early 970s, at the Council of Winchester when Edgar was king, the Rule of Benedict would be imposed on all monastic houses.

NOTES

1. Mayr-Harting, *The Coming of Christianity*, 110.
2. Eata was later made bishop of Lindisfarne, but the see of York came to prominence as the pre-eminent see of the region.
3. Cavill, *Anglo-Saxon Christianity*, 93.
4. Mayr-Harting, *The Coming of Christianity*, 111.
5. For further information regarding the role of the pope in the first millennium, see Küng, "The Roman System" in Küng's *Can We Save the Catholic Church?* 65–105.
6. Yorke, *The Conversion of Britain*, 12.
7. In the Preface to the second edition of Mayr-Harting's, *The Coming of Christianity*: "I refer at least twice to Aidan as a bishop in the Irish tradition, and so perhaps he was," 6.
8. Thomas F. X. Noble, "Rome in the Seventh Century," in Lapidge, *Archbishop Theodore*, 76.
9. Mayr-Harting, *The Coming of Christianity*, 132.

10. As we saw in chapter 6, Benedict Biscop did not begin to build up his impressive center of learning at Wearmouth until after 674.

11. Lyndsey had recently been annexed by Northumbria, and its bishop is included here as one of the three bishops who were to cover Northumberland when Wilfrid left in 678. It had not, however, been part of Wilfrid's original diocese. Thus, it would be correct to say that Wilfrid's diocese had been divided into two. "On Wilfrid's expulsion, Bosa became Bishop of all Deira with his seat at York. Eata superintended Bernicia either from Lindisfarne or Hexham, and Eadhaeth became first Bishop of Lindsey. . . . The original intention was to make two new bishoprics in Wilfrid's diocese for Bernicia and Deira; the other diocese was to be the newly acquired province of Lindsey, and so was not, in spite of Eddius, part of Wilfrid's old diocese at all." Colgrave, *The Life of Bishop Wilfrid*, 168.

12. Yorke, *Nunneries and the Anglo-Saxon Houses*, 163.

13. Bede, *Ecclesiastical History*, III.29, 197–98; Beda, *Historia Ecclesiastica, Liber Tertius*, 29, CXVII.

14. Adams, *The King of the North*, 298–99.

15. Colgrave, *The Life of Bishop Wilfrid*, 49.

16. Colgrave, *The Life of Bishop Wilfrid*, 117.

17. "St. Wilfrid," New Advent *Catholic Encyclopedia* at http://www.newadvent.org/cathen/15621c.htm. Accessed January 31, 2017.

Chapter Fourteen

Hild Departs This Life

Hild died in 680 at the considerable age of sixty-six. As we have seen, she had been a vowed religious for thirty-three years, during which time she had gone from small beginnings with a handful of companions under the tutelage of Aidan to become a driving force behind the Christian expansion known as the Golden Age of Northumbria. She had led, inspired, and organized her community of men and women to evangelize the people of Northumbria. She had inspired missionary zeal in those whom she educated. She had provided pastoral care and Christian instruction for the workers on the vast monastic estates, which over time she had built up.

Under Hild's leadership, the Abbey at Whitby had become the main center of learning in the north of England, before the rise of Wearmouth and Jarrow. Within the walls of Whitby, she built up a highly successful seminary, producing five bishops; she had perhaps founded the first school of Anglo-Saxon poetry; and she had overseen the Scriptorium as it produced the theological and scriptural texts that fueled the entire enterprise. The innovative sacramental customs that she and the Irish missionaries practiced, particularly in relation to reconciliation, fed into developments that were taking place across the whole of the western world—developments that were to become integral and indistinguishable parts of the one Catholic tradition.

HILD, THE ABBESS, DIES SAINT

At the time of her death, Hild was highly regarded by the whole English Church; she was acknowledged, by peasantry and nobility alike, to be a person of exceptional holiness and an outstanding spiritual guide. She was held in high esteem by all factions. Take, for example, the way in which Eddius,

Wilfrid's biographer and ardent supporter, recounted the coming together of the various parties to the Whitby synod:

> On a certain occasion in the days of Colman, Bishop of York and Metropolitan, while Oswui [Oswy] and Alhfrith [Alfrith] his son were reigning, the abbots and priests and men of all ranks in the orders of the Church gathered together in a monastery called Whitby, in the presence of the holy mother and most pious nun Hild, as well as of the kings and two bishops, namely Colman and Agilberht [Agilbert], to consider the question of the proper date for the keeping of Easter.[1]

Given the evident friction between Hild and Wilfrid, one might think that Eddius would have rather muted his praise for Hild and perhaps downplayed her importance. Yet Eddius ignores all the women present at Whitby except Hild, but of Hild he recounts that the bishops, the kings, abbots, priests, and men of all ranks and orders gathered not "at Hild's monastery", but "in Hild's presence." The implication is that Hild was the person of highest rank into whose presence the others assembled. She, "the most pious nun," is the "holy mother."

That Bede acknowledged Hild's holiness is evident throughout the account of her life, but particularly from the way in which he describes the years leading up to her death. Typically a holy death is preceded by trials sent by God so that the soul might be made perfect in weakness (*uirtus eius in infirmatate perfeceretur*). Bede describes how Hild was struck by a recurrent and virulent fever that continued to afflict her for six years (*Percussa etenim febribus acri coepit ardore fatigari, et per sex cotinuos annos eadem molestia laborare non cessebat*). He goes on to say that throughout all this time, she continued to give thanks to God, and both publicly and in private to instruct those committed to her care that they should serve God obediently when good health and give thanks to God when afflicted by illness and suffering. In this she was an example to all.

Finally he describes her actual death in the seventh year of her suffering.

> In the seventh year of her infirmity, as her suffering penetrated her whole body, she arrived her last day. And around cockcrow, having received food for the journey—holy communion—when the handmaids of Christ who were in the same monastery had been summoned, she urged them to preserve the peace of the gospel with each other and indeed with all others. As she spoke these words of exhortation, joyfully she saw death, or rather, in the words of the Lord, she passed from death to life.

> *VIIo ergo suae infirmitatis anno, conuerso ad interanea dolore, ad diem peruenit ultimum, et circa galli cantum, percepto uiatico sacrosanctae communionis, cum arcessitis ancellis Christi, quae erant in eodem monasterio, de seruanda*

> *eas inuicem, immo cum omnibus pace euangelica ammoneret; inter uerba exhortationis laeta mortem uidit, immo, ut uerbis Domini loquar, de morte transuit ad uitam.*[2]

As we have already seen, Hild lived at a time when sickness was more or less a way of life. Hygiene was extremely poor, the benefits of the burgeoning medical studies had yet to make any practical improvement to medical care, and Hild had lived through one of the fiercest plagues to have swept through Europe. Moreover at sixty-six years of age, she was an old woman. It would seem most likely that in the final years of life she suffered from illnesses of one sort or another. Yet this is not really Bede's main concern.

What Bede gives us here is a classic account of the last years of a saint. The years of sickness represent Hild's final trial on earth before being made worthy to enter straightaway into the heavenly kingdom. During this time of trial, she never wavered, either in her duty to God or in her duty to those committed to her charge. The main message embedded in this idealized version of her last years is that her strength was made perfect in weakness; her virtue was perfected in her infirmity. She died in the seventh year of her suffering (seven, of course, being the perfect number). Hild died a saint.

Bede then goes on to recount Hild's actual deathbed scene and the reported visions that accompanied her death. At the break of dawn, she received her last holy communion, or viaticum. She then summoned the other members of her community and urged them to act peaceably among themselves and toward all others as the Gospel demanded. Here we might make a comparison with Caedmon's deathbed scene. Missing from Hilda's last moments is the penitential element we find with Caedmon, when those around the deathbed are reconciled to him, and he to those around him. Perhaps because Hild had been made perfect in her weakness, penitence was deemed unnecessary. At any rate, abbess to the last, responsible for the reconciliation of the monastic community, Hild entreats those around her to be reconciled to each other and to maintain the peace of reconciliation with those around them.

VISIONS

Two visions are recorded that were said to have taken place at the time of Hild's death. The first occurred at Hackness, according to Bede, some thirteen miles from Whitby. Hild had founded the monastery there only that year, and the Prioress was Frigyth. Also living there was a woman, Begu, who had been a vowed religious for more than thirty years, and it was Begu who had the vision.

Lying in the sisters' dormitory she heard the sound of the bell that would be rung when one of the sisters died to wake them and call them to prayer. Thinking that she was awake, she saw a powerful light flood in through the roof that had been opened up. Then she saw Hild's soul carried up to heaven in the midst of this light, guided by angels. When she did awake, she realized this must have been a dream or a vision. She went immediately to Frigyth, the Prioress, and in great distress informed her that Hild had gone from this life, explaining the wondrous manner of her departing.

Frigyth roused all the sisters from their sleep, and they gathered in the church, where they spent the whole night reciting the psalter and praying for Hild's soul. At daybreak, some brothers from Whitby arrived at Hackness with the news of Hild's death. It transpired that Begu had received her vision at the very hour of Hild's passing.

The second vision occurred at Whitby itself in a remote part of the monastery where novices lived separately from those who had taken their vows. Novices were those who were testing their vocation and receiving instruction before being admitted as full members of the community. The sister who had the vision is not named by Bede but is said to have loved Hild dearly.

Bede tells us less about this vision, and the reactions it prompted, but in its essentials it follows the same pattern as Begu's vision. Like Begu, this nun who loved Hild dearly saw Hild's soul ascend to heaven in the company of angels; she then woke those around her and told them to pray for Hild's soul; the vision was received at the very hour of Hild's death, even though Hild's death was not known by the rest of her community until early the next morning.

A number of Hild's community would have been gathered round her actual deathbed, but plainly not all, because by this time the community had grown out of all proportion from the small group with whom Hild had begun the consecrated life on the banks of the river Wear. No doubt as well as reaching Hackness, word had gone out to all the monastic estate lands that the Holy Mother Hild had departed this life.

In death, Hild gained the Latinized version of her name, Hilda, as it was written into the official Church calendar for the celebration of her feast. Her feast day is November 17, the day in which she went from this life to enter fully into the eternal feast of heaven.

NOTES

1. Colgrave, *The Life of Bishop Wilfrid*, 21.
2. Beda, *Historia Ecclesiastica, Liber Quartos*, 21 [23] CLIII. My translation.

Chapter Fifteen

Hild and Aelffled

It would seem likely that both Eanfled and Aelffled, who succeeded Hild as abbesses of Whitby, had been among those who attended Hild's deathbed, assuming that they were not away on some business at the time.[1] It was Aelffled and her mother, Eanfled, who took over the running of the abbey on Hild's death. Aelffled, we remember, had been given into Hild's care as an infant. Eanfled, as was common practice, had followed her daughter into the monastery on the death of her husband in 670, and Eanfled's son, Ecgfrith, succeeded to the throne of Northumbria.

There is little or nothing known about Eanfled after her entry; other than the fact that when Hild died she was Abbess, ruling jointly with Aelffled. More is known about Aelffled, partly from Bede's *Ecclesiastical History* and more from his *Life of Cuthbert* of 721.[2] The great saint Cuthbert was Prior (second to the Abbot) at Lindisfarne after the Whitby synod and a close friend and confident of Aelffled. Then there is a further significant source for Aelffled in Eddius's *Life of Wilfrid*.[3]

HILD IS ECLIPSED BY AELFFLED

A surprising feature of the years following Hild's death is that her two successors do not seem to have been actively promoting Hild's status as a saint or even attempting to safeguard her memory. This is all the more remarkable because Bede's account of Hild's life, his description of her fortitude in her final years of severe sickness, together with the visions that accompanied her death, leave the reader in no doubt that Bede considered her exceptional sanctity to be evident to all those who knew her. It is even more surprising when we remember that Aelffled had been under Hild's protection for her entire life since babyhood. Yet as Barbara Yorke points out, at Whitby itself, Hild's memory seems to have been eclipsed by that of Aelffled.

A stone cross dating from the late eighth or ninth century appears to commemorate Aelffled, but nothing similar has been found to commemorate Hild. In itself this is hardly conclusive, given the utter devastation that was to befall the area in the course of the Danish invasions. More telling, however, is the fact that Hild receives no mention in the *Life of Gregory*, which was written at Whitby, during the time when Aelffled was abbess. Nor does Hild appear in the Northumbrian *liber vitae*.[4]

This *liber vitae* (book of lives), later incorporated into the *Liber Vitae Dunelmensis* (*Durham Book of Lives*), probably originated during the reign of King Ecgfrith. The section for queens and abbesses begins with the names of Oswy's first queen, Raegnmaeld, and second queen, Eanfled, who later became abbess. The next name is Iurminburg, the queen of Eanfled's son, Ecgfrith, followed by the name of Eanfled's daughter, Aelffled, princess and abbess. There is uncertainty regarding the fourth name; the best guess suggests that it applied to another abbess of royal birth. Nowhere does Hild's name appear, though she was both princess and abbess, famous in her time, and belonged to this period.

If, as supposed, the *Liber Vitae* was begun in Ecgfrith's reign, which ran from 670 to 685, then it looks likely that the omission of Hild's name, which can hardly have been accidental, was sanctioned by Aelffled. Aelffled's position at Whitby would have been strengthened even during Hild's lifetime by the arrival of her mother, the widowed queen, and by Hild's failing health during the last years of her life. Her position was further consolidated by the fact that her brother, who was expanding his rule beyond Northumbria, was secure on the throne. The question arises as to whether, as her position strengthened and Hild's health failed, differences arose between the two women—whether Aelffled diverged from the path that Hild had set out.

To examine further why Aelffled may have been unwilling to commemorate Hild, we need to turn to family affiliations. Here we find that, although Hild and Aelffled were closely related (both were granddaughters of the great King Edwin), in the struggle for supremacy between Bernicia and Deira, they had been on different sides. Under Edwin, the Deiran royal family gained the upper hand in the struggle to gain control of the whole of Northumbria, and it was to Edwin and the Deiran royal family that Hild owed her allegiance. When Oswy secured the kingship, however, it was the Bernician line that was in the ascendancy. And Aelffled was the daughter of Oswy.

It is likely that Hild would have understood the necessity to bolster the Bernician family line. Since Edwin's death at the hands of Penda's forces, it had fallen to the Bernician line, under Oswald and his successors, to defend

Christianity and support the monasteries. And as we have seen, Hild was capable of working in harmony with both political houses.

AELFFLED HAS WILFRID RESTORED TO YORK

There is a further reason why we might question whether Aelffled diverged from the course set out by Hild, and that is the part that Aelffled played at the Synod of Nidd in 706. It is quite clear from Eddius's account of Wilfrid's life, that it was primarily Aelffled who was responsible for the decision finally to restore him restored to his see in Northumbria. Given the history between Hild and Wilfrid, it might seem surprising that Aelffled, who had been in Hild's care since infancy, should be arguing the case *for* Wilfrid. Could this be linked to Aelffled's seeming unwillingness to commemorate Hild and to the matter of family affiliations? Once again, the relationship between Hild and Aelffled is called into question, and specifically, the question is did they clash in their attitude toward Wilfrid.

It would be possible to make an argument that Aelffled was a long-time supporter of Wilfrid. As a young man, from an unhappy home situation, desiring to spend his life in God's service, Wilfrid was making every effort to make his way in the Church when he was sent to the royal court of Aelffled's mother, Queen Eanfled. Eanfled provided for him the protection and support that he needed. She first arranged for him to stay for some years at Lindisfarne. Subsequently when Wilfrid had wanted to travel to Rome, Eanfled continued her efforts on his behalf. First she sent him to Erconberht, King of Kent, where he had to wait for a year. Then at Eanfled's request, Erconberht found a guide for Wilfrid: Biscop Baducing, later Benedict Biscop, the monk who had nurtured Bede, and who at that time was himself setting out for Rome.[5] Thus, Eanfled, and now seemingly Aelffled herself, were very much Wilfrid's long-term sponsors.

Yet Hollis sheds a different light on the reasons for Aelffled's support for Wilfrid. Hollis regards Theodore as the driving force behind Wilfrid's reinstatement and points to a letter that Theodore wrote to Aelffled, urging her to support Wilfrid. Having laid aside his own hostility, Theodore "evidently regarded Aelffled as one of Wilfrid's foremost ranking enemies, whose favour needed to be won if Wilfrid was to be allowed to return to his see."[6] This would suggest that Hild and Aelffled had been at one in their antipathy toward Wilfrid.

In support of the argument that Hild and Aelffled were of one mind, it is significant that although Wilfrid had his former see restored to him at the Synod of Nidd, it was not the case that he regained the sole control of the vast

Northumbrian diocese centered on York. The decrees from Rome, although they had insisted that Wilfrid should be restored, had also stipulated that there should be other bishops appointed and that Wilfrid should work peacefully with them. This last point was significant.

The relations between Wilfrid and the other bishops had been far from peaceful for decades. So why did he finally agree to work peacefully with the other bishops? According to the *Catholic Encyclopedia*, it was because he had finally forced the other bishops to acknowledge the rulings from Rome: "he decided to accept, as the principle of Roman authority had been vindicated."[7] More likely, he was worn out by recent illness and a lifetime of conflict, and maybe, even, he wanted to make peace before his death, which occurred four years later. Wilfrid's uncharacteristic desire to live peaceably might well have been a factor in Aelffled's willingness to plead his cause.

Perhaps the main reason for thinking that Hild and Aelffled maintained a harmonious relationship throughout their years together is that the sources stress that both were "peace-makers," or "peace-weavers." Aelffled's credentials as peace-weaver are evident from her role at the Synod of Nidd. Eddius clearly attributes to Aelffled's intervention the "complete peace" achieved at this synod among Wilfrid, all the bishops, and the king and his council after decades of bad blood.[8]

Hild's capacity for peace-making has been evident time and again in the telling of her story. We have only to think of her ability to be accepted by and maintain a good relationship with King Oswy, whose father Ethelfrith had been killed by her childhood protector and great-uncle, Edwin. Hild was a Deiran princess, and Oswy was a Bernician king. Most strikingly in the years that led up to the Whitby synod, Hild had commanded the respect of those who favored Irish ways as well as those who wanted to adopt Roman ones. Then in the years after the synod she appears to have maintained good relations with all, except Wilfrid, yet even Eddius, Wilfrid's biographer, calls her "holy mother."[9]

In all probability, had Hild still been alive in 706, she too would have been willing to have Wilfrid reinstated to his bishopric because the reach of his powers as bishop had been much reduced, but more importantly because Wilfrid had been willing to live in peace with the other bishops.

When it comes to the question of how Whitby fared under Aelffled and indeed to what extent Aelffled, like Hild, was a leading figure in the Church, a closer examination of what is reported to have taken place at the synod of Nidd proves informative. This is how Eddius describes the scene as the pre-eminent leaders of the Church gathered at Nidd to decide Wilfrid's future:

> The king and his chief men, three of his bishops and their abbots, as well as the blessed abbess Aelffled, always the comforter and best counsellor of the whole province, all gathered together in one place near the river Nidd and on its eastern side. Archbishop Berhtwald also and Bishop Wilfrid arrived together on the same day.[10]

What a rich scene this conjures up: One woman of royal birth, the head of what was still one of the most important religious institutions in the whole of the North of England, standing alone among the prelates of the Church in the presence of the king. The king was Osred, Aldfrith's son. Aldfrith, and therefore by extension Osred, in large part owed his throne to Aelffled's efforts.

It seems highly unlikely that Aelffled would have attended the synod without other women from her community. The fact that Eddius does not think them worth mentioning makes it all the more significant that he puts Aelffled right up there with the other leaders of the Church. Yet it is not simply Aelffled's presence at Nidd and Eddius's high praise that marked Aelffled out as a formidable participant in the leadership of the Church. It is quite clear from Eddius that hers was the voice that prevailed.

In the course of the synod, Archbishop Berhtwald read letters from Rome to himself and to Wilfrid, both in their original Latin and in translation. The other bishops were then offered a choice: either they make peace with Wilfrid and restore to him what he formerly ruled, or they go all together to Rome for judgment. Anyone who refused to do either was to be excommunicated, and, if a bishop or priest, stripped of holy orders. The bishops resisted. It was then that Aelffled spoke. She claimed that it had been the dying will of King Aldfrith that the decrees of the Apostolic See with regard to Wilfrid be respected. By this time Aelffled seems to have been at the height of her powers. As we will see, with Cuthbert's help she had installed her half-brother, Aldfrith, on the Northumbrian throne; now she testifies to his dying will, which unsurprisingly coincides nicely with her own.

Following Aelffled's intervention on behalf of Wilfrid the decision was made:

> When she had finished her speech, Berhtfrith the aforesaid chief man of the king made answer: "This is the will of the king and of his chief men, that we obey the mandates of the Apostolic See and the commands of King Aldfrith in all things."[11]

Hollis believes that "Eddius's account of the role of Aelffled at the synod of Nidd contains the merest hint of what must have been a very eminent and influential position."[12] Yet as Eddius describes the proceedings, although Aelffled's report of the king's dying wish was the critical deciding factor, the bishops found it necessary to discuss further among themselves, before finally agreeing to reinstate Wilfrid. Hollis thinks that Eddius deliberately downplays Aelffled's importance

> After these words were finished, the bishops separated from the rest and began to take counsel together; sometimes the archbishop consulted with them and sometimes the prudent virgin Aelffled. The end of this holy council was that all the bishops and the king with his counsellors made a complete peace with Bishop Wilfrid, which they kept until the end of their lives.[13]

AELFFLED'S STATUS UNDERMINED

Hollis interprets Eddius's account of the events at Nidd as giving a glimpse of the actual authority exercised by Aelffled, while ensuring that she is seen to be under the control of the bishops. She then sees Bede's hostility toward female leadership more openly expressed as Bede rewrites an earlier, anonymous, *Life of Cuthbert* to make clear her lowly status in relation to Cuthbert.

> Though Eddius gives the impression that, as brides of the Lamb, the powers of royal women were safely under episcopal control, Bede's rewriting of Aelffled's role in the *Life of Cuthbert* reflects, in its considerable hostility to her as an intimate of the bishop-saint, sharp competitive strains concerning women's participation in the ecclesiastical sphere.[14]

Although Bede's account of Hild's life is colored by the limitations that, in his view, appropriately restrict women's activities in the Church, he nonetheless presents a portrait of a supremely holy woman, whose contribution to the mission of the Church was quite outstanding. With regard to Hild's successor, Aelffled, Bede is less generous in his praise. In particular in his *Life of Cuthbert* of 721 Bede is at pains to stress the subordinate status of the relationship between Aelffled and Cuthbert.

On one occasion, Aelffled sent a request to Cuthbert that they should meet as she was anxious to talk to him. The matter under discussion was the question of succession in Northumbria in the event of King Ecgfrith's death. Cuthbert seemed to share Aelffled's concern, and the two were evidently collaborators in the political arena. Cuthbert, who had left Lindisfarne for a quieter life of prayer on the island of Farne, left his retreat to meet Aelffled on the Island of Coquet.

Ecgfrith, we remember is Aelffled's brother and apparently had no children. The concern would have been to ensure a smooth takeover of power on his death and to install a monarch who would be sympathetic to the ideals of

Whitby and Lindisfarne. It seems that as a result of this meeting, Cuthbert, through his various contacts, managed to locate a half-brother of Aelffled's in an Irish monastery. This half-brother, Aldfrith, was the illegitimate son of Oswy and Fina.[15] Between them, Aelffled and Cuthbert were able to secure the throne of Northumbria for Aldfrith.

The point at which Bede is most obviously at pains to stress the subordinate status of Aelffled in relation to Cuthbert is during the course of the discussion on the Island of Coquet, Bede has Aelffled falling at Cuthbert's feet.

> On another occasion also the same most reverend Aelfflaed, virgin and mother of the virgins of Christ, sent and asked the man of God, adjuring him in the name of the Lord that he would deign to visit her and talk over matters of importance. . . . Having got into conversation with him, and having heard much from him on the matters about which she was asking him, suddenly in the midst of their talk, she fell at his feet and adjured him by the terrible awe-inspiring name of the King of Heaven and of His angels, that he would tell her how long Ecgfrith her brother would live and rule over the kingdom of the English.
>
> *Alio item tempore misit eadem reuerentissima uirgo et mater uirginum Christi Elfled, rogauitque uirum Dei adiurans in nomine Domini ut eum uidere, et de necessariis mereretur alloqui. . . Cuius potita colloquiis, cum multa ab eo quae sciscitabatur audiret, ecce repente in medio sermone aduoluta pedibus eius, adiurauit eum per nomen illud terribile ac uenerabile superni regis et angelorum eius, ut diceret illi quam longo tempore uicturus esset Egfridus frater illius et regnum gubernaturus Anglorum.*[16]

In fact in describing the scene as Cuthbert comes out of seclusion to plot the succession with Aelffled, Bede is close to his original source, an anonymous *Life of Cuthbert* written around 700:

> Furthermore there was a certain nun, a virgin and royal abbess called Aelfflaed who humbly asked the hermit of God in the name of the Lord to cross the sea and meet her at Coquet Island. The handmaiden of God on bended knees began to ask him many things.
>
> *Preterea sanctimonialis uirgo et regalis Aelfleda abbatissa sanctum anachoritam Dei humiliter in nomine Domini in obuiam sibi nauigare ad Cocpaedesae petiuit. Cui ancilla Dei flectens genua, multa interrogare cepit.*[17]

Perhaps Bede's is not so different from the original *Life*, which has Aelffled falling to her knees, rather than falling at Cuthbert's feet. It is probably understandable that in any *Life* dedicated to bearing witness to Cuthbert's outstanding sanctity, Aelffled should be given a lowly status in relation to the great miracle-working saint. Nonetheless, it is noticeable that in his version

Bede is most careful to mention Aelffled as little as possible and, above all, avoid reminiscences that might indicate any friendship or equality between the her and Cuthbert.

FRIENDSHIPS AND EQUALITY: CUTHBERT AND TRUMWINE

The anonymous author was writing a mere thirteen years after Cuthbert's death in 687. Either the author himself or one of Cuthbert's fellow monks acting as the author's source would have been close to the events as they occurred. For the telling of another story by the anonymous author, one that we have already encountered in chapter 9, it was Aelffled herself who was the source, and here a different picture emerges in terms of the relationship, one might say friendship, between Aelffled and Cuthbert.

The anonymous author tells how the Abbess Aelffled herself told the story of how she was feasting with Cuthbert at Ovington [Osingadun], in his diocese, when Cuthbert went into an ecstatic trance, dropping his knife on the table. Then "unheard by the others," she asked what it was that had been revealed. He described the vision in which he saw the soul of one of Aelffled's company being carried into heaven. When she asked who it was that had died, he replied: "You will name him to me to-morrow when I am celebrating mass!" A messenger was sent to her monastery to discover who had just died, but all in the monastery were found to be alive. Eventually it was learned that it was one of the brothers in the shepherds' huts who had fallen from the top of a tree and died. As soon as Aelffled learned this, she ran breathless into where Cuthbert was celebrating Mass, arriving at prayer "Remember, Lord, thy servants," and straight away declared the brother's name, Hadwald.[18]

In the homely meal-time scene during which Cuthbert received his vision, the body language could hardly be more different from that of the previous story, when Aelffled is reported to have fallen to her knees. Now we may imagine Cuthbert and Aelffled sitting opposite each other, eating and conversing together. Recognizing that Cuthbert is having a vision, Aelffled leans in toward him across the table. In lowered tones, Cuthbert confides his vision to her. He tells her that she will be the one to discover who it is who has died, and that immediately she is to join the Liturgy on the following day, at whatever point it has reached, and give the name of the deceased.

How good it would be to have the exact details of the way in which that Liturgy played out. It was Cuthbert who was consecrating the Church, yet it is clear that Aelffled's role was by no means negligible. Her part was so crucial that she was required to interrupt proceedings at any point on this occasion, giving the name of the person who had died. At the very least she was not required to keep silent; what more she did we may never know, but we do know that she was an active participant with a significant role.

Hild's friendship with Trumwine is recorded by Bede. It was to Aelffled and to Whitby that this bishop, caught up in the vagaries of war, turned when he needed somewhere to shelter. Having settled others for whom he had responsibility in various monasteries where he had contacts, he chose to settle himself at Whitby with a few of his followers.

> Entrusting others, wherever he was able to the monasteries of his friends, he himself chose a place of lodging in the oft-mentioned monastery of the servants and handmaids of God, which is called Streanaeshalch. And there for several years with a few of his own people he led a life of strict monasticism, to the advantage not only of himself but of many others.
>
> *Eosque, ubicumque poterat, amicis per monasteria commendams, ipse in saepedicto famulorum famularumque Dei monasterio, quod uocatur Streanaeshalch, locum mansionis elegit; ibique cum paucis suorum in monachica districtione uitam non sibi solummodo, sed et multis utilem, plurimo annorum tempore duxit.*[19]

Bishop Trumwine had been forced to flee his seat at Abercorn in Pictish territory after the Picts defeated King Ecgfrith in battle. Where he could Trumwine found a place of safety for those on the losing side in various monasteries. Trumwine himself sought protection at Whitby, where he lived a life of austerity. In the same passage Bede goes on to say that when bishop Trumwine arrived, the devout teacher Aelffled found Trumwine to be both a great solace in her own life, and a great help in governing the monastery (*Sed, adueniente illuc episcopo, maximum regendi auxilium, simul et suae uitae solacium deuota Deo doctrix inuenit*).

What, then are we to make of the help that the bishop gave to the abbess in governing the monastery?

After the death of Hild, the Whitby abbess continued to be a powerful force in the land, and the Whitby Abbey continued to be a prestigious center of learning, despite the increasing importance of the new school at Canterbury under the direction of Archbishop Theodore and the great scholar Abbot Hadrian and, of course, the rise of Wearmouth/Jarrow as a major educational establishment. Bede, called Aeffled a "teacher," a title he denied to Hild. An important *Life of Gregory* was written at Whitby during Aelffled's tenure, and although the actual author of the *Life* is unknown, it could well have been written by one of the women in the monastery. Women continued to study at a high level and to be influential figures in Church affairs.

When Trumwine was afforded shelter at Whitby in 685, his residency there was not a case of a bishop interfering in the running of a monastery. Rather it was the case of a bishop seeking sanctuary in a community well under the authority of a powerful woman. Aelffled acquiesced to his request, allowing him and some of his own companions to join her community, and it seems likely that the solace she received from his presence in the abbey was reciprocated.

It is not known whether Whitby continued as a double monastery for the whole period of Aelffled's rule. Stephanie Hollis argues that "if we take seriously the implication of his [Bede's] *Life of Cuthbert*, the double monastery at Whitby had already been dissolved in the time of Aelffled, for he describes her as ruling over a sizeable company of women."[20] Bede calls Aelffled the venerable handmaiden of Christ, "who to the joys of virginity added a maternal and pious care of no small company of the handmaidens of Christ / *quae inter gaudia uirginitatis non paucis famularum Christi agminibus maternae pietatis curam adhibebat.*"[21] But restricting Aelffled's pious care to women may simply have been Bede unwilling to acknowledge Aelffled's status in relation to Trumwine and his companions.

Despite the omission of Hild's name from the *Life of Gregory* and from the Northumbrian *Liber Vitae*, in the event, it was Aelffled's memory that was eclipsed by Hild's. Despite the best efforts of Eddius and Bede to obscure the authority of both Hild and Aelffled, they cannot hide the fact that both women were evidently powerful church figures, and in many respects, on an equal footing with bishops. Aelffled was certainly one of the great Church leaders of her day; leader of a great monastery, director of what was still one of the most important centers of learning; a coworker and confidante of Cuthbert; the protector of bishop Trumwine; a king-maker; a bishop-maker in relation to Wilfrid; and a peace-maker. Yet it was Hild's life that shone more brightly in Christian memory and which so captivated Bede.

NOTES

1. It is clear that Aelffled at least was heavily involved in both ecclesial and political activities in what were turbulent times, and the claustration of nuns, that is to say keeping them within the confines of monastery, had yet to be imposed.
2. Bede had previously written a *Life of Cuthbert* in verse around 716, and there was an earlier anonymous version from around 700, which was a significant source for Bede. The two lives are available in Colgrave, *Two Lives of Saint Cuthbert.*
3. Colgrave, *Life of Wilfrid.*
4. Yorke, *Nunneries and the Anglo-Saxon Royal Houses*, 164.

5. Colgrave, *Life of Wilfrid*, 9.
6. Hollis, *Anglo-Saxon Women*, 183.
7. "St. Wilfrid," New Advent *Catholic Encyclopedia.*
8. Colgrave, *Life of Wilfrid*, 133.
9. Colgrave, *Life of Wilfrid*, 21.
10. Colgrave, *Life of Wilfrid*, 129.
11. Colgrave, *Life of Wilfrid*, 133.
12. Hollis, *Anglo-Saxon Women*, 181
13. Colgrave, *Life of Wilfrid*, 133.
14. Hollis, *Anglo-Saxon Women*, 179
15. Williamson, *Kings & Queens of Britain*, 215.
16. "Bede's Life of St. Cuthbert," in Colgrave, *Two Lives of Saint Cuthbert*, ch. XXIV, 234–35.
17. "Anonymous Life of St. Cuthbert," in Colgrave, *Two Lives of Saint Cuthbert*, Bk. III, ch. VI, 102–3.
18. "Anonymous Life of St. Cuthbert," Book IV, ch. X. 127.
19. Beda, *Historia Ecclesiastica, Liber Quartos*, 24 [26] CLX. My translation.
20. Hollis, *Anglo-Saxon Women*, 268.
21. "Bede's Life of St. Cuthbert," in Colgrave, *Two Lives of Saint Cuthbert*, ch. XIII, 230–31.

Chapter Sixteen

Further Developments

Aelffled, who had succeeded Hild as Abbess at Whitby, died in 714. No records have been found that provide information regarding life in the monastery between 714 and its destruction by Danish invaders in 867. Henrietta Leyser is probably correct when she suggests a gradual decline.

> Already in Aelfflaed's time, there were changes afoot. Though described by Bede as a teacher, it is unlikely that her [Aelffled's] role in this respect measured up in any way to Hilda's. The need had passed. The arrival of Archbishop Theodore in 669 with Abbot Hadrian, and the opening of their new school at Canterbury, heralded a new era. Theodore's known disapproval of double monasteries, moreover, even though he took no active measures against them, can have done nothing to improve their morale. One by one their functions were usurped; kings came to rely less on the charisma gained from the sanctity of their great abbesses, more on unction bestowed by bishops and on masses said by priest-monks.[1]

Nonetheless, if Whitby was in gradual decline during Aelffled's rule, that was not the case with regard to all the double monasteries in England. During this same period, the monastery at Ely was founded by Etheldreda in 673.

THE BRIEF BRILLIANCE OF THE ABBESSES OF ELY

As we saw in chapter 5, the double monastery at Ely was founded by its first Abbess, Etheldreda, in 673. Thus, it was founded precisely during Hild's declining years, and during that period when Theodore, Archbishop of Canterbury, was known for his disapproval of the double monastery as a suitable vehicle for the monastic life. The main source for the lives of its first abbesses, Etheldreda, Sexburga, Erminilda, and Werburga is the *Liber Eliensis* (Book of Ely), a work in three parts, compiled by a monk from Ely in the later twelfth century. The first part of the *Liber Eliensis* covers the founding of Ely monastery by Etheldreda—a double house under female leadership. It follows the story of Ely to its destruction by the Danes and what happened immediately afterward. Joan Morris records that according to the *Liber Eliensis*:

> after the death of these four great abbesses, the monastery continued as before in ever greater fervour under the rule of these holy women (*beatarum regimine ferminarum),* until the Danish invasion in 866.[2]

The title of paragraph 38 of the *Liber Eliensis* regarding what happened after the death of these four named abbesses reads:

> As for divine worship at Ely, it flourished under the regime of these holy women until it was laid waste by Danish fire and sword.[3]

> *Quod apud Ely cultus divini operis sub sanctarum floruit regimine ferminarum donec igne et ferro vastatur a Danis*

As the paragraph begins, it tells how after the death of the truly saintly Etheldreda, Sexburga, Erminilda, and Werburga, the service of God was rarely wanting at the church in Ely, under the regime of these holy women. On the contrary, divine worship, rather than growing lukewarm, became ever more passionate and more devoted. For many years the monastery grew and flourished, keeping the rule and safeguarding the monastic way of life.

> *Post decessum vero sanctarum [Etheldreda, Sexburga, Erminilda] atque [Werburga] ecclesia Elge [Ely] minime vacabat ab opera Dei, immo virtu divini culsus sub beatarum regimine ferminarum, not tepescente sed magis ac magis in ea fervescente fervore discipline regularis ac custodia monastice professionis, multis annorum evolventibus orbitis floruit.*[4]

Despite this upbeat assessment of the *Liber Eliensis*, Jo Ann Kay McNamara says that "Ely's history after the first generation of royal abbesses is lost to record."[5] Werburga, the last of these royal abbesses, died in 699 or 700; thus, there is a gap in the records similar to the gap in the Whitby records after Aelffled of Whitby died in 714. At the Second Council of Nicea in 787double monasteries were banned altogether under Canon 20, though this ruling was not incorporated into the rulings of English Church councils.[6]

Also mirroring the Whitby experience, after Ely's destruction by the Vikings, the still valuable estate was taken over by Benedictine monks. "When the wealthy monastery was reconstituted after the Viking invasions, a community of Benedictine monks attached to the episcopal see took over the dower of Saint Etheldreda and enjoyed its revenues."[7] Here again we find a pattern that mirrors events at Whitby. Whitby had remained a valuable estate, even after the sacking of its monasteries and outlying houses by the Danes, "retaining the ownership of around forty ruined oratories."[8] Like Ely, it was reclaimed as a monastery by monks, in this case, monks from Evesham, who refounded the abbey in 1078 as a Benedictine house for men. Its haunting ruins, some of which date back to the thirteenth century, still stand today on the cliff top at Whitby. (See figure 16.1.)

Thus, it would seem as if, as soon as the dust had settled at the ruined monasteries of Whitby and Ely, the opportunity was taken to bar women religious from their precincts and to replace the abbesses of these great double houses with abbots, who ruled only monks.

AS BISHOPS CLAIMED GOVERNANCE

Hild had been the brightest of lights, the shining jewel in the Golden Age of Northumbria. As Aelffled took over her mantel, and as Etheldreda was only

Figure 16.1. The ruins of the Whitby Abbey, rebuilt in Gothic style over a period of 200 years from 13th to 15th centuries.
Photograph by Cherry_Girl on iStock.

beginning to establish the great double monastery at Ely, the opportunities for women to follow in their footsteps were already in the process of being closed down. In the years that immediately followed the Whitby synod, the move toward episcopal rather than monastic structures of governance had begun to gain some ground in Anglo-Saxon England. However, it was not until 735, well after Hild's death, that York became the prestigious center envisaged by Gregory I and Theodore. With the appointment of Egbert as its first archbishop,[9] power moved decisively from the abbess to the bishop.

The move was of course detrimental to women. As we have seen, at a time when the monastery had fulfilled many of the functions of the parish or diocese, abbesses like Hild had legitimately fulfilled the role of bishop in many areas of Church life. These powers were gradually stripped from them as measures were enforced to enhance the prestige of the bishop. The powers of the bishop were more rigorously defined and claimed as exclusive to them, and only men could be ordained bishop. Underlying the whole process was the patriarchal assumption, common throughout the Christian world, but embedded especially in Roman thinking, that women were to be ruled by men.

It was above all in the double monastery that women in the seventh century had continued the tradition, dating back to Jesus himself, of working alongside men as equals in the apostolic mission. In the primitive Church, the leadership roles of women like Pricilla, an outstanding coworker of Paul, or Phoebe, minister of the church at Cenchreae,[10] stemmed from the still-remembered practice of Jesus himself.[11] By the time of the conversion of the Roman Empire in the early fourth century, patriarchal thinking had reasserted itself in Christian life, and where it could, it had extended its reach throughout the Church. In this way, the memory of women's inclusion was to a large extent lost to history.

Where the memory still persisted, as in Anglo-Saxon England, women's full inclusion in the Church's mission came under pressure, as the full weight of patriarchal thinking was imported across the Channel by the likes of Augustine and Theodore. It would seem that it had been expedient to allow Hild and others to continue as monastic heads until the episcopacy could be built up to sufficient strength for their replacement. We already know that Theodore may have acted in concert with Hild against the troublesome Wilfrid. Maybe Theodore's good relationship with Hild, and the high regard in which she was held, explained his failure to act against the double monasteries, despite his express disapproval. It is somewhat ironic that through her teaching Hild was instrumental in boosting the number of bishops, while Aelffled and her family secured the rise to power of Wilfrid.

THE SYNOD OF HERTFORD

Theodore successfully increased the bishoprics around the country, and the bishops themselves gained strength and prestige from the development in Roman thinking on the exalted status of the bishop. Inevitably, the competing jurisdictions of the bishop and the monastic head, whether male or female, were the cause of friction, and clarification was needed. As the powers of the abbesses were incrementally reduced, the double monasteries they headed would have been particularly vulnerable; as would the communities of men who wished to retain Irish practices. Even those who wished to retain connections to the Irish communities headed by Colman were subject to hostility from Wilfrid, now a bishop.

The synod in in Hertford in 673 addressed this issue. (It was incidentally at this synod that the submission to Rome formulated at Whitby was extended to the entire Anglo-Saxon England.) Canon 3 determined that no bishop should interfere in the monasteries or take anything from them by force. "*Ut, quaeque monasteria Deo consecrata sunt, nulli episcoporum liceat ea in aliquo inquietare, nec quicquam de eorum rebus uiolenter abstrahere.*"[12] In this, the council was reiterating a long-established custom dating back to Anthony, Pachomius, and Benedict and reaffirmed by papal Bull by John IV in 641.[13]

Although this afforded some protection for female monastics, it was the marking off of the many less prestigious ordained ministries from male priestly ordination that undermined the status of women for centuries to come. As the powers of the ordained priesthood were clarified and claimed as exclusive, the functions that women had previously, and quite legitimately, carried out were systematically usurped.

As well as curtailing the interference of bishops in monasteries, the Synod of Hertford was designed to reign in other extensions of their juridical reach. Canon 2 determined that a bishop should confine himself to the affairs of his own diocese and not interfere in dioceses other than his own. "*Ut nullus episcoporum parrochiam alterius inuadat, sed contentus sit gubernatione creditae sibi plebis.*"[14] This canon was probably aimed at Wilfrid, who, since his return to England after his episcopal ordination in Gaul, had already begun to found a whole chain of monasteries from his base at Ripon. Wilfrid had no qualms about cutting across the boundaries of kingdoms and dioceses.

In addition to the increase of his monastic holdings, Wilfrid's rule as bishop of York was causing consternation. For the three or four years preceding the Hertford synod, Wilfrid had been restored to the vast Northumbrian diocese with its center at York. Here, as we have seen, he built up a massive power base, including a standing army, to the consternation of the royal family, King Ecgfrith, Queen Iurminburg, and Archbishop Theodore alike.

THE IMPOSITION OF THE BENEDICTINE RULE

Although bishops were forbidden to interfere directly in the affairs of any given monastery, other factors were nonetheless restricting the freedom of the abbess within her own monastery. We have noted in previous chapters the flexibility enjoyed by the monastic head to formulate a rule suitable to the particular circumstances of her monastery. Such flexibility would be drastically reduced with the eventual imposition of the Benedictine rule across all monasteries.

Wilfrid's monasteries, spreading rapidly across Britain in the late seventh century, followed the Benedictine rule. As we have seen, Bede, Wilfrid's later contemporary, was greatly in favor of the Benedictine rule and keen to see its universal acceptance. In the telling of Hild's remarkable achievements, he may well have exaggerated the continuity of her rule from Hartlepool to Whitby. Nearly two centuries after Hild's death, the Rule of Benedict was prescribed for all the monastic communities of England.

Stephanie Hollis argues that the time of Alfred the Great (871–899) marked the diminishment of the status of the abbesses, as well as their removal from public affairs: "from the reign of Alfred onwards, the literature reveals an increase in the prestige and authority of male ecclesiastics and a reduction in the status of women, particularly monastic women, and this parallels the overall tendency of canon law."[15]

This marked loss of prestige occurred within a decade or two of the final destruction of the monastery at Whitby, built up to such dazzling heights by Hild. Physically and legislatively, much of her ministry was erased from history.

It was at the Council of Winchester, held under King Edgar's supervision in the early 970s, that the Rule of Benedict was prescribed for the whole of England. The purpose of this council was the reform of the monasteries, many of which were in a state of decay. One of Edgar's bishops was Aethelwold, "a scholar and dynamic teacher who inspired a series of decaying monasteries to adopt the Benedictine Rule as their standard of life."[16] Aethelwold had himself translated the Benedictine rule from Latin to Anglo-Saxon English.

Doubtless the reforms under Edgar brought a new energy and a greater piety to monastic life, but they served to consolidate further the perception that women were to be subject to male authority. It was not simply that the creativity of women like Hild was thus stifled, but the strict hierarchy of the sexes that operated in the Benedictine Rule served to formalize the second-class status of women in the Church.

LONGER TERM

The purpose of this book has been to uncover the sacramental responsibilities that were legitimately exercised by Hild and women like her; to demonstrate that she was a Church leader with governing, liturgical, and pastoral responsibilities that were in many instances on a par with priests and bishops and that these activities were not an aberration, but fully part of the Catholic tradition, which has its roots in the practice of Jesus himself. It is not within the remit of this book to chart the progressive loss of these responsibilities from the eighth century onward.

Suffice to say that Wimborne in Dorset, founded somewhere between 702 and 705 by Cuthburga, was one of the last double monasteries in Anglo-Saxon England to be headed by a woman.[17] It was from Wimborne that Leoba was sent by the Abbess Tetta to lead a party of thirty nuns to join Boniface's mission in Germany. According to Sarah Foot, in her exhaustive study of consecrated women in early medieval Britain, the last Anglo-Saxon double monastery for which there is certain evidence was that headed by a certain Abbess Aethelthryth. We know of Aethelthryth through a letter she received from Alcuin in 796.

Mixed houses seem to have lingered on into the late ninth century, but the ones we know about were headed not by an abbess but by an abbot. Foot finds, however, that "there is no evidence for any mixed congregation in England beyond the early years of the tenth century."[18]

DEVELOPMENTS IN CONTINENTAL EUROPE

My focus all along has been on the many roles that Hild had undertaken as the Abbess of her double monastery at Whitby. Joan Morris, writing a history of women with the jurisdiction of bishops, reminds us that "a great number of communities headed by abbesses with independent jurisdiction exempt from bishops were spread throughout Italy, Spain, France, Germany, Poland, Austria, England, and Ireland."[19] From its origins in Gaul and Anglo-Saxon England, the functions of the abbess spread to other areas of Western Europe as they became Christianized.

There was a revival of sorts of the double monastery in the twelfth and thirteenth centuries. However, against a background of the growing restrictions placed on women's activities, "later medieval double houses such as those founded by Gilbert of Sempringham. . . were always governed by men."[20]

NOTES

1. Leyser, *Medieval Women*, 37.
2. Morris, *Against Nature and God*, 25.
3. My translation.
4. *Liber Eliensis* edited by E. O. Blake (Camden Third Series Volume XCII, London 1962). Paragraph 38, p. 52.
5. McNamara, *Sisters in Arms*, 166.
6. According to Foot, *Veiled Women*, 66: "those communities that were already in existence were to be permitted to continue provided that they followed the recommendations of St. Basil."
7. McNamara, *Sisters in Arms*, 166.
8. Leyser, *Medieval Women*, 25, cites A. Thacker, "Monks, Preaching and Pastoral Care in Early Anglo-Saxon England," in *Pastoral Care Before the Parish*, eds. J. Blair and R. Sharpe (London: Leicester University Press, 1992), 143–44.
9. Yorke, *The Conversion of Britain*, 151
10. See Elisabeth Schüssler Fiorenza "Women in the Pauline Churches," in *Feminism and Theology*, eds. Janet Martin Soskice and Diana Lipton (Oxford: Oxford University Press, 2003), 208–13.
11. See, for example, Elizabeth Schüssler Fiorenza, *Discipleship of Equals: A Critical Feminist Ekklesia-logy of Liberation* (London: SCM, 1993), 104–16.
12. Bede, *Ecclesiastical History*, IV 5. 214; Beda, *Historia Ecclesiastica, Liber Quartos*, 5, CXXIX.
13. Morris, *Against Nature and God*, 18.
14. Bede, *Ecclesiastical History*, IV 5. 214; Beda, *Historia Ecclesiastica, Liber Quartos*, 5, CXXIX.
15. Hollis, *Anglo-Saxon Women*, 1.
16. MacCulloch, *History of Christianity*, 364.
17. Stanford, *The She-Pope*, 49.
18. Foot, *Veiled Women I*, 63.
19. Morris, *Against Nature and God*, 3.
20. Foot, *Veiled Women I*, 49.

Chapter Seventeen

The Untold Story

For the most amazing flowering of Christian culture, the seventh and eighth centuries are justifiably regarded as Golden Age of Northumbria. It was essentially in the fertile ground of the monasteries that this amazing flowering took place.

As a glittering Northumbrian phenomenon, this golden age was short-lived. By the ninth century, the vitality of monastic life in this part of Britain was in decline. The management of the large monastic estates had been so effective that their lands and other assets were coveted by others who had the power to take them. Not only did the Viking raids cause devastation, but secular rulers and bishops claimed or claimed back the lands that had provided the monasteries with their livelihood and enabled them to flourish.

Nonetheless, it would be mistaken to think with the close of this golden age that the culture, the learning, the pastoral care, and the deep piety that marked it out as golden were also lost. In fact much of what came to be considered characteristic of the Roman communion was drawn initially from practices that developed outside Rome's sphere of influence, including the monasteries of the Anglo-Saxons.[1]

A rich Northumbrian tributary of Christian practice fed into the mainstream of Christian tradition to be passed on down the ages. Thus, we may justifiably claim that some of the pious practices promulgated by Hild and certain lines of theological thinking that she promoted and perhaps even helped to develop now continue unattributed within the Roman tradition because Bede has Hild right at the source of this tributary. It was Hild who was likened to a sparkling jewel, which lit up the whole of Britain with the splendor of its light.

SUPPRESSION AND DISTORTION

The light that Hild had sparked would pervade the whole of Britain. Her teaching, thought, and practice fed into the mainstream of Roman tradition. Yet Hild is barely mentioned, or left out altogether, when later history attempts to record the historical figures whose lives were instrumental in producing the Golden Age of Northumbria and its rich heritage. It is only by appreciating the circumstances of this omission that Hild can as it were be recovered from obscurity.

The history that has come down to us is permeated and distorted by the later assumption that the task of leadership had been entrusted by God exclusively to bishops (male), priests (male), and male deacons. Thus, when later writers discuss the work of the abbeys in general, they assume them to have been in the charge of abbots.

With a little research, it has been possible to ascertain that in Anglo-Saxon England, there was virtually no difference in local canon law between the monasteries, no matter whether they housed women or men or both or in what ratio. That is to say, with very few exceptions, what the abbot did, so did the abbess. Historical research also tells us what this male-focused telling did not know or chose to leave out: that the powerful double monasteries of the early Middle Ages were mostly headed by women and that it was these women's agency and influence that maintained and enriched the Christian tradition we have today.

A further layer of distortion has come from the practice of reading the sacramental theology of the second millennium into that of the first. By taking the later perspective, it has been possible to look at women's agency in the first millennium and to claim that they did not "administer the sacraments." Yet when this later perspective is applied to the men, as well as the women of Hild's time, what we discover is that it is not just the case that Hild did not administer the sacraments, but certain of the sacraments, according to second-millennium definitions, would not have been available at all. Yet what has been uncovered of Hild's time points to an extraordinarily rich sacramental life—a sacramental life in which both women and men participated, in many ways interchangeably, as active channels of God's grace.

The way in which Hild and other holy women administered confession, for example, was simply the way that it was administered in her part of the world and in their time. The fact that the part played by Hild and other gifted women confessors has been written out of the tradition continues to be a considerable loss to the Church to this day. To take but one example: according to the 1983 Code of Canon Law, only bishops can lift the excommunication imposed on those responsible for an abortion. Nonetheless, in September 2015 Pope Francis I, with considerable sensitivity to the distressing plight of women he had met, issued an instruction that not just bishops, but all priests during the Year of Mercy (December 8, 2015 to November 20, 2016) would be authorized to grant absolution for the sin of abortion.

The same sensitivity should extend to once again allowing female as well as male confessors. "It is surely not difficult to imagine a situation in which a woman who has felt compelled to have an abortion might reasonably baulk at the idea of confession to a man."[2] I am thinking here of girls forced into prostitution through poverty or an abusive marriage through family honor and of the victims of gang rape. Ignorance of our history allows sensitive pastoral practice to be rejected out of hand, while misogyny, casting the woman as the sinner whose sin cannot be absolved in the normal way, is allowed free reign.

It is known that there was no distinction between the role of the abbess and that of abbot in Britain in the fifth to seventh centuries. If the abbot acted as confessor then so did the abbess. Hild, thus, had what is now understood as the power to forgive sins in the name of Jesus Christ. Representing Christ "in the sacrament of penance in the true sense,"[3] she and other women, participated in this power as it was exercised up to and including her own time.

These facts have been written out of the telling of its history by a Church that in reserving this power to men only has appealed to an unswerving tradition going right back to Jesus. When hierarchs of the Roman Catholic Church appeal to the tradition of the Church, they should acknowledge that not only the primitive Church, where women undoubtedly had leadership responsibilities, but also the early medieval period, when women like Hild exercised huge responsibility—both are an authentic part of that tradition. Patriarchy has been incidental to Christianity, not an essential component.

To read the history of the first millennium through the lens of the strictures of the second is to arrive at a false understanding of the practice of Jesus himself and of the tradition he initiated. Specifically, it serves to eradicate the part that Hild and women like her played in the sacramental life of the Church.

Uncovering these facts, on the other hand, could open the way not only to a more balanced and more pastoral practice, but to a practice that reflects more authentically the mind of Jesus himself, who included women in his mission in a way quite remarkable for his time.

TOWARD A FULLER ACCOUNT OF THE CHRISTIAN TRADITION

The decision taken at Whitby should not be regarded as a question of catholicity or schism. Although it was certainly sensible to settle on an agreed date for Easter, it would have been perfectly possible for other aspects of Celtic Liturgy to have continued alongside Roman ones and for the two sections of the church to have remained in communion with each other. The practices of the Celtic church, such as the full engagement of women in its mission, were legitimate practices, echoing the diversity of ministry in the early Church, and as such, are integral to Catholic tradition. That such traditions have been largely written out of a version that sought to downgrade women's contribution to the life of the church makes them no less authentic and no less in keeping with the mind of Christ as made known to his earliest followers.

ROLE REVERSAL

Traveling around Northumbria some years ago, I was struck by the sense that this is the territory not so much of Hild, as of Bede. Simply as a tourist, one gets the impression that Bede's fame is greater than Hild's, his status more prestigious. Simply as a student of Church history, when one considers the question of who is source for whom, the most obvious answer is that Bede is the source for Hild. The story of Hild's life is one among a great many stories of the lives of saints that Bede has recorded. Yet the more I have researched other records that shed light on Hild's life, the more I have found that a different answer presents itself.

Counterintuitively, it seems to me that Hild is a significant source for Bede's life. Before looking at the evidence to substantiate this claim, I will first take a brief look at the various reasons why the Bede–Hild relationship tends to be looked at the other way round and why Bede is routinely thought of as the major figure in the Anglo-Saxon era, and Hild as the lesser figure for whom Bede is the source.

Bede actually wrote more biblical commentaries than historical texts, and he was an expert scholar in other areas, such as the complicated calculations required to work out the correct dating of Easter. Yet above all Bede's fame is a result of his groundbreaking work as a historian. So much of the earliest history of the English people comes to us through him!

Bede wrote his *Ecclesiastical History of the English People* late in life. He was already writing in an era that had reduced to a secondary status the agency of women in the life of the Church. Anglo-Saxon England had moved in a matter of decades from a situation where the importance of female as well as male leaders was taken for granted in the Church, to a situation where the leadership of women was being deliberately blotted out of the official version of history. Bede just about straddled both worlds but belonged for the most part in the latter.

Bede was no doubt greatly influenced by Benedict Biscop because he spent his entire life from the age of seven in the two Northumbrian monasteries founded by Biscop, Wearmouth, and Jarrow. Biscop made several visits to Rome and was captivated by the beauty of Italian churches, going to great lengths to bring their splendor to his two monasteries. Bede, too, was passionate about Rome and the authority of the Holy See.

As a scrupulous adherent of Roman ways he was naturally swayed regarding the uncompromising line that Rome was taking when it came to the upgrading bishops in relation to priests and the downgrading of women in relation to both. The steady encroachment of patriarchal thinking was the backdrop to his many years of adult life. It can be seen in his telling of Hild's life in the *Ecclesiastical History*, the truly great work of his old age.

Yet there is another side to Bede, which would have been open to other influences in his early formative years. From his sermons we discover that he was not merely a brilliant scholar, but a contemplative scholar, thoroughly immersed in the mysteries of faith. And it is in his spiritual life, in his immersion in the life of prayer, where Hild's influence would have been at play. Bede acknowledges this himself, though obliquely, for he has Hild right at the source of the rich Northumbrian tributary of Christian practice that fed into the mainstream of Christian tradition of which he himself was part.

And as we saw in chapter 5, given the circumstances of Bede's childhood, it would have been virtually impossible for him not to have been influenced, one way or another, by the great celebrity of the Northumbrian world of his time, Hild of Whitby, who died when he was about seven years of age, and whom he described as "mother of all." So great was her fame, that her death must have been one of the abiding memories of his childhood—surely a formative event for a young child himself embarking on the religious life and in the very area in which Hild had begun her own life as a vowed religious.

It was perhaps only twenty-two or twenty-three years after Hild's departure from the monastery on north bank of the River Wear that Bede arrived at the monastery of Wearmouth. The head of that monastery, and presumably one of the most formative influences on the child at such an impressionable age, was Benedict Biscop. Through Biscop, Bede would have learned something of Hild's early ministry.

Biscop himself had spent the first twenty-five years of his life, from 62 to 53, as a nobleman of Northumbria before leaving for Rome with Wilfrid. In his teens, Biscop would have known King Oswald and how he had brought Aidan from Iona to Lindisfarne. As a young man he would have known that Aidan had called Hild back to Northumbria to set up her first community on the north bank of the River Wear, and he would still have been in Northumbria when she moved from there to Hartlepool.

Subsequently Bede lived to see Whitby put into the shade by his own institution at Jarrow, and by Canterbury as a center for learning. He would have seen Wilfrid, whom Hild opposed, rise to dominate the monastic landscape. Bede saw Wilfrid build and restore the churches of York, Ripon, and Hexham and achieve the most impressive monastic expansion in the whole of Anglo-Saxon England with every monastery under his personal control. He saw Wilfrid establish the authority of the Roman See in England, an achievement that was viewed favorably by Bede. Yet for all this Bede's account of Wilfrid's life was not altogether favorable.

On the other hand, his treatment is wholly sympathetic of two central Irish figures: Aidan, who ventured out from Iona to set up the missionary hub at Lindisfarne, and Colman, who retreated from there back to Lindisfarne rather than abandon the practices of his beloved father in faith, Columba. And as for Hild, Bede has Hild right at the source of the rich Northumbrian tributary of Christian practice that fed into the mainstream of Christian tradition which has been passed on down the ages.

There is one further connection that puts Bede firmly in the tradition of Hild's monasticism. It was John, bishop of Hexham, who ordained Bede, first as deacon and then as priest. And John had received his priestly training under Hild.

Mayr-Harting seems to be talking about something similar to the role reversal suggested when he says:

> It is easy to confuse what Rome gave with what she received. There was much in the way of worship and devotion, monastic custom, and ideas which was being developed outside Rome (some of it amongst the Anglo-Saxons) at this time, and which later came to be considered as characteristic of the Roman communion.[4]

As one of the most influential monastic leaders in Anglo-Saxon England, it must be assumed Hild's teaching, thought and practice retained their place as "characteristic of the Roman communion." For the sake of a more authentic telling of the tradition and a greater conformity with the mind of Christ, it is high time that the shadow of patriarchy that has so effectively blotted out Hild's role as one of the great spiritual mothers of the early medieval period was removed, so that her brilliant light might shine out more fully in the tradition that she helped to shape.

NOTES

1. Mayr-Harting, *The Coming of Christianity*, 4.
2. Anne Inman, *The Tablet* 12 September 2015 "Letters" 17.

3. Marrou, "The Conversion of Northern Europe," 455, in a discussion of the Chapter of Faults talks of "the association of the Superior in the sacrament of penance in the true sense." See chapter 7, Hild the Confessor.

4. Mayr-Harting, *The Coming of Christianity*, 4.

Glossary

The definitions show my understanding of the words as they are used in the context of this book.

Anglo-Saxons: Dominant population in eastern and southeastern Britain descended from Angles, Saxons, and Jutes, Germanic tribes who had crossed the North Sea from Denmark (Jutland) and the Netherlands.

apostles: Those followers of Jesus in the New Testament period who were "sent" to preach the Good News of the Kingdom of God.

apostolic: In line with the mission of the apostles.

ascetic: One who practices an extreme form of self-denial out of love for Jesus Christ.

asceticism: The practice of extreme self-denial.

Bernicia: That part of Northumbria which was North of the Tees.

Bretwalda: A king who had gained authority over all the other kings in the various territories of Anglo-Saxon England; an overlord.

British: Those who were descended from the inhabitants of Britain when Britain was part of the Roman Empire.

Celtic Church: The term "Celtic Church" is often used interchangeably with the term "Irish Church." In the early medieval period, the Irish inhabited an area known as Dal Riata.

Celts: People of central and western Europe, who, from at least the fourth century BCE shared a language, and to some extent, a culture. Through trade networks, some of the inhabitants Britain and Ireland took on a Celtic identity.

claustration: The shutting up of vowed religious behind the closed walls of the monastery.

convivium: A Latin word meaning "feast."

Dalriada (Dàl Riata): The seventh-century Celtic/Irish kingdom of southwest Scotland and parts of Ulster.

Deira: That part of Northumbria that was South of the Tees.

Didache: A short, authoritative anonymous set of Christian teachings dating from the late first century.

Easter: The most important feast of the Christian year, celebrating the resurrection of Jesus Christ from the dead.

ecclesial: Of the Church.

episcopacy: Collective term for bishops.

Extreme Unction: The anointing of a person at the point of death. Formerly the name given to what is now called the Sacrament of the Sick.

Frankia: Roughly what is now France and what in Roman times was part of the larger territory of Gaul.

Gaul: An area comprising modern-day France, parts of Belgium, western Germany, and northern Italy, inhabited by Celtic tribes.

habit: Religious dress worn by vowed religious.

hagiography: Writings about holy people. Gk. *hagios* = "holy"; *graph* = "to write".

harp: Small stringed instrument that accompanied the singing of the sagas; in Old English, *hearpa*; also known as the lyre.

hierarchy: The ruling all-male clergy of the Catholic Church graded according to rank.

last rites: Sacramental rites reserved for those in danger of death.

lector: Reader/one who reads aloud from Scripture during the Liturgy.

litany: A series of petitionary prayers, led by one person, with a fixed response from the rest of those present.

Liturgy: Formal worship; derives from the Greek *ergon* meaning "work" and *litos* meaning "belonging to the people." It has connotations of paying one's dues to God.

lyre: *See* harp.

ministry: A specific service performed as part of the Church's mission.

missal: Mass book containing prayers and readings necessary to offer the Mass.

miter: Distinctive form of headdress worn by bishops, abbots, and abbesses and still today worn by bishops.

monastery: The dwelling place of a group of people living together under religious vows. In the seventh century, the monastery might house just three or four people or a very considerable number. The word "monastery" covered many different arrangements.

Orthodox: Churches of Eastern Europe that are distinguished from the Latin Churches of Western Europe.

orthodox: Conforming to the true teachings of the faith as determined by the Church authorities.

patriarchal: A society in which all power is invested in a male head, the patriarch or father, with a clear ranking of classes of people, and where men rule over women and children.

Picts: Indigenous peoples of northern and Eastern Scotland in the Anglo-Saxon period.

Psalms: Ancient poetic prayers of the Hebrews, intended to be sung, recorded in the Bible, used by Jesus, e.g. Matthew 26:30; 27:46.

reeve: The official who oversaw the running of the estate.

religious: Men or women who have taken religious vows.

reliquary: A container for holy relics.

Rule: A set of regulations for a particular community of vowed religious. The Rule would be written down and would be read aloud to the community as a reminder of how they should live.

sacaramentary: A book containing the prayers used by the celebrant to administer any of the sacraments.

sacristy: A small room inside the church where special vestments are kept for use in the Liturgy and where robing takes place. *See* vestry.

saga: A long narrative telling of the heroic deeds of the ancestors of a particular people, notably the Germanic tribes of Scandinavia.

schismatic: Creating a schism or split; breaking away from the true Church.

Scotti: Roman name for Irish tribes who lived in southwest Scotland.

Scriptorium: The room in a monastery where books were copied, most notably the Bible, and the works of the early Church theologians and ascetics.

See: A geographical area over which a particular bishop has jurisdiction.

staff: A stick in the shape of a shepherd's crook held by a bishop, an abbot, or an abbess, signifying their role as shepherd, just as Christ was shepherd to the flock. The staff is still used by bishops today, as the symbol of their authority.

synod: Another name for a council.

thegn: A lord who had been granted land by the king in return for military service.

tonsure: A particular style of haircut, with part of the head shaved, for men who enter a religious order.

vestry: A small room inside the church where special vestments are kept for use in the Liturgy and where robing takes place. *See* sacristy.

vernacular: The language of the people.

Viaticum: Holy communion given to a person at the point of death as food for the journey (*via*).

Vikings: Sea-faring tribes from Scandinavia who began raids on Britain in the eighth century.
Welsh: Population of Wales and other parts of southern England whose ancestors went back to the Roman occupation of Britain.
witan: The council of advisers to an Anglo-Saxon king.

Bibliography

Adams, Max. *The King of the North: The Life and Times of Oswald of Northumbria.* London: Head of Zeus Ltd., 2013.

BaedaeVenerabilis. *Historiam Ecclesiasticam Gentis Anglorum Historiam Abbatum Epistolam AD Ecgberctum* Carolus Plummer, A. M. Tomus Prior Oxon II E. Typographeo Clarendoniano. 1896.

Beda Venerabilis. *Historia Ecclesiastica Gentis Anglorum.* Printed in Great Britain by Amazon.

Bede. *Bede: Ecclesiastical History of the English People, with Bede's Letter to Egbert and Cuthbert's Letter on the Death of Bede.* Translated by Leo Sherley-Price, revised by R. E. Latham, translation of the minor works, new Introduction and Notes by D. H. Farmer. London: Penguin, 1990.

———. *Bede's Life of St. Cuthbert*, translated by Simon Webb. LangleyPress, 2014. Kindle.

———. *Historia Ecclesiastica Gentis Anglorum: Latin and English and Vocabulary*, developed by Paul Hudson. SPQR Study Guides Book 20. Kindle.

Bitel, Lisa M. *Isle of the Saints: Monastic Settlement and Christian Community in Early Ireland.* Ithaca, NY: Cornell University Press, 1990.

Blair, John. *The Church in Anglo-Saxon Society*. Oxford: Oxford University Press, 2006.

Blake, E.O., ed. *Liber Eliensis*, Camden Third Series, Volume XCII. London 1962.

Bradley, Ian. *Celtic Christianity: Making Myths and Chasing Dreams.* Edinburgh: Edinburgh University Press, 1999.

Bradley, S. A. J. "Introduction" and "Notes." In *Anglo-Saxon Poetry*, translated and edited by S. A. J. Bradley, xi–xxii and passim. London: Everyman, 2003.

———, ed. and trans. *Anglo-Saxon Poetry*. London: Everyman, 2003.

Brooks, Beda. *The World of Saint Mildred c. 660–730: A Study of an Anglo-Saxon Nun in the Golden Age of the English Church.* Bath, England: Downside Abbey Publications, 1996.

Brown, H. E. *For God Alone: The Lives of the Early English Saints: St. Hilda and St. Elfleda of Whitby*. Phoenix: Leonine Publishers, 2016.

Catholic Encyclopedia. http://www.newadvent.org/cathen/

Cavill, Paul. *Anglo-Saxon Christianity: Exploring the Earliest Roots of Christian Spirituality in England.* London: HarperCollins, 1999.

Cobb, Peter G. "The Architectural Setting of the Liturgy." In *The Study of Liturgy*, edited by Cheslyn Jones, Geoffrey Wainwright, and Edward Yarnold, 473–87. London: SPCK, 1978.

Colgrave, Bertram. "Introduction." In *The Earliest Life of Gregory the Great: By an Anonymous Monk of Whitby*, translated by Bertram Colgrave, 1–70. Cambridge: Cambridge University Press, 1985.

———. "Notes." In *The Life of Bishop Wilfrid by Eddius Stephanus*, translated by Bertram Colgrave, 151–87. Cambridge: Cambridge University Press, 1985.

Colgrave, Bertram, trans. *The Earliest Life of Gregory the Great: By an Anonymous Monk of Whitby.* Cambridge: Cambridge University Press, 1985.

———. *The Life of Bishop Wilfrid by Eddius Stephanus.* Cambridge: Cambridge University Press, 1985.

———. *Two Lives of Saint Cuthbert: A Life by an Anonymous Monk and Bede's Prose Life*. Copied by St. Pius X Press.

———. *Two Lives of Saint Cuthbert: A Life by an Anonymous Monk of Lindisfarne and Bede's Prose Life*. Cambridge: Cambridge University Press, 1940, 1985.

Cramp, Rosemary. *Wearmouth and Jarrow Monastic Sites.* Swindon: English Heritage, 2005.

Cubitt, Catherine. *Anglo-Saxon Church Councils: c. 650–c. 850.* London: Leicester University Press, 1995.

Cusack, Carole M. *The Rise of Christianity in Northern Europe, 300–1000.* London: Cassell, 1999.

Dix, Gregory. *The Shape of the Liturgy.* London: A. & C. Black, 1986.

Farmer, D. H. "Introduction" and "Notes." In *Bede: Ecclesiastical History of the English People*, translated by Leo Sherley-Price, revised by R. E. Latham, 19–38; 361–78. London: Penguin, 1990.

Fell, Christine. "Hild, Abbess of Streonaeshalch." In *Hagiography and Medieval Literature: A Symposium*, edited by H. Bekker-Nielsen et al., 76–99. Odense: Odense University Press, 1981.

———. *Women in Anglo-Saxon England and the Impact of 1066.* London: British Museum Publications, 1984.

Fiorenza, Elisabeth Schüssler. "The Twelve and the Discipleship of Equals." In *Discipleship of Equals: A Critical Feminist Ekklesia-logy of Liberation,* by Elisabeth Schüssler Fiorenza, 104–16. London: SCM, 1993.

———. "Women in the Pauline Churches." In *Feminism and Theology*, edited by Janet Martin Soskice and Diana Lipton, 203–26. Oxford: Oxford University Press, 2003.

Foot, Sarah. *Monastic Life in Anglo-Saxon England c. 600–900.* Cambridge: Cambridge University Press, 2009.

———. *Veiled Women I.* Aldershot, UK: Ashgate Publishing, 2000.

Frend, W. H. C. *The Early Church*. London: SCM, 1991.

Gascoigne, Bamber. *Christianity: A History*. New York: Carrol and Graf, 2003.

Godfrey, J. "The Place of the Double Monastery in the Anglo-Saxon Minster System." In *Famulus Christi: Essays in Commemoration of the Thirteenth Centenary of the Birth of the Venerable Bede*, edited by G. Bonner, 344–50. London, 1976.

Gregory, Bishop of Nyssa. *The Life of Saint Macrina*, translated by Kevin Corrigan. Toronto: Peregrina Publishing, 1989/1987.

Gregory the Great. *The Book of Pastoral Rule and Selected Epistles of Pope St. Gregory I (The Great)*, translated by James Barmby and edited by Paul A. Böer. Veritatis Splendor Publications MMXII. Kindle.

Gregory of Tours. *The History of the Franks*. Translated with an introduction by Lewis Thorpe. London: Penguin Books, 1974.

———. *The History of the Franks.* Translated with an introduction by Lewis Thorpe. Penguin Books,1974. Kindle.

Haines, Dorothy. *Sunday Observance and the Sunday Letter in Anglo-Saxon-England.* Cambridge: D. S. Brewer, 2010.

Heath, Cyril, *The First Unity: The Story of the Synod of Hertford A.D. 673*, with forewords by His Grace the Archbishop of Canterbury and by His Eminence the Roman Catholic Archbishop of Westminster. 1971

Heine, Susanne. "Women, Tasks and Ministries." In *Women and Early Christianity* by Susanne Heine, 86–92. London: SCM Press, 1987.

Hollis, Stephanie. *Anglo-Saxon Women and the Church: Sharing a Common Fate.* Woodbridge, Suffolk: Boydell Press, 1992.

Hunter Blair, Peter. "Whitby as a Centre of Learning in the Seventh Century." In *Learning and Literature in Anglo-Saxon England*, edited by Michael Lapidge and Helmut Gneuss, 3–32. Cambridge: Cambridge University Press, 1985.

———. *The World of Bede*. London, 1970.

Inman, Anne. "Lessons from the Reformation: When Papal Power Trumps Legitimate Debate." *The Pastoral Review* 13, no. 6 (November/December 2017): 20–27.

———. "Women Deacons in Anglo-Saxon England." *The Pastoral Review* 13, no.1 (January/February 2017): 42–46.

Jackson, Deirdre. *Medieval Women.* London: The British Library, 2015.

John Paul II. *Ordinatio Sacerdotalis: Apostolic Letter to the Bishops of the Catholic Church on Reserving Priestly Ordination to Men.* Vatican City: Libreria Editrice Vaticana, 1994.

Kelly, J. N. D. *Early Christian Doctrines.* London: A & C Black, 1977.

Knowles, David. *The Monastic Order in England: A History of its Development from the Times of St. Dunstan to the Fourth Lateran Council 940–1216.* Cambridge: Cambridge University Press, 1963.

Küng, Hans. "The Roman System." In *Can We Save the Catholic Church? We Can Save the Catholic Church!* 65–105. London: William Collins, 2013.

Lapidge, Michael. "The Career of Archbishop Theodore." In *Archbishop Theodore: Commemorative Studies on his Life and Influence*, edited by Michael Lapidge, 1–29. Cambridge: Cambridge University Press, 1995.

Levison, Wilhelm. *England and the Continent in the Eighth Century*. Oxford: Clarendon Press, 1998.

Leyser, Henrietta. *Medieval Women: A Social History of Women in England 450–1500*. London: Phoenix Press, 2002.

MacCulloch, Diarmaid. *A History of Christianity*. London: Penguin, 2010.

Macy, Gary. *A Hidden History of Women's Ordination: Female Clergy in the Medieval West*. Oxford: Oxford University Press, 2008.

Marrou, Henri. "Towards the Conversion of Northern Europe." In *The Christian Centuries: The First Six Hundred Years*, edited by Jean Danielou and Henri Marrou, 451–58. London: Darton, Longman and Todd, 1978.

Mayr-Harting, Henry. *The Coming of Christianity to Anglo-Saxon England*, 2nd ed. University Park: Pennsylvania State University Press, 1991.

McBrien, Richard. *Catholicism: New Study Edition*. New York: HarperCollins, 1994.

McGrath, Alister, E. *Christian Theology: An Introduction*. Oxford: Blackwell, 1997.

McNamara, Jo Ann Kay. *Sisters in Arms: Catholic Nuns through Two Millennia*. Cambridge, MA: Harvard University Press, 1996.

Morris, Joan. *Against Nature and God*. London: Mowbrays, 1973.

Mundahl-Harris, Sylvia. *St. Hilda and Her Times*. Whitby: Caedmon of Whitby, 1997.

Neuner, J., and J. Dupuis, eds. *The Christian Faith, in the Doctrinal Documents of the Catholic Church*. Collins 1986,

Nicholson, Joan, "*Feminae Gloriosae: Women in the Age of Bede*." In *Medieval Women*, edited by D. Baker, 15–29. Oxford: Ecclesiastical History Society/Blackwell, 1978.

O'Loughlin, Thomas. *Celtic Theology: Humanity, World and God in Early Irish Writings*. London: Continuum, 2000.

Platt, Colin. *The Monastic Grange in Medieval England: A Reassessment*. London: Macmillan, 1969.

Plummer, C. ed. "*Vita Prima Sancti Brendani*." In *Vitae Sanctorum Hiberniae Book I*. Oxford, 1910.

Plummer, C. ed. "*Vita Sancte Ite Virginis*." In *Vitae Sanctorum Hiberniae Book II*. Oxford, 1910.

Ramirez, Janina. *The Private Lives of the Saints: Power, Passion and Politics in Anglo-Saxon England*. London: W. H. Allen, 2016.

Roberts, Alice. *The Celts: Search for a Civilization*. London: Heron Books, 2016.

Schmitt, Miriam, and Linda Kulzer, eds. *Medieval Women Monastics: Wisdom's Wellsprings*. Collegeville, MN: Liturgical Press, 1996.

Schüssler Fiorenza, Elisabeth. *Discipleship of Equals: A Critical Feminist Ekklesialogy of Liberation*. London: SCM, 1993.

———. "Women in the Pauline Churches." In *Feminism and Theology*, edited by Janet Martin Soskice and Diana Lipton, 208–13. Oxford: Oxford University Press, 2003.

Simpson, Ray. *Hilda of Whitby: A Spirituality for Now*. Abingdon, Oxford: The Bible Reading Fellowship, 2014.

Smith, Julie Ann. *Ordering Women's Lives: Penitentials and Nunnery Rules in the Early Medieval West.* Aldershot, UK: Ashgate Publishing, 2001

Stanford, Peter. *The She-Pope.* London: Arrow, 1998.

Stenton, Frank. *Anglo-Saxon England.* Oxford: Oxford University Press, 1971.

Swan, Laura. *The Forgotten Desert Mothers: Sayings, Lives, and Stories of Early Christian Women.* New York: Paulist Press, 2001.

Swanton, M. J. *A Fragmentary Life of St. Mildred and other Kentish Royal saints.* 15–27 *Archaeologica Cantiana*, XCI, 1975.

Tanner, Norman. *New Short History of the Catholic Church.* London: Bloomsbury, 2014.

Taylor, Joan E. "Two by Two: The Ark-Etypal Language of Mark's Gospel." In *The Body in Biblical, Christian and Jewish Texts*, edited by Joan E. Taylor, 58–82. London: Bloomsbury Publishing, 2014.

Trevelyan, G. M. *A Shortened History of England.* London: Penguin, 1987.

Ward, Benedicta. *A True Easter: The Synod of Whitby 664 AD.* Oxford: SLG Press, 2008.

Webb, J. F., trans, Farmer, D. H., ed. *The Age of Bede*. Penguin Books, 2004. Kindle.

Williamson, David. *Kings & Queens of Britain.* Leicester, UK: Webb and Bower, 1991.

Wood, Michael. *In Search of the Dark Ages.* London: BBC Publishing, 2005.

Yorke, Barbara. *The Conversion of Britain 600-800.* London: Pearson and Longman, 2006.

———. *Nunneries and the Anglo-Saxon Royal Houses.* London: Continuum, 2003.

Young, Simon. *A.D. 500: A Journey Through the Dark Isles of Britain and Ireland.* London: Phoenix, 2005.

Index

Page references for figures are italicized.

About the Author

Anne E. Inman gained her B.Th. (Southampton), her M.Th. (the former Heythrop College, London University), and PhD (Heythrop), through part-time study while bringing up her two sons and running a business jointly with her husband. For twenty years, she lectured in theology at various universities, including Birkbeck College, University of London, and the University of Notre Dame (Indiana) London Centre, before retiring from teaching in 2014. She was Director of Education for Parish Service, London, for four years until 2013. Her book *Evidence and Transcendence: Religious Epistemology and the God-World Relationship* was published in 2008, and she contributed to *Anselm: A Man Born out of Due Time* (2013). She is a member of the Catholic Theological Association of Great Britain (having twice served on its committee) and the European Society for Catholic Theology. Her most recent writings look at the ministry of women and the development of sacramental theology in the early medieval period. Inman puts the case that, even in the Roman Catholic tradition, the offices of teaching, sanctifying, and governing the faithful have not always been reserved to men alone.

Lightning Source UK Ltd.
Milton Keynes UK
UKHW020632260920
370546UK00003B/47

9 781978 700666